THE
GEODEMOGRAPHIC
POCKET BOOK

a portrait of Britain's products, towns, counties and marketplaces

1998

CACI Information Services

IN ASSOCIATION WITH

NTC PUBLICATIONS LTD

Calderdale College

1090196

THE GEODEMOGRAPHIC POCKET BOOK

1998 Edition

ISBN   1 84116 004 0

NTC Publications Ltd • Farm Road • Henley-on-Thames
Oxfordshire RG9 1EJ • United Kingdom
Tel: (01491) 411000   •   Fax: (01491) 571188

Comments and suggestions for future editions of this pocket book are welcomed. Please contact: Editor, The Geodemographic Pocket Book, NTC Publications Ltd at the above address.

Printed and bound in Great Britain by Biddles Ltd, Guildford and King's Lynn.

NOTES

(i) Constituent figures in the tables may not add up to the totals, due to rounding.

(ii) For full definitions readers are referred to the sources given at the foot of each table.

(iii) Some topics are mentioned in more than one table but the information is not necessarily from the same source. Any differences are likely to be due to difference in definition, method of calculation, or periods covered.

ACKNOWLEDGEMENTS

The publishers would like to thank all those who have contributed to this compilation of statistics, in particular the coproducers of the book – CACI Information Services – whose contribution and support have been invaluable, and Target Group Index (TGI) whose data are featured extensively in Chapters 4, 5 and 6.

Other contributors, including Government departments, whose help is gratefully acknowledged, are listed below:

British Market Research Bureau (BMRB) International Limited
Family Expenditure Survey
General Household Survey
General Register Offices (GRO) for Scotland and Northern Ireland
GfK Marketing Services Limited
Government Actuary's Department
National Readership Survey (NRS)
NOP Financial
Office for National Statistics (ONS)
Verdict Research Limited

CACI Information Services Ltd is an international high technology services corporation. Founded in 1962, The company currently employs over 2,500 people in 45 offices worldwide. Since 1975 CACI has operated in the UK where it has established itself as a market leader in its three primary areas of operation: market analysis, information systems and direct marketing. The company's corporate objective is the effective interpretation of information to help clients understand and increase the efficiency of their business.

NTC Publications Ltd, part of the Information Sciences Group, is a specialist provider of professional publishing, market research, industry forecasting, database management and marketing services. Its business – often in collaboration with leading trade associations, government bodies, research companies, advertising agencies, service organisations and industry – is to provide information to business and management professionals; researched, packaged and disseminated according to the user's needs.

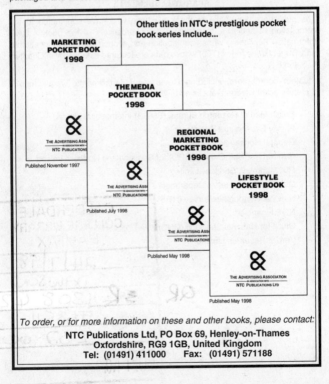

Other titles in NTC's prestigious pocket book series include...

MARKETING POCKET BOOK 1998

THE ADVERTISING ASSOCIATION
NTC PUBLICATIONS
Published November 1997

THE MEDIA POCKET BOOK 1998

THE ADVERTISING ASSOCIATION
NTC PUBLICATIONS
Published July 1998

REGIONAL MARKETING POCKET BOOK 1998

THE ADVERTISING ASSOCIATION
NTC PUBLICATIONS
Published May 1998

LIFESTYLE POCKET BOOK 1998

THE ADVERTISING ASSOCIATION
NTC PUBLICATIONS LTD
Published May 1998

To order, or for more information on these and other books, please contact:
NTC Publications Ltd, PO Box 69, Henley-on-Thames
Oxfordshire, RG9 1GB, United Kingdom
Tel: (01491) 411000   Fax: (01491) 571188

FOREWORD

CACI, the first Census agency, has been operating in the UK since 1975. We are the UK's leading marketing solutions provider with three primary areas of operation: market analysis, information systems and direct marketing. Products range from standard demographic reports and customised projects to PC-based solutions.

CACI has specialist consultants who work with major players in industry sectors which include Finance, Retail, Leisure, Automotive, Media, Telecommunications Healthcare and Local Government.

CACI's leading consumer classifications include:

☐ **ACORN** – First developed in 1978, it remains the most respected and reliable tool for segmenting today's GB population in terms of their consumer and lifestyle characteristics. ACORN combines geography with demographic data from the 1991 Census to classify the GB population into 17 groups which are subdivided into 54 types. This provides a matrix of consumer characteristics which is comprehensive enough to define the real potential for marketing and planning operations.

CACI has developed an entire family of ACORN classifications which use Census data together with other data sources. These include:

- **Financial*ACORN** – targeting consumers by their likelihood to purchase various financial products;

- **PayCheck** – a classification which profiles household income at postcode level;

- **Scottish*ACORN** – targeting Scottish neighbourhoods by socio-economic type;

- **UK*ACORN** – targeting Northern Irish neighbourhoods by socio-economic type.

☐ **Lifestyles *UK*** – CACI's sophisticated new database targeting 44 million consumers at individual level using any number of combinations from 300 lifestyle selections.

Lifestyles *UK* is a comprehensive list selection and profiling tool which also enables users to tag their existing database with key lifestyle variables. This can be used to gain a better understanding of existing customers and to target prospects more effectively. Lifestyles *UK* can also provide marketing solutions to help with cross-selling, customer retention strategies or calculating the lifetime value of customers.

CACI's PC-based Solutions include:

InSite – the leading PC-based Geographic Information System built by CACI. A combined database and mapping package, InSite is tailored to the needs of today's strategic planning and target marketing professionals. InSite allows data to be held on customers, outlets and competitors as well as information about the population at large, their lifestyles and purchasing behaviour. Analysis can be carried out on this information for any geographical area of the UK. InSite is fully compatible with the Windows 95 operating system and other Microsoft applications.

CACI's Services

These services include:

- **Market Analysis Services:** Helping businesses assess consumer potential in relation to the performance of existing sites and in support of expansion and rationalisation decisions.

- **Direct Marketing:** Targeting names and addresses for effective mailing and door-to-door distribution as well as database management and enhancement.

- **Marketing Database Solutions:** Finding solutions and adding value to marketing databases through consultancy and expertise.

- **FieldForce Planning:** Organising sales territories to match geographical sales opportunities and objectives.

- **AreaData Service:** A fast and cost effective service providing data on demographics, buying and spending habits, for any geography in Great Britain.

- **Sampling Services:** Defining efficient and representative area selections for quality sample frames.

- **Information Systems:** Advanced bespoke business systems to help you manage data more proactively and profitably.

For more information on CACI's products and services please contact:
The Marketing Department • CACI Limited
CACI House • Kensington Village • Avonmore Road • London W14 8TS
Tel: (0171) 602 6000 • Fax: (0171) 603 5862
e-mail: marketing@caci.co.uk

CONTENTS

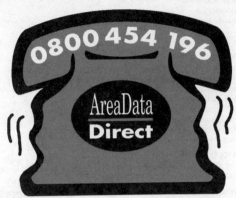

CHAPTER 1

AN INTRODUCTION TO GEODEMOGRAPHICS

The Geodemographic Pocket Book is intended as a practical guide for anyone who needs to look at and compare (in statistical terms) Britain's towns, counties, conurbations and local authority areas.

The book illustrates graphically the considerable variations that exist in levels of wealth and purchasing behaviour across the diverse geographic and demographic groups within Britain.

How Britain is Divided

Britain can be divided up and analysed as geographic or demographic entities in a number of ways, each of which is useful for a number of purposes. For example, Britain is broken down into the following general administrative areas:

British Administrative/Census Areas (1991)

	Counties	Districts	Wards	Enumeration Districts
Great Britain	**67**	**459**	**10,933**	**151,719**
England	47	366	8,985	147,644
Wales	8	37	945	6,600
Scotland	12	56	1,003	38,254
Households (average)	331,778	44,780	1,976	148

Note: In Scotland: Regions (9) and Island Areas (3) rather than Counties; Pseudo Postcode Sectors rather than Wards; and Output Areas rather than Enumeration Districts.

Sources: ONS; GRO(S).

Britain can also be divided into more specific postal areas:

PAF Data – UK Postal Geography

	Postcode Area	Postcode District	Postcode Sector	Postcode Unit
Number in the UK	121	2,900	9,000	1,600,000
Households (average)	192,000	7,930	2,550	14.5
Example postcode	**HP**	**15**	**6**	**QG**
	Outward Code		Inward Code	

These two simple geographies are extensively used for marketing purposes. By combining them with Census data, market research data and other data it is possible to analyse the British population in very considerable detail.

The methods – now widely used – by which the various data sets and geographies are linked together are known as 'Geodemographics'. The geodemographic information in this book is based on data from CACI Information Services, including the ACORN geodemographic classification, and the British Market Research Bureau's (BMRB) Target Group Index (TGI) Survey.

GEODEMOGRAPHICS

Locality Marketing

Geodemographics work on the well-proven principle that people who live in similar 'neighbourhoods' are likely to have similar behavioural, purchasing and lifestlye habits. By effectively codifying people by key characteristics, geodemographic classifications can offer great accuracy in the targeting of customers on both a demographic and geographic basis.

In Britain, most geodemographic information is derived from the Census. By linking the results of the Census with data from other sources it has become possible to 'profile' consumers by geographical area. Other data sources which can be used in geodemographic classifications include:

- market research data;
- the Postcode Address File (PAF) – the official Royal Mail file of all addresses in Great Britain;
- the Electoral Roll (ER);
- credit-related data – provided by credit referencing bureaux;
- other data (e.g. companies' own in-house customer data, industry specific data, etc.).

Of these, market research data and the Postcode Address File (PAF) are perhaps the most important. Market research data provides the bases from which geographic and demographic comparisons can be made, while PAF data allows for demographic classification to an average residential 'area' of 15 households. This compares to Census data where the smallest recorded residential areas average approximately 150 households.

Uses of Geodemographic Classifications

The principal uses of geodemographic classifications include:

- Consumer profiling by geographical area – establishing *how a product may sell* in a certain area.
- Identification of product use across geographical areas – establishing *who is buying a certain product*.
- Defining the market potential of existing customer databases/mailing lists – *targeting potential customers* from consumers of other products.

As such, geodemographics provide a vital tool for many key marketing and site location operations which demand a close understanding of the consumer potential in a database or an area.

They allow sellers/suppliers to <u>differentiate</u> between different groups of buyers/users – and establish which groups of people are key target users, which groups are potential users and which groups are non-users. This offers opportunities for specific targeting of likely customers and the potential for increasing return on investment.

A Description of the Tables in this Chapter

The two tables in this chapter demonstrate different breakdowns of the British population in terms of a number of key geodemographic profiles.

Table 1 shows the ACORN profile of CACI's 1998 population projections for Great Britain. The table shows the 17 ACORN Groups and 54 ACORN Types

(plus 1 'unclassified') in the ACORN classification which is derived from the Government's 1991 Census of Great Britain.

Table 2 shows the Financial*ACORN profile of CACI's 1998 population projections for Great Britain. The table shows the 4 Categories, 12 Groups and 51 Types (plus 1 'unclassified') in the Financial*ACORN classification which is derived from the Government's 1991 Census of Great Britain and data from NOP's Financial Research Survey (FRS).

DATA SOURCES USED IN THE GEODEMOGRAPHIC POCKET BOOK

ACORN

Developed by CACI, the ACORN geodemographic classification system categorises consumers into 54 socio-economic Types, which aggregate up to 17 Groups, according to the characteristics of the residential area in which they live.

The ACORN classification is built using key data from the 1991 Census. The ACORN Types are created where clusters of common characteristics form across this data.

Target Group Index (TGI)

The British Market Research Bureau's (BMRB) Target Group Index (TGI) is an annually updated consumer survey based on a sample of over 25,000 adults in the UK. The survey records information on over 400 consumer products (from food to finance) and some 3,500 different named brands.

Using ACORN with TGI Product Data

Combining ACORN with the responses to the TGI's consumer survey panels gives access to a refined resource for targeting customers. Any product covered by the TGI survey can be assigned an ACORN Type based on the highest volume penetration for that product. Equally, for any one of the ACORN Types it is possible to establish which TGI products have highest volume penetration.

For a detailed introduction to the subject please refer to 'Targeting Customers – How to Use Geodemographic and Lifestyle Data in Your Business', by Peter Sleight. Published by NTC Publications Ltd (Tel: 01491 411000).

TABLE 1: CACI ACORN PROFILE OF GREAT BRITAIN

Table 1 shows the ACORN profile of CACI's 1998 population projections for Great Britain. The table shows the 17 ACORN Groups and 54 ACORN Types (plus 1 'unclassified') in the ACORN classification which is derived from the Government's 1991 Census of Great Britain.

ACORN Categories	ACORN Groups	ACORN Types		CACI's 1998 Population Projections		Corresponding Social Grade
				Number	Percent of Total	
A THRIVING	**1 Wealthy Achievers, Suburban Areas**	1.1	Wealthy suburbs, large detached houses	1,476,022	2.6	AB
		1.2	Villages with wealthy commuters	1,839,635	3.2	AB
		1.3	Mature affluent home owning areas	1,559,402	2.7	ABC1
		1.4	Affluent suburbs, older families	2,132,677	3.7	ABC1
		1.5	Mature well-off suburbs	1,729,608	3.0	ABC1
	2 Affluent Greys, Rural Communities	2.6	Agricultural villages, home-based workers	930,036	1.6	ABC2D
		2.7	Holiday retreats, older people, home-based workers	400,866	0.7	ABC2D
	3 Prosperous Pensioners, Retirement Areas	3.8	Home owning areas, well-off older residents	812,289	1.4	ABC1
		3.9	Private flats, elderly people	544,382	0.9	ABC1
	4 Affluent Executives, Family Areas	4.10	Affluent working families with mortgages	1,226,163	2.1	ABC1
		4.11	Affluent working couples with mortgages, new homes	721,361	1.3	ABC1
		4.12	Transient workforces, living at their place of work	201,841	0.4	*
B EXPANDING	**5 Well-Off Workers, Family Areas**	5.13	Home owning family areas	1,491,918	2.6	ABC1
		5.14	Home owning family areas, older children	1,723,980	3.0	C1C2
		5.15	Families with mortgages, younger children	1,274,799	2.2	C1C2
	6 Affluent Urbanites, Town & City Areas	6.16	Well-off town & city areas	639,115	1.1	AB
		6.17	Flats & mortgages, singles & young working couples	425,189	0.7	ABC1
		6.18	Furnished flats & bedsits, younger single people	253,662	0.4	ABC1
C RISING	**7 Prosperous Professionals, Metropolitan Areas**	7.19	Apartments, young professional singles & couples	656,986	1.1	ABC1
		7.20	Gentrified multi-ethnic areas	558,364	1.0	ABC1
	8 Better-Off Executives, Inner City Areas	8.21	Prosperous enclaves, highly qualified executives	431,240	0.7	ABC1
		8.22	Academic centres, students & young professionals	371,655	0.6	ABC1
		8.23	Affluent city centre areas, tenements & flats	254,396	0.4	ABC1
		8.24	Partially gentrified multi-ethnic areas	409,135	0.7	ABC1
		8.25	Converted flats & bedsits, single people	498,647	0.9	*

	Group	Type	Description	Population	%	Social grade
D SETTLING	**9** Comfortable Middle Agers, Mature Home Owning Areas	9.26	Mature established home owning areas	1,901,159	3.3	ABC1
		9.27	Rural areas, mixed occupations	1,998,784	3.5	*
		9.28	Established home owning areas	2,310,649	4.0	C1
		9.29	Home owning areas, council tenants, retired people	1,529,541	2.7	ABC1
	10 Skilled Workers, Home Owning Areas	10.30	Home owning areas, council tenants, retired people	1,529,541	2.7	C2
		10.31	Home owners in older properties, younger workers	1,746,408	3.0	C1C2
		10.32	Home owning areas with skilled workers	1,762,344	3.1	C2DE
E ASPIRING	**11** New Home Owners, Mature Communities	11.33	Council areas, some new home owners	2,186,023	3.8	C2DE
		11.34	Mature home owning areas, skilled workers	1,770,286	3.1	C2DE
		11.35	Low rise estates, older workers, new home owners	1,607,672	2.8	C2DE
	12 White Collar Workers, Better-Off Multi-Ethnic Areas	12.36	Home owning multi-ethnic areas, young families	647,676	1.1	C1
		12.37	Multi-occupied town centres, mixed occupations	1,041,973	1.8	*
		12.38	Multi-ethnic areas, white collar workers	617,435	1.1	C1
F STRIVING	**13** Older People, Less Prosperous Areas	13.39	Home owners, small council flats, single pensioners	1,090,322	1.9	C2DE
		13.40	Council areas, older people, health problems	972,699	1.7	C2DE
	14 Council Estate Residents, Better-Off Homes	14.41	Better-off council areas, new home owners	1,378,827	2.4	C2DE
		14.42	Council areas, young families, some new home owners	1,710,052	3.0	C2DE
		14.43	Council areas, young families, many lone parents	899,111	1.6	C2DE
		14.44	Multi-occupied terraces, multi-ethnic areas	489,064	0.8	C2DE
		14.45	Low rise council housing, less well-off families	1,015,161	1.8	C2DE
		14.46	Council areas, residents with health problems	1,098,493	1.9	C2DE
	15 Council Estate Residents, High Unemployment	15.47	Estates with high unemployment	649,273	1.1	DE
		15.48	Council flats, elderly people, health problems	382,712	0.7	C2DE
		15.49	Council flats, very high unemployment, singles	494,008	0.9	DE
	16 Council Estate Residents, Greatest Hardship	16.50	Council areas, high unemployment, lone parents	1,053,942	1.8	DE
		16.51	Council flats, greatest hardship, many lone parents	515,727	0.9	DE
	17 People In Multi-Ethnic, Low-Income Areas	17.52	Multi-ethnic, large families, overcrowding	369,374	0.6	DE
		17.53	Multi-ethnic, severe unemployment, lone parents	574,309	1.0	DE
		17.54	Multi-ethnic, high unemployment, overcrowding	303,014	0.5	DE
			Unclassified	290,089	0.5	
			TOTAL	**57,558,628**	**100.0**	

Note: * Corresponding social grades represent national average.

Source: ONS & GRO(S) © Crown Copyright 1991. All rights reserved.

5

TABLE 2: Financial*ACORN PROFILE OF GREAT BRITAIN

Table 2 shows the Financial*ACORN profile of CACI's 1998 population projections for Great Britain. The table shows the 12 Financial*ACORN Groups and 52 Financial*ACORN Types (plus 1 'unclassified') in the Financial*ACORN classification which is derived from the Government's 1991 Census of Great Britain and data from NOP's Financial Research Survey (FRS).

Financial*ACORN Categories	Financial*ACORN Groups	Financial*ACORN Types	CACI's 1998 Population Projections Number	Percent of Total
	1 Wealthy Equityholders	1.1 Mature couples & families, extensive financial portfolio	351,486	0.6
		1.2 Professional families, with life assurance, loans & mortgages	298,826	0.5
		1.3 Older families, active in loans & deposit accounts	349,654	0.6
		1.4 Older couples, low on pension plans & high on stocks & shares	419,525	0.7
		1.5 Middle aged couples, making sensible investments, few loans	1,027,728	1.8
		1.6 Older families with average loans & ample investments	592,680	1.0
		1.7 Mature couples, insurance, life assurance & deposit accounts	1,258,134	2.2
		1.8 Older couples, equities, pension plans & other savings	368,835	0.6
		1.9 Senior citizens with carefully planned savings & investments	459,266	0.8
		1.10 Middle aged, preferring investments in tax exempt savings	496,457	0.9
		1.11 Younger single executives, investing, saving & using credit	401,559	0.7
		1.12 Professional singles & couples, using credit & debit cards	401,220	0.7
A FINANCIALLY SOPHISTICATED	**2 Affluent Mortgageholders**	2.13 Younger couples & families, very active across financial range	303,035	0.5
		2.14 Families with children, credit & debit cards & investing heavily	294,496	0.5
		2.15 Older families, deposit/savings accounts, above average shares	928,209	1.6
		2.16 Young & middle aged couples investing in tax exempt savings	834,525	1.4
		2.17 Young singles & couples, planning ahead, personal pensions	307,563	0.5
		2.18 Families, personal pensions, life assurance, tax exempt savings	360,425	0.6
		2.19 Young couples & families, above av. mortgages & life assurance	777,110	1.4
		2.20 Young adults in couples, settling down with mortgages & loans	451,767	0.8
		2.21 Families & younger couples, mortgages but wary of investments	565,102	1.0
	3 Comfortable Investors	3.22 Older Couples, wide range of investments, especially in shares	843,071	1.5
		3.23 Middle aged couples with ample personal pensions	348,580	0.6
		3.24 Older couples, av. on credit/loans, keen on tax exempt savings	1,169,111	2.0
		3.25 Traditional couples, tax exempt savings & personal pensions	1,249,547	2.2

B FINANCIALLY INVOLVED

4 Better-Off Borrowers

Code	Description	Population	%
4.26	Young families with children, using loans & mortgages	561,238	1.0
4.27	Younger families & couples, high spending, new commitments	605,666	1.1
4.28	Young singles & couples, keen on loans & personal pensions	1,477,883	2.6
4.29	Families, av. financial activity but above average mortgages	3,013,138	5.2
4.30	Younger people, setting up home	1,701,683	3.0
4.31	Family groups, especially younger families, borrowing heavily	181,706	0.3

5 Prosperous Savers

Code	Description	Population	%
5.32	Older families & couples with careful savings & investments	1,162,108	2.0
5.33	Mature singles & couples enjoying high share ownership	1,082,437	1.9
5.34	Older couples, deposit accounts, tax exempt savings, shares	1,551,530	2.7
5.35	Young, low life assurance but high denationalised stocks	1,186,111	2.1
5.36	Retired, active in shares, credit cards, deposit accounts	1,234,250	2.1
5.37	Pensioners, very high share ownership, few loans & mortgages	672,662	1.2

C FINANCIALLY MODERATE

6 Younger Spenders

Code	Description	Population	%
6.38	Young adults, very active in credit cards & some investments	1,066,618	1.9
6.39	Younger single people using cash and debit cards, few loans	358,856	0.6

7 Settled Pensioners

Code	Description	Population	%
7.40	Older people, average activity across the financial range	2,602,197	4.5
7.41	Elderly singles & couples, some savings, generally average	2,592,604	4.5

8 Working Families

Code	Description	Population	%
8.42	Younger couples, few children, mortgages & average savings	3,504,335	6.1
8.43	Families of all ages with children, using above average loans	1,420,795	2.5

9 Thrifty Singles

Code	Description	Population	%
9.44	Young adults, average spending & few savings or mortgages	1,061,319	1.8
9.45	Young singles & couples, low spending & negligible savings	1,212,659	2.1

D FIN. INACTIVE

10 Middle Aged Assured

Code	Description	Population	%
10.46	Middle aged & older singles, above average life assurance	2,379,707	4.1
10.47	Middle aged couples, above av. life assurance, few investments	639,266	1.1

11 Older Cash Users

Code	Description	Population	%
11.48	Older singles, retired or unemployed, negligible credit	2,959,175	5.1
11.49	Families & single people, below av. use of financial products	2,803,393	4.9
12.50	Young families, very low activity in mortgages & credit cards	4,075,497	7.1
12.51	Families with children, very little saving or spending	1,301,340	2.3

	Population	%
Unclassified	292,544	0.5
TOTAL	**57,558,628**	**100.0**

Source: ONS & GRO(S) © Crown Copyright 1991. All rights reserved.

7

CHAPTER 2

DEMOGRAPHIC SUMMARY TABLES

RESIDENT POPULATION OF THE UNITED KINGDOM, MID 1996

By Nation

Thousands

	Total	Males	Females
England	49,089.1	24,129.3	24,959.8
Wales	2,921.1	1,428.1	1,493.0
Scotland	5,128.0	2,485.8	2,642.2
Great Britain	**57,138.2**	**28,043.2**	**29,095.0**
Northern Ireland	1,663.3	812.5	850.8
United Kingdom	**58,801.5**	**28,855.7**	**29,945.8**

By Sex and Age

Years of age	Total		Males		Females	
	'000s	%	'000s	%	'000s	%
0– 4	3,763.4	6.4	1,929.3	6.7	1,834.1	6.1
5– 9	3,905.3	6.6	2,002.2	6.9	1,903.1	6.4
10–14	3,689.6	6.3	1,894.5	6.6	1,795.1	6.0
15–19	3,522.3	6.0	1,809.6	6.3	1,712.6	5.7
20–24	3,802.8	6.5	1,950.0	6.8	1,852.7	6.2
25–29	4,577.6	7.8	2,339.2	8.1	2,238.3	7.5
30–34	4,842.6	8.2	2,465.5	8.5	2,377.1	7.9
35–39	4,289.3	7.3	2,166.1	7.5	2,123.2	7.1
40–44	3,803.6	6.5	1,906.3	6.6	1,897.2	6.3
45–49	4,129.7	7.0	2,065.0	7.2	2,064.8	6.9
50–54	3,465.9	5.9	1,726.6	6.0	1,739.4	5.8
55–59	2,986.4	5.1	1,478.3	5.1	1,508.0	5.0
60–64	2,772.2	4.7	1,354.5	4.7	1,417.7	4.7
65–69	2,646.3	4.5	1,242.1	4.3	1,404.1	4.7
70–74	2,412.0	4.1	1,068.3	3.7	1,343.7	4.5
75–79	1,823.7	3.1	732.0	2.5	1,091.8	3.6
80–84	1,301.6	2.2	452.9	1.6	848.6	2.8
85+	1,067.2	1.8	272.9	0.9	794.3	2.7
Total	**58,801.5**	**100.0**	**28,855.7**	**100.0**	**29,945.8**	**100.0**

Population Projections

Thousands

	1996	Projections				
		1997	2001	2011	2021	2031
0–14	11,358	11,373	11,291	10,405	10,124	9,799
15–29	11,903	11,708	11,169	11,667	10,910	10,146
30–44	12,935	13,135	13,684	12,040	11,449	11,420
45–59	10,582	10,694	11,232	12,654	12,917	11,005
60–74	7,830	7,769	7,712	9,213	10,542	11,925
75+	4,192	4,261	4,383	4,516	5,186	6,427
Males	28,856	28,949	29,312	30,011	30,375	30,114
Females	29,946	29,991	30,160	30,483	30,754	30,606
Total	**58,802**	**58,941**	**59,472**	**60,493**	**61,130**	**60,720**

Sources: ONS; General Register Offices for Scotland and Northern Ireland; NTC.

RESIDENT POPULATION OF CONURBATIONS, MID 1996

	'000s	Percent of GB Population
Greater London	7,074	12.4
West Midlands incl. Birmingham 1,021, Dudley 312, Coventry 307, Walsall 263, Wolverhampton 245	2,643	4.6
Greater Manchester incl. Manchester 431, Wigan 310, Stockport 291, Bolton 265, Salford 229	2,576	4.5
West Yorkshire incl. Leeds 727, Bradford 483, Kirklees 389	2,109	3.7
Central Clydeside incl. Glasgow City 673, Motherwell 143	1,616	2.8
Merseyside incl. Liverpool 468, Wirral 329, Sefton 290	1,420	2.5
South Yorkshire incl. Sheffield 530, Doncaster 292	1,305	2.3
Tyne and Wear incl. Sunderland 294, Newcastle upon Tyne 282	1,127	2.0

Sources: ONS; General Register Office for Scotland.

RESIDENT POPULATION OF SELECTED DISTRICTS, MID 1996

	'000s		'000s		'000s
Bristol	400	Harrogate	148	Stratford-on-Avon	111
Leicester	295	Middlesbrough	147	Exeter	108
Nottingham	284	Rochester	145	Scarborough	108
Kingston upon Hull	267	Newbury	144	Stroud	108
Plymouth	256	Reading	142	Cheltenham	107
Stoke-on-Trent	254	Maidstone	141	Gloucester	107
Derby	234	Blackburn	140	Winchester	106
Southampton	215	Poole	139	Carlisle	103
Milton Keynes	197	Canterbury	137	Mansfield	102
Northampton	192	Lancaster	137	Chesterfield	101
Portsmouth	190	Oxford	137	Darlington	101
Warrington	189	Preston	135	Worthing	99
Luton	182	St Albans	130		
Stockton-on-Tees	179	Norwich	126	Cardiff	315
Southend-on-Sea	172	Guildford	125	Swansea	230
Wycombe	164	Stafford	125	Newport	137
Basildon	163	Torbay	123		
Bournemouth	161	Warwick	123	Edinburgh	449
Peterborough	159	Newcastle-u-Lyme	122	Aberdeen	217
Chelmsford	157	Chester	119	Dundee City	150
Brighton	156	Cambridge	117	Kirkcaldy	148
Colchester	154	Ipswich	114	Falkirk	143
Blackpool	153	Salisbury	113		
Macclesfield	153	Slough	111	Belfast	297

Sources: ONS; General Register Offices for Scotland and Northern Ireland.

GOVERNMENT OFFICE REGIONS

POPULATION

	Mid-1996 estimates	
	'000s	%
North East	2,601	4.6
North West	6,940	12.1
Yorks & Humb.	5,036	8.8
East Midlands	4,142	7.2
West Midlands	5,317	9.3
Eastern	5,293	9.3
London	7,074	11.9
South East	7,895	12.7
South West	4,842	7.7
Wales	2,921	5.1
Scotland	5,128	9.0
Great Britain	**57,138**	**100.0**

Note: The population of Northern Ireland ('000s) in 1996 was 1,663.

Sources: ONS; General Register Offices for Scotland and Northern Ireland.

■ Conurbations

□ Unitary Authority Areas

SCOTLAND

Highland

Moray

Grampian

Angus

Perth & Kinross

Fife

Stirling

Argyll & Bute

Strathclyde

Dumfries and Galloway

Scottish Borders

Cumbria

Northumberland

Durham

Tyne & Wear

NORTH EAST

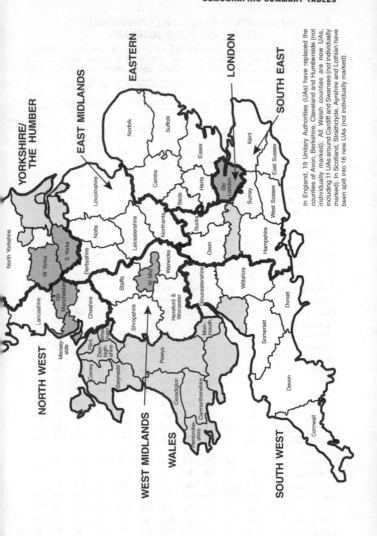

In England, 19 Unitary Authorities (UAs) have replaced the counties of Avon, Berkshire, Cleveland and Humberside (not individually marked). All Welsh counties are now UAs, including 11 UAs around Cardiff and Swansea (not individually marked). In Scotland, Strathclyde, Ayrshire and Lothian have been split into 16 new UAs (not individually marked).

DISTRIBUTION OF INCOME LEVEL OF HOUSEHOLDS BY COUNTY AND METROPOLITAN AREA

Figures are indexes derived from the difference between the income level of households by area compared to Great Britain as a whole, using CACI's PayCheck classification for 1998. The GB average for each income level is 100.

	Up to £4,999	£5,000 to £9,999	£10,000 to £14,999	£15,000 to £19,999	£20,000 to £24,999	£25,000 to £29,999	£30,000 to £34,999	£35,000 to £39,999	£40,000 to £44,999	£45,000 to £49,999	£50,000 plus
Metropolitan Areas											
Inner London	86	79	83	90	98	109	120	132	145	158	203
Outer London	68	72	82	94	108	120	132	143	153	162	182
Gtr. Manchester	117	112	106	100	95	91	87	84	81	78	70
Merseyside	132	119	108	98	90	84	79	75	71	68	60
South Yorkshire	142	129	113	98	86	76	69	63	58	55	46
Tyne and Wear	147	133	113	96	83	73	66	61	57	54	47
West Midlands	126	118	109	100	92	85	79	74	71	67	60
West Yorkshire	115	111	106	101	96	92	88	84	81	78	70
English Counties											
Avon	94	98	102	103	104	103	101	99	97	95	90
Bedfordshire	74	80	91	102	111	118	122	125	127	128	125
Berkshire	56	63	77	93	111	128	143	157	169	179	199
Buckinghamshire	55	64	77	93	110	126	142	156	169	181	210
Cambridgeshire	80	88	96	103	109	112	114	114	114	113	108
Cheshire	87	91	95	99	104	108	112	115	117	118	118
Cleveland	137	125	110	97	88	81	76	70	66	61	50
Cornwall and the Isles of Scilly	125	123	116	105	94	82	72	63	56	50	38
Cumbria	98	107	109	107	103	97	91	85	80	74	60
Derbyshire	106	108	107	104	100	96	91	86	82	78	68
Devon	111	116	114	107	98	89	80	72	65	59	47
Dorset	98	103	106	106	104	99	94	89	84	80	68
Durham	131	125	112	99	89	80	74	68	64	60	51
East Sussex	102	99	100	101	101	100	99	99	98	98	96
Essex	81	84	91	99	106	113	118	123	126	129	133
Gloucestershire	86	93	100	105	107	108	107	105	103	100	93
Hampshire	80	87	95	102	108	112	114	116	117	117	114
Hereford and Worcester	92	96	100	103	104	104	104	103	101	100	94
Hertfordshire	63	69	80	94	108	123	136	149	160	170	193
Humberside	119	119	111	102	94	86	79	74	69	64	54
Isle of Wight	127	122	115	104	93	82	73	65	58	53	40
Kent	87	91	97	102	106	109	110	111	110	110	107
Lancashire	106	108	107	103	100	95	91	87	83	79	70
Leicestershire	99	101	103	103	103	101	98	95	92	89	81

	Up to £4,999	£5,000 to £9,999	£10,000 to £14,999	£15,000 to £19,999	£20,000 to £24,999	£25,000 to £29,999	£30,000 to £34,999	£35,000 to £39,999	£40,000 to £44,999	£45,000 to £49,999	£50,000 plus
English Counties (cont.)											
Lincolnshire	99	101	103	103	103	101	98	95	92	89	81
Norfolk	107	109	109	106	101	94	88	81	76	70	58
Northamptonshire	83	91	98	104	107	109	110	109	108	107	104
Northumberland	115	113	107	101	95	91	86	83	79	77	69
North Yorkshire	91	98	103	105	105	103	101	98	95	93	86
Nottinghamshire	120	115	108	101	94	88	83	79	75	72	64
Oxfordshire	64	74	87	100	112	122	130	136	140	144	150
Shropshire	101	105	106	105	102	98	94	89	86	82	72
Somerset	98	106	109	108	103	97	91	85	80	75	63
Staffordshire	103	107	107	104	100	96	92	88	84	80	71
Suffolk	94	100	104	106	105	103	99	94	90	86	75
Surrey	50	57	71	88	108	128	149	169	188	205	249
Warwickshire	87	92	97	102	105	107	108	109	110	110	112
West Sussex	80	85	93	101	108	113	118	121	123	124	124
Wiltshire	76	86	97	106	112	115	115	114	111	109	98
Welsh Counties											
Clwyd	108	110	108	105	100	94	88	82	77	72	61
Dyfed	122	120	114	105	94	85	76	68	62	56	43
Gwent	118	116	110	102	94	88	82	77	72	69	60
Gwynedd	131	121	112	102	92	83	75	68	62	56	45
Mid Glamorgan	129	125	115	102	91	81	72	65	58	53	41
Powys	110	114	113	107	99	90	82	74	68	63	50
South Glamorgan	102	103	103	102	100	98	96	94	93	91	86
West Glamorgan	119	118	112	104	95	87	79	72	66	60	48
Scottish Counties											
Borders	106	111	110	105	99	92	86	81	77	73	63
Central	107	106	104	101	99	96	94	92	89	87	80
Dumfries and Galloway	115	116	112	106	98	89	80	73	66	60	46
Fife	108	109	107	103	99	94	90	86	82	79	69
Grampian	91	93	97	100	103	106	108	109	110	110	108
Highland	110	112	109	105	99	93	86	80	74	69	56
Lothian	96	100	100	100	101	101	101	102	102	101	99
Strathclyde	127	119	107	98	90	85	81	78	75	72	65
Tayside	115	115	109	102	95	89	84	80	76	73	63
Orkney	122	113	108	102	96	90	84	78	73	68	55
Shetland	61	75	90	105	118	126	131	132	131	128	111
Western Isles	105	109	110	108	103	96	88	80	73	66	50

CHARACTERISTICS OF HOUSEHOLD POPULATION[1]

(a) Number of households in Great Britain: 23,390,000 (March 1997)

(b) Size of households, 1996

	%
1 person	27
2 persons	34
3 persons	16
4 persons	15
5 persons	5
6 or more persons	2
	100

Average (mean) h/h size:	1996	2.43
	1971	2.91

(c) Sex of head of household, 1995

	%
Male	74
Female	26
	100

43% of the female heads of household are over 60 and living alone.

(d) Marital status by sex, 1996

	Men	Women
16 and over	%	%
Married	61	55
Cohabiting	7	7
Single	22	17
Widowed/divorced, etc.	9	20
	100	100

(e) Female housewives with/without children under 15, 1997

	%	%
With children, (total)		30.3
0–23 months	6.1	
0–4 years	13.7	
4–15 years	16.5	
Without children		69.7
		100.0

(f) Working status of housewives (female)[2], 1997

	%	%
Working full-time		
30+ hours per week	26.9	
Working part-time		
8–29 hours per week	18.9	
Working full- or part-time		45.8
Not working; and part-time under 8 hours per week		54.2
		100.0

(g) Number of economically active persons in household, 1996–97

	%
No person	32.7
1 person	27.9
2 persons	32.2
3 or more persons	7.2
	100.0

(h) Retired/non-retired h'holds[3], 1996–97

	%
Retired, (total)	41.4
Dependent on state pensions	19.3
Other	22.2
Non-retired	58.6
	100.0

(i) Static/non-static households, 1997/Q1

	%	%
Static		98
Non-static, (total)		2
Newly weds' h'holds	0.2	
Movers into:		
– new homes	0.1	
– other movers	1.6	
		100

Notes: [1] (g), (h) refer to the UK; (b), (c), (d), (e), (f), (i) to Great Britain.
   [2] According to the Family Expenditure Survey 1996-97, 16% of households have working married women with dependent children.
   [3] Households consisting of one adult or one man and one woman only.

Sources: (a), (i):   GfK Marketing Services Ltd.
   (b), (c), (d): General Household Survey.
   (e), (f):   National Readership Survey (NRS Ltd.) January – December 1997.
   (g), (h):   Family Expenditure Survey 1996-97.

CHAPTER 3

HOUSEHOLD INCOME

PayCheck – Classifying Household Income Levels

PayCheck is a classification which profiles income at postcode level, using information from CACI's lifestyle database, in conjunction with Census and market research data to increase statistical reliability.

Income reflected by PayCheck is gross family income including income from saving and investments. It provides the mean, mode and median income for every postcode in the UK, broken down into bands which increase from £0-£100,000+ in groupings of £5,000.

PayCheck can be aggregated to profile other geographies, e.g. Enumeration Districts, counties, outlets or catchment areas. PayCheck can also be used to income code in-house database records and any subsequent names and addresses added to it.

This chapter provides a listing of the 459 local authority districts/unitary authorities (UA) ranked by income indexed against the UK. The index is calculated by dividing the mean income for each area by the mean income for the UK and multiplying by 100. An index score of 100 is equivalent to the UK average.

Rank	Local Authority District/ Unitary Authority	Household Income Index	Rank	Local Authority District/ Unitary Authority	Household Income Index
1	City of London	204	30 =	Hammersmith & Fulham	133
2 =	Kensington & Chelsea	154	32 =	Wandsworth	132
2 =	Richmond upon Thames	154	32 =	Eastwood	132
4	Elmbridge	153	34 =	Hertsmere	131
5	Chiltern	152	34 =	Runnymede	131
6	Surrey Heath	151	34 =	Bracknell Forest	131
7	South Bucks	150	34 =	Mid Sussex	131
8	Westminster, City of	147	38 =	Newbury	130
9	Hart	146	38 =	Epping Forest	130
10	Wokingham	145	38 =	South Oxfordshire	130
11 =	St Albans	144	41 =	Sevenoaks	129
11 =	Windsor & Maidenhead	144	41 =	Merton	129
13	Woking	141	43 =	Macclesfield	128
14	Epsom & Ewell	140	43 =	Basingstoke & Deane	128
15 =	Mole Valley	138	45 =	Aylesbury Vale	127
15 =	Tandridge	138	45 =	Spelthorne	127
17	Bearsden & Milngavie	137	45 =	Vale of White Horse	127
18 =	Reigate & Banstead	136	45 =	East Hampshire	127
18 =	Waverley	136	45 =	Ealing	127
18 =	Barnet	136	45 =	Dacorum	127
18 =	Wycombe	136	51	Sutton	126
18 =	Brentwood	136	52 =	Redbridge	125
18 =	East Hertfordshire	136	52 =	Chelmsford	125
24 =	Bromley	135	52 =	Hillingdon	125
24 =	Kingston upon Thames	135	52 =	Horsham	125
26 =	Guildford	134	52 =	Croydon	125
26 =	Uttlesford	134	52 =	Tunbridge Wells	125
26 =	Camden	134	58	South Cambridgeshire	124
26 =	Harrow	134	59 =	Mid Bedfordshire	123
30 =	Three Rivers	133	59 =	Winchester	123

Rank	Local Authority District/ Unitary Authority	Household Income Index	Rank	Local Authority District/ Unitary Authority	Household Income Index
61	North Hertfordshire	122	105 =	Greenwich	112
62 =	Kincardine & Deeside	121	105 =	Wealden	112
62 =	Welwyn Hatfield	121	105 =	Cotswold	112
64 =	Daventry	120	115 =	Eastleigh	111
64 =	Haringey	120	115 =	Waltham Forest	111
64 =	Broxbourne	120	115 =	Harrogate	111
67 =	Tonbridge & Malling	119	118 =	Chester	110
67 =	South Northamptonshire	119	118 =	Fylde	110
67 =	Harborough	119	118 =	Selby	110
67 =	Test Valley	119	118 =	Vale Royal	110
67 =	Watford	119	118 =	Tewkesbury	110
67 =	Lambeth	119	118 =	Castle Morpeth	110
67 =	Hounslow	119	118 =	Braintree	110
67 =	Rutland	119	118 =	Ribble Valley	110
67 =	Rochford	119	118 =	Wansdyke	110
76 =	Havering	118	118 =	Wychavon	110
76 =	Brent	118	128 =	Stockport	109
76 =	South Bedfordshire	118	128 =	Trafford	109
76 =	Huntingdonshire	118	130 =	Tower Hamlets	108
76 =	Rushcliffe	118	130 =	East Northamptonshire	108
81 =	Gordon	117	130 =	Strathkelvin	108
81 =	Maldon	117	130 =	Cambridge	108
81 =	Congleton	117	134 =	Blaby	107
81 =	Islington	117	134 =	Derbyshire Dales	107
81 =	Milton Keynes	117	134 =	Southwark	107
86 =	West Oxfordshire	116	134 =	Crawley	107
86 =	Stratford-on-Avon	116	134 =	Melton	107
86 =	Bexley	116	134 =	Gravesham	107
86 =	Bromsgrove	116	134 =	Stafford	107
90 =	Solihull	115	141 =	High Peak	106
90 =	Enfield	115	141 =	East Cambridgeshire	106
90 =	Rushmoor	115	141 =	Stroud	106
90 =	Maidstone	115	141 =	Hinckley & Bosworth	106
94 =	Lichfield	114	141 =	North East Fife	106
94 =	Reading	114	141 =	Babergh	106
94 =	Fareham	114	141 =	Chichester	106
94 =	Northavon	114	141 =	Lewes	106
98 =	Cherwell	113	141 =	Monmouth	106
98 =	Lewisham	113	141 =	Malvern Hills	106
98 =	Castle Point	113	141 =	Colchester	106
98 =	Slough	113	141 =	Tynedale	106
98 =	Warwick	113	141 =	Warrington	106
98 =	North Wiltshire	113	141 =	Thurrock	106
98 =	Shetland	113	155 =	Oadby & Wigston	105
105 =	North Bedfordshire	112	155 =	Southend-on-Sea	105
105 =	South Staffordshire	112	155 =	Cheltenham	105
105 =	Kennet	112	155 =	Bury	105
105 =	Hambleton	112	155 =	Chorley	105
105 =	Dartford	112	155 =	Woodspring	105
105 =	Basildon	112	155 =	Hackney	105
105 =	Beverley	112	155 =	Hove	105

Rank	Local Authority District/ Unitary Authority	Household Income Index	Rank	Local Authority District/ Unitary Authority	Household Income Index
163 =	Stirling	104	204 =	Perth & Kinross	99
163 =	East Dorset	104	204 =	Richmondshire	99
163 =	Mid Suffolk	104	216 =	Wellingborough	98
163 =	Thamesdown	104	216 =	Canterbury	98
163 =	Stevenage	104	216 =	Dumbarton	98
163 =	Luton	104	216 =	Crewe & Nantwich	98
163 =	South Ribble	104	216 =	Mendip	98
163 =	Edinburgh City	104	216 =	Wyre	98
163 =	Gillingham	104	216 =	Clydesdale	98
163 =	North Warwickshire	104	216 =	Worcester	98
163 =	Aberdeen City	104	216 =	Copeland	98
174 =	Ashford	103	216 =	Durham	98
174 =	Oxford	103	226 =	Teesdale	97
174 =	Worthing	103	226 =	Rother	97
174 =	South Norfolk	103	226 =	Holderness	97
174 =	Bridgnorth	103	226 =	Forest Heath	97
174 =	Broadland	103	226 =	Havant	97
174 =	Vale of Glamorgan	103	226 =	North Shropshire	97
181 =	South Herefordshire	102	226 =	Redditch	97
181 =	Tweeddale	102	226 =	Amber Valley	97
181 =	Salisbury	102	226 =	Cumbernauld & Kilsyth	97
181 =	Rugby	102	226 =	Kyle & Carrick	97
181 =	South Lakeland	102	236 =	Ryedale	96
186 =	South Kesteven	101	236 =	West Devon	96
186 =	St Edmundsbury	101	236 =	Shrewsbury & Atcham	96
186 =	East Lothian	101	236 =	Broxtowe	96
186 =	Poole	101	236 =	Eden	96
186 =	Northampton	101	236 =	Purbeck	96
186 =	West Wiltshire	101	236 =	Isles of Scilly	96
186 =	Swale	101	236 =	Adur	96
186 =	New Forest	101	236 =	Alyn & Deeside	96
186 =	Charnwood	101	236 =	Cardiff	96
186 =	Ellesmere Port & Neston	101	236 =	Brecknock	96
186 =	South Derbyshire	101	236 =	Wirral	96
186 =	Rochester upon Medway	101	236 =	Boothferry	96
186 =	Kettering	101	236 =	Glyndwr	96
199 =	Brighton	100	250 =	Peterborough	95
199 =	West Lancashire	100	250 =	Ettrick & Lauderdale	95
199 =	Craven	100	250 =	Sefton	95
199 =	Delyn	100	250 =	South Hams	95
199 =	Glanford	100	250 =	Midlothian	95
204 =	Kingswood	99	250 =	Rossendale	95
204 =	Staffordshire Moorlands	99	250 =	Banff & Buchan	95
204 =	Bath	99	250 =	Shepway	95
204 =	Wyre Forest	99	250 =	West Lothian	95
204 =	East Kilbride	99	250 =	North Dorset	95
204 =	Arun	99	250 =	Dover	95
204 =	Newham	99	250 =	North Kesteven	95
204 =	Gedling	99	250 =	Dunfermline	95
204 =	Harlow	99	263 =	Calderdale	94
204 =	North West Leicestershire	99	263 =	Nairn	94

Rank	Local Authority District/ Unitary Authority	Household Income Index	Rank	Local Authority District/ Unitary Authority	Household Income Index
263 =	Forest of Dean	94	314 =	Stockton-on-Tees	90
263 =	Kirklees	94	314 =	Fenland	90
263 =	Newark & Sherwood	94	314 =	Ogwr	90
263 =	East Staffordshire	94	314 =	Western Isles	90
263 =	Taff-Ely	94	314 =	East Devon	90
263 =	North East Derbyshire	94	314 =	Leominster	90
263 =	Inverness	94	314 =	Moray	90
263 =	Southampton	94	314 =	St Helens	90
263 =	Renfrew	94	314 =	Caradon	90
263 =	Leeds	94	314 =	Rochdale	90
263 =	Eastbourne	94	314 =	Tameside	90
263 =	South Somerset	94	327 =	Carmarthen	89
277 =	Gloucester	93	327 =	King's Lynn & W. Norfolk	89
277 =	Taunton Deane	93	327 =	Alnwick	89
277 =	Bolton	93	327 =	Exeter	89
277 =	Bristol	93	327 =	Wrexham Maelor	89
277 =	The Wrekin	93	327 =	Chester-le-Street	89
277 =	Corby	93	327 =	Wigan	89
277 =	Erewash	93	327 =	Preston	89
277 =	Caithness	93	327 =	Orkney	89
277 =	Allerdale	93	327 =	Oldham	89
277 =	Bournemouth	93	327 =	Weymouth & Portland	89
277 =	West Dorset	93	327 =	Bassetlaw	89
277 =	Newport	93	327 =	Ipswich	89
289 =	Gosport	92	327 =	Wakefield	89
289 =	Sedgemoor	92	341 =	Portsmouth	88
289 =	Barking & Dagenham	92	341 =	Tendring	88
289 =	Lancaster	92	341 =	Berwickshire	88
289 =	Clackmannan	92	341 =	Lochaber	88
289 =	Teignbridge	92	341 =	Stewarty	88
289 =	Falkirk	92	341 =	Halton	88
289 =	Newcastle-under-Lyme	92	341 =	York	88
289 =	Nuneaton & Bedworth	92	341 =	Swansea	88
289 =	Tamworth	92	341 =	Cunninghame	88
299 =	Bradford	91	350 =	Birmingham	87
299 =	Dudley	91	350 =	Annandale & Eskdale	87
299 =	Carlisle	91	350 =	Waveney	87
299 =	West Lindsey	91	350 =	Kilmarnock & Loudon	87
299 =	Ross & Cromarty	91	350 =	Hereford	87
299 =	Hamilton	91	350 =	North Norfolk	87
299 =	Mid Devon	91	350 =	Blyth Valley	87
299 =	Darlington	91	350 =	Aberconwy	87
299 =	Christchurch	91	350 =	Coventry	87
299 =	South Holland	91	350 =	Lliw Valley	87
299 =	East Yorkshire	91	350 =	South Shropshire	87
299 =	Breckland	91	361 =	Carrick	86
299 =	Oswestry	91	361 =	North Tyneside	86
299 =	Cannock Chase	91	361 =	Blackpool	86
299 =	Derby	91	361 =	Kirkcaldy	86
314 =	Nithsdale	90	361 =	Dinefwr	86
314 =	Angus	90	361 =	Suffolk Coastal	86

Rank	Local Authority District/ Unitary Authority	Household Income Index	Rank	Local Authority District/ Unitary Authority	Household Income Index
361 =	Colwyn	86	413 =	Wolverhampton	81
361 =	Radnorshire	86	413 =	Middlesbrough	81
361 =	Inverclyde	86	413 =	Skye & Lochalsh	81
361 =	South Pembrokeshire	86	413 =	Dwyfor	81
371 =	Walsall	85	413 =	Restormel	81
371 =	Chesterfield	85	413 =	Sutherland	81
371 =	Hastings	85	413 =	Barrow-in-Furness	81
371 =	Great Yarmouth	85	423 =	Torridge	80
371 =	Arfon	85	423 =	Scunthorpe	80
371 =	Ynys Mon-Isle of Anglesey	85	423 =	Barnsley	80
371 =	Preseli Pembrokeshire	85	423 =	Mansfield	80
371 =	Berwick-upon-Tweed	85	423 =	Lincoln	80
371 =	Langbaurgh-on-Tees	85	423 =	Meirionnydd	80
371 =	Torfaen	85	429 =	Leicester	79
371 =	Roxburgh	85	429 =	Glasgow City	79
371 =	Blackburn	85	429 =	Ashfield	79
371 =	Neath	85	429 =	Liverpool	79
371 =	Torbay	85	429 =	Gateshead	79
371 =	Burnley	85	429 =	Nottingham	79
371 =	East Lindsey	85	429 =	Monklands	79
371 =	Montgomeryshire	85	429 =	Bolsover	79
371 =	Hyndburn	85	437 =	Manchester	78
389 =	Salford	84	437 =	Wigtown	78
389 =	Thanet	84	437 =	South Tyneside	78
389 =	Sedgefield	84	437 =	Hartlepool	78
389 =	Medina	84	437 =	Penwith	78
389 =	North Devon	84	437 =	Merthyr Tydfil	78
394 =	Dundee City	83	437 =	Knowsley	78
394 =	Badenoch & Strathspey	83	437 =	Clydebank	78
394 =	Scarborough	83	437 =	Great Grimsby	78
394 =	Argyll & Bute	83	437 =	Rhymney Valley	78
394 =	Newcastle upon Tyne	83	437 =	Derwentside	78
394 =	Ceredigion	83	448 =	Sunderland	77
394 =	Port Talbot	83	448 =	Sandwell	77
394 =	Wear Valley	83	448 =	Stoke-on-Trent	77
394 =	Rhuddlan	83	451 =	Wansbeck	75
394 =	Islwyn	83	451 =	Blaenau Gwent	75
394 =	South Wight	83	451 =	Cynon Valley	75
394 =	Sheffield	83	454	Rhondda	74
394 =	Plymouth	83	455	Cleethorpes	73
394 =	Norwich	83	456 =	Kingston upon Hull	72
394 =	Boston	83	456 =	Cumnock & Doon Valley	72
409 =	West Somerset	82	458	Pendle	71
409 =	Motherwell	82	459	Easington	69
409 =	Rotherham	82			
409 =	Kerrier	82			
413 =	Doncaster	81			
413 =	North Cornwall	81			
413 =	Llanelli	81			

CHAPTER 4

A PORTRAIT OF BRITAIN'S SIXTEEN LARGEST MARKETPLACES

1. GREATER LONDON

Derived using **CACI's Population Projections for 1998**   Data refers to **adults** except where indicated

Base: All GB		Total for Area	As a Percentage of: Area	GB Base	Index (GB av.=100)
Total Resident Population		7,106,768	100.0	100.0	100
of whom female		3,616,510	50.9	50.8	100
By age	*of whom female (%)*				
0– 4	48.8	520,201	7.3	6.5	113
5– 9	49.0	470,922	6.6	6.6	101
10–14	48.8	422,631	5.9	6.3	94
15–19	49.2	436,810	6.1	6.2	100
20–24	50.1	463,974	6.5	5.9	111
25–34	49.7	1,318,305	18.5	15.4	120
35–44	49.2	1,114,096	15.7	14.3	110
45–54	50.7	832,516	11.7	13.1	89
55–64	51.0	605,749	8.5	9.9	86
65–74	53.5	480,959	6.8	8.4	81
75+	65.4	440,605	6.2	7.4	84
Cost of Car (of only or most recently obtained car)					
Up to £2,999		1,192,291	20.9	22.9	91
£3,000– £4,999		660,334	11.6	13.5	86
£5,000– £6,999		564,038	9.9	11.1	89
£7,000– £9,999		500,138	8.8	11.1	79
£10,000–£19,999		718,198	12.6	12.8	99
£20,000+		83,959	1.5	1.1	131
Owner of a Company Car		471,630	8.3	7.7	108
Income Level of Households[1]					
Up to £4,999		242,675	8.2	10.9	75
£5,000– £9,999		360,555	12.1	16.3	75
£10,000–£14,999		442,149	14.9	18.1	82
£15,000–£19,999		430,929	14.5	15.7	92
£20,000–£24,999		368,534	12.4	12.0	104
£25,000–£29,999		292,060	9.8	8.5	116
£30,000–£34,999		221,392	7.5	5.9	127
£35,000–£39,999		163,642	5.5	4.0	139
£40,000–£44,999		119,363	4.0	2.7	150
£45,000–£49,999		86,574	2.9	1.8	160
£50,000+		241,605	8.1	4.3	191
Use of Multiple Stores in Last Year					
Dept. stores (not groceries)		4,689,687	82.4	78.5	105
Ladies' outfitters		2,844,007	50.0	53.5	93
Gentlemen's outfitters		3,371,608	59.2	64.0	93
DIY		3,293,741	57.9	60.5	96
Furniture, appliances, durables		3,521,097	61.8	64.6	96
Shoes		3,765,582	66.1	70.1	94

Data refers to **adults** except where indicated

Base: All GB	Total for Area	As a Percentage of: Area	GB Base	Index (GB av.=100)
Visits to Licensed Premises (at least weekly)				
Pubs	1,341,618	23.6	26.3	90
Licensed clubs	380,801	6.7	11.6	58
Wine bars	98,179	1.7	1.4	123

Annual Personal Expenditure		Data refers to **adults** except where indicated		
Base: All GB	Total Spend in Area (£m)	Spend Per Person in: Area (£)	GB Base (£)	Index (GB av.=100)
Convenience Goods				
Cigarettes, tobacco	1,308	184.1	184.1	100
Food	5,813	818.0	806.4	101
Household goods	1,205	169.5	174.1	97
Newspaper, magazines, etc.	489	68.8	67.0	103
Alcohol (off-licence)	927	130.5	122.5	107
Total	**9,742**	**1,370.8**	**1,354.2**	**101**
Comparison Goods				
Personal				
Children's, infantswear	364	51.2	52.4	98
Footwear	474	66.7	63.6	105
Menswear	728	102.4	97.5	105
Womenswear	1,220	171.6	171.2	100
Total	**2,785**	**391.9**	**384.8**	**102**
Home				
Brown goods	465	65.4	65.0	101
White goods	477	67.1	74.7	90
Furniture, floorcoverings	888	125.0	137.8	91
H'hold textiles, soft furnishings	357	50.2	50.6	99
Total	**2,187**	**307.7**	**328.0**	**94**
Leisure				
Books	240	33.8	29.3	115
DIY, gardening	941	132.4	143.8	92
Eating out	1,582	222.6	181.0	123
Photographic	265	37.3	26.2	142
Records, tapes, CDs, videos	316	44.5	41.9	106
Sports equipment	340	47.8	47.8	100
Toys, games, cycles, prams	192	27.0	30.9	87
Total	**3,874**	**545.2**	**500.9**	**109**

© CACI Limited, 1998.   Tel: 0171 602-6000 (London) / 0131 557-0123 (Edinburgh).
Note: [1] PayCheck data. Please see Chapter 3 for details.
Sources: © BMRB International Limited, 1997.
Buying potential information modelled using data from TGI 4/96–3/97.
© Verdict Research Limited, 1997.
Buying potential information modelled using data from Verdict Research.

2. GREATER MANCHESTER

Derived using CACI's Population Projections for 1998   Data refers to **adults** except where indicated

Base: All GB		Total for Area	As a Percentage of: Area	As a Percentage of: GB Base	Index (GB av.=100)
Total Resident Population		2,590,672	100.0	100.0	100
of whom female		1,313,261	50.7	50.8	100
By age	*of whom female (%)*				
0– 4	48.7	176,997	6.8	6.5	106
5– 9	48.7	184,230	7.1	6.6	109
10–14	48.7	177,013	6.8	6.3	108
15–19	48.8	166,876	6.4	6.2	105
20–24	48.7	157,339	6.1	5.9	103
25–34	48.7	407,412	15.7	15.4	102
35–44	49.4	365,126	14.1	14.3	99
45–54	49.6	327,941	12.7	13.1	96
55–64	50.3	250,700	9.7	9.9	97
65–74	54.2	202,092	7.8	8.4	93
75+	66.3	174,946	6.8	7.4	91
Cost of Car (of only or most recently obtained car)					
Up to £2,999		513,274	25.0	22.9	109
£3,000– £4,999		248,523	12.1	13.5	89
£5,000– £6,999		194,677	9.5	11.1	85
£7,000– £9,999		224,572	10.9	11.1	98
£10,000–£19,999		185,145	9.0	12.8	71
£20,000+		15,343	0.7	1.1	66
Owner of a Company Car		130,260	6.3	7.7	83
Income Level of Households[1]					
Up to £4,999		133,154	12.7	10.9	117
£5,000– £9,999		190,651	18.2	16.3	112
£10,000–£14,999		200,900	19.2	18.1	106
£15,000–£19,999		164,662	15.7	15.7	100
£20,000–£24,999		119,104	11.4	12.0	95
£25,000–£29,999		80,935	7.7	8.5	91
£30,000–£34,999		53,382	5.1	5.9	87
£35,000–£39,999		34,797	3.3	4.0	84
£40,000–£44,999		22,655	2.2	2.7	81
£45,000–£49,999		14,822	1.4	1.8	78
£50,000+		31,133	3.0	4.3	70
Use of Multiple Stores in Last Year					
Dept. stores (not groceries)		1,550,959	75.6	78.5	96
Ladies' outfitters		1,140,532	55.6	53.5	104
Gentlemen's outfitters		1,408,315	68.6	64.0	107
DIY		1,232,277	60.0	60.5	99
Furniture, appliances, durables		1,372,568	66.9	64.6	104
Shoes		1,479,661	72.1	70.1	103

Data refers to **adults** except where indicated

Base: All GB	Total for Area	As a Percentage of: Area	GB Base	Index (GB av.=100)
Visits to Licensed Premises (at least weekly)				
Pubs	584,464	28.5	26.3	108
Licensed clubs	276,179	13.5	11.6	116
Wine bars	37,261	1.8	1.4	130

Annual Personal Expenditure — Data refers to **adults** except where indicated

Base: All GB	Total Spend in Area (£m)	Spend Per Person in: Area (£)	GB Base (£)	Index (GB av.=100)
Convenience Goods				
Cigarettes, tobacco	611	235.8	184.1	128
Food	2,099	810.2	806.4	100
Household goods	445	171.9	174.1	99
Newspaper, magazines, etc.	173	66.8	67.0	100
Alcohol (off-licence)	335	129.3	122.5	106
Total	**3,663**	**1,413.9**	**1,354.2**	**104**
Comparison Goods				
Personal				
Children's, infantswear	144	55.5	52.4	106
Footwear	164	63.3	63.6	99
Menswear	247	95.4	97.5	98
Womenswear	431	166.5	171.2	97
Total	**986**	**380.6**	**384.8**	**99**
Home				
Brown goods	161	62.1	65.0	96
White goods	191	73.6	74.7	99
Furniture, floorcoverings	343	132.4	137.8	96
H'hold textiles, soft furnishings	139	53.7	50.6	106
Total	**834**	**321.7**	**328.0**	**98**
Leisure				
Books	71	27.4	29.3	93
DIY, gardening	353	136.1	143.8	95
Eating out	453	174.7	181.0	97
Photographic	73	28.2	26.2	108
Records, tapes, CDs, videos	106	41.0	41.9	98
Sports equipment	125	48.1	47.8	101
Toys, games, cycles, prams	90	34.8	30.9	112
Total	**1,270**	**490.3**	**500.9**	**98**

© CACI Limited, 1998.   Tel: 0171 602-6000 (London) / 0131 557-0123 (Edinburgh).
Note: ¹ PayCheck data. Please see Chapter 3 for details.
Sources: © BMRB International Limited, 1997.
Buying potential information modelled using data from TGI 4/96–3/97.
© Verdict Research Limited, 1997.
Buying potential information modelled using data from Verdict Research.

3. MERSEYSIDE

Derived using **CACI's Population Projections for 1998**   Data refers to **adults** except where indicated

Base: All GB	Total for Area	As a Percentage of: Area	As a Percentage of: GB Base	Index (GB av.=100)
Total Resident Population	1,421,001	100.0	100.0	100
of whom female	732,458	51.5	50.8	101
By age *of whom female (%)*				
0– 4	48.6	91,504	6.4	6.5	100
5– 9	48.7	96,100	6.8	6.6	103
10–14	48.9	96,453	6.8	6.3	107
15–19	48.9	91,322	6.4	6.2	104
20–24	48.8	83,637	5.9	5.9	100
25–34	49.6	210,238	14.8	15.4	96
35–44	50.6	201,797	14.2	14.3	99
45–54	50.6	176,054	12.4	13.1	94
55–64	51.7	144,315	10.2	9.9	102
65–74	54.8	125,623	8.8	8.4	105
75+	66.9	103,958	7.3	7.4	99
Cost of Car (of only or most recently obtained car)				
Up to £2,999	267,735	23.5	22.9	103
£3,000– £4,999	128,859	11.3	13.5	84
£5,000– £6,999	103,924	9.1	11.1	82
£7,000– £9,999	125,606	11.0	11.1	99
£10,000–£19,999	91,178	8.0	12.8	63
£20,000+	8,754	0.8	1.1	68
Owner of a Company Car	71,604	6.3	7.7	82
Income Level of Households[1]				
Up to £4,999	81,776	14.4	10.9	132
£5,000– £9,999	110,433	19.4	16.3	119
£10,000–£14,999	110,987	19.5	18.1	108
£15,000–£19,999	87,513	15.4	15.7	98
£20,000–£24,999	61,408	10.8	12.0	90
£25,000–£29,999	40,749	7.2	8.5	84
£30,000–£34,999	26,377	4.6	5.9	79
£35,000–£39,999	16,941	3.0	4.0	75
£40,000–£44,999	10,900	1.9	2.7	71
£45,000–£49,999	7,065	1.2	1.8	68
£50,000+	14,575	2.6	4.3	60
Use of Multiple Stores in Last Year				
Dept. stores (not groceries)	851,645	74.9	78.5	95
Ladies' outfitters	614,773	54.1	53.5	101
Gentlemen's outfitters	771,449	67.9	64.0	106
DIY	671,000	59.0	60.5	97
Furniture, appliances, durables	759,238	66.8	64.6	103
Shoes	806,079	70.9	70.1	101

Data refers to **adults** except where indicated

Base: All GB	Total for Area	As a Percentage of: Area	GB Base	Index (GB av.=100)
Visits to Licensed Premises (at least weekly)				
Pubs	318,630	28.0	26.3	106
Licensed clubs	165,358	14.5	11.6	125
Wine bars	17,100	1.5	1.4	108

Annual Personal Expenditure   Data refers to **adults** except where indicated

Base: All GB	Total Spend in Area (£m)	Spend Per Person in: Area (£)	GB Base (£)	Index (GB av.=100)
Convenience Goods				
Cigarettes, tobacco	360	253.5	184.1	138
Food	1,174	826.2	806.4	102
Household goods	244	171.6	174.1	99
Newspaper, magazines, etc.	97	68.1	67.0	102
Alcohol (off-licence)	181	127.7	122.5	104
Total	**2,056**	**1,447.0**	**1,354.2**	**107**
Comparison Goods				
Personal				
Children's, infantswear	83	58.3	52.4	111
Footwear	94	66.0	63.6	104
Menswear	132	92.7	97.5	95
Womenswear	247	173.6	171.2	101
Total	**555**	**390.6**	**384.8**	**102**
Home				
Brown goods	92	64.8	65.0	100
White goods	111	77.9	74.7	104
Furniture, floorcoverings	189	133.0	137.8	97
H'hold textiles, soft furnishings	76	53.3	50.6	105
Total	**468**	**329.0**	**328.0**	**100**
Leisure				
Books	40	27.9	29.3	95
DIY, gardening	195	137.0	143.8	95
Eating out	245	172.3	181.0	95
Photographic	38	26.4	26.2	100
Records, tapes, CDs, videos	59	41.8	41.9	100
Sports equipment	70	49.3	47.8	103
Toys, games, cycles, prams	51	36.1	30.9	117
Total	**698**	**490.8**	**500.9**	**98**

© CACI Limited, 1998.   Tel: 0171 602-6000 (London) / 0131 557-0123 (Edinburgh).
Note: [1] PayCheck data. Please see Chapter 3 for details.
Sources: © BMRB International Limited, 1997.
          Buying potential information modelled using data from TGI 4/96–3/97.
          © Verdict Research Limited, 1997.
          Buying potential information modelled using data from Verdict Research.

4. SOUTH YORKSHIRE

Derived using **CACI's Population Projections for 1998**   Data refers to **adults** except where indicated

Base: All GB	Total for Area	As a Percentage of: Area	As a Percentage of: GB Base	Index (GB av.=100)
Total Resident Population	1,304,796	100.0	100.0	100
of whom female	658,794	50.5	50.8	99
By age *of whom female (%)*				
0– 4 48.8	83,214	6.4	6.5	99
5– 9 48.6	86,395	6.6	6.6	101
10–14 48.8	81,874	6.3	6.3	99
15–19 48.3	77,773	6.0	6.2	97
20–24 48.1	75,543	5.8	5.9	99
25–34 47.7	207,186	15.9	15.4	103
35–44 48.7	186,469	14.3	14.3	100
45–54 49.7	167,063	12.8	13.1	97
55–64 50.8	131,061	10.0	9.9	101
65–74 53.9	111,321	8.5	8.4	102
75+ 65.1	96,897	7.4	7.4	101
Cost of Car (of only or most recently obtained car)				
Up to £2,999	226,781	21.5	22.9	94
£3,000– £4,999	121,777	11.6	13.5	85
£5,000– £6,999	122,780	11.7	11.1	105
£7,000– £9,999	102,859	9.8	11.1	88
£10,000–£19,999	108,851	10.3	12.8	81
£20,000+	5,633	0.5	1.1	48
Owner of a Company Car	62,325	5.9	7.7	77
Income Level of Households[1]				
Up to £4,999	82,754	15.4	10.9	142
£5,000– £9,999	112,654	21.0	16.3	129
£10,000–£14,999	109,330	20.4	18.1	113
£15,000–£19,999	82,157	15.3	15.7	98
£20,000–£24,999	54,859	10.2	12.0	86
£25,000–£29,999	34,772	6.5	8.5	76
£30,000–£34,999	21,625	4.0	5.9	69
£35,000–£39,999	13,425	2.5	4.0	63
£40,000–£44,999	8,398	1.6	2.7	58
£45,000–£49,999	5,319	1.0	1.8	55
£50,000+	10,523	2.0	4.3	46
Use of Multiple Stores in Last Year				
Dept. stores (not groceries)	768,825	73.0	78.5	93
Ladies' outfitters	577,360	54.8	53.5	103
Gentlemen's outfitters	693,619	65.9	64.0	103
DIY	644,071	61.1	60.5	101
Furniture, appliances, durables	665,646	63.2	64.6	98
Shoes	742,516	70.5	70.1	101

Data refers to **adults** except where indicated

Base: All GB	Total for Area	As a Percentage of: Area	GB Base	Index (GB av.=100)
Visits to Licensed Premises (at least weekly)				
Pubs	332,597	31.6	26.3	120
Licensed clubs	159,208	15.1	11.6	130
Wine bars	12,989	1.2	1.4	88

Annual Personal Expenditure

Data refers to **adults** except where indicated

Base: All GB	Total Spend in Area (£m)	Spend Per Person in: Area (£)	GB Base (£)	Index (GB av.=100)
Convenience Goods				
Cigarettes, tobacco	266	203.6	184.1	111
Food	1,059	811.4	806.4	101
Household goods	228	174.6	174.1	100
Newspaper, magazines, etc.	85	65.3	67.0	97
Alcohol (off-licence)	160	122.4	122.5	100
Total	**1,797**	**1,377.3**	**1,354.2**	**102**
Comparison Goods				
Personal				
Children's, infantswear	62	47.7	52.4	91
Footwear	79	60.6	63.6	95
Menswear	128	98.1	97.5	101
Womenswear	211	162.0	171.2	95
Total	**481**	**368.4**	**384.8**	**96**
Home				
Brown goods	87	66.7	65.0	103
White goods	107	81.8	74.7	110
Furniture, floorcoverings	211	161.8	137.8	117
H'hold textiles, soft furnishings	71	54.4	50.6	108
Total	**476**	**364.8**	**328.0**	**111**
Leisure				
Books	35	26.7	29.3	91
DIY, gardening	192	146.9	143.8	102
Eating out	224	172.0	181.0	95
Photographic	36	27.8	26.2	106
Records, tapes, CDs, videos	53	40.9	41.9	98
Sports equipment	61	46.4	47.8	97
Toys, games, cycles, prams	43	33.1	30.9	107
Total	**644**	**493.7**	**500.9**	**99**

© CACI Limited, 1998.   Tel: 0171 602-6000 (London) / 0131 557-0123 (Edinburgh).
Note: ¹ PayCheck data. Please see Chapter 3 for details.
Sources: © BMRB International Limited, 1997.
Buying potential information modelled using data from TGI 4/96–3/97.
© Verdict Research Limited, 1997.
Buying potential information modelled using data from Verdict Research.

5. TYNE AND WEAR

Derived using **CACI's Population Projections for 1998**   Data refers to **adults** except where indicated

Base: All GB	Total for Area	As a Percentage of: Area	As a Percentage of: GB Base	Index (GB av.=100)
Total Resident Population	1,128,971	100.0	100.0	100
of whom female	577,607	51.2	50.8	101
By age *of whom female (%)*				
0– 4	48.7	69,812	6.2	6.5	96
5– 9	48.6	73,010	6.5	6.6	99
10–14	49.0	72,336	6.4	6.3	101
15–19	48.9	73,719	6.5	6.2	106
20–24	48.6	67,771	6.0	5.9	102
25–34	49.1	170,484	15.1	15.4	98
35–44	49.6	164,798	14.6	14.3	102
45–54	49.9	141,702	12.6	13.1	96
55–64	51.4	111,304	9.9	9.9	99
65–74	54.9	102,568	9.1	8.4	108
75+	66.0	81,467	7.2	7.4	98
Cost of Car (of only or most recently obtained car)				
Up to £2,999	187,297	20.5	22.9	89
£3,000– £4,999	94,787	10.4	13.5	77
£5,000– £6,999	90,155	9.9	11.1	89
£7,000– £9,999	88,342	9.7	11.1	87
£10,000–£19,999	94,535	10.3	12.8	81
£20,000+	1,673	0.2	1.1	16
Owner of a Company Car	44,869	4.9	7.7	64
Income Level of Households[1]				
Up to £4,999	75,877	16.0	10.9	147
£5,000– £9,999	102,088	21.6	16.3	133
£10,000–£14,999	96,599	20.4	18.1	113
£15,000–£19,999	70,990	15.0	15.7	96
£20,000–£24,999	46,741	9.9	12.0	83
£25,000–£29,999	29,452	6.2	8.5	73
£30,000–£34,999	18,326	3.9	5.9	66
£35,000–£39,999	11,437	2.4	4.0	61
£40,000–£44,999	7,216	1.5	2.7	57
£45,000–£49,999	4,621	1.0	1.8	54
£50,000+	9,548	2.0	4.3	47
Use of Multiple Stores in Last Year				
Dept. stores (not groceries)	701,378	76.8	78.5	98
Ladies' outfitters	508,380	55.6	53.5	104
Gentlemen's outfitters	604,885	66.2	64.0	103
DIY	466,401	51.0	60.5	84
Furniture, appliances, durables	590,790	64.7	64.6	100
Shoes	645,878	70.7	70.1	101

Data refers to **adults** except where indicated

Base: All GB	Total for Area	As a Percentage of: Area	GB Base	Index (GB av.=100)
Visits to Licensed Premises (at least weekly)				
Pubs	303,238	33.2	26.3	126
Licensed clubs	185,977	20.4	11.6	175
Wine bars	19,185	2.1	1.4	150

Annual Personal Expenditure   Data refers to **adults** except where indicated

Base: All GB	Total Spend in Area (£m)	Spend per Person in: Area (£)	GB Base (£)	Index (GB av.=100)
Convenience Goods				
Cigarettes, tobacco	225	199.6	184.1	108
Food	933	826.6	806.4	103
Household goods	190	168.7	174.1	97
Newspaper, magazines, etc.	77	68.0	67.0	101
Alcohol (off-licence)	128	113.6	122.5	93
Total	**1,554**	**1,376.6**	**1,354.2**	102
Comparison Goods				
Personal				
Children's, infantswear	61	54.1	52.4	103
Footwear	75	66.2	63.6	104
Menswear	107	95.1	97.5	97
Womenswear	199	175.9	171.2	103
Total	**442**	**391.3**	**384.8**	102
Home				
Brown goods	79	69.7	65.0	107
White goods	71	62.8	74.7	84
Furniture, floorcoverings	162	143.5	137.8	104
H'hold textiles, soft furnishings	55	49.0	50.6	97
Total	**367**	**324.0**	**328.0**	99
Leisure				
Books	26	23.0	29.3	78
DIY, gardening	144	127.6	143.8	89
Eating out	206	182.1	181.0	101
Photographic	28	24.3	26.2	93
Records, tapes, CDs, videos	44	39.0	41.9	93
Sports equipment	57	50.4	47.8	105
Toys, games, cycles, prams	38	33.2	30.9	107
Total	**541**	**479.5**	**500.9**	96

© CACI Limited, 1998.   Tel: 0171 602-6000 (London) / 0131 557-0123 (Edinburgh).
Note: [1] PayCheck data. Please see Chapter 3 for details.
Sources: © BMRB International Limited, 1997.
Buying potential information modelled using data from TGI 4/96–3/97.
© Verdict Research Limited, 1997.
Buying potential information modelled using data from Verdict Research.

6. WEST MIDLANDS

Derived using **CACI's Population Projections for 1998**   Data refers to **adults** except where indicated

Base: All GB	Total for Area	As a Percentage of: Area	GB Base	Index (GB av.=100)
Total Resident Population	2,631,931	100.0	100.0	100
of whom female	1,333,338	50.7	50.8	100
By age *of whom female (%)*				
0– 4	48.9	185,793	7.1	6.5	109
5– 9	48.9	187,416	7.1	6.6	109
10–14	48.8	178,703	6.8	6.3	107
15–19	49.0	174,989	6.6	6.2	108
20–24	48.6	158,786	6.0	5.9	103
25–34	49.0	409,930	15.6	15.4	101
35–44	49.2	361,011	13.7	14.3	96
45–54	49.7	314,316	11.9	13.1	91
55–64	50.3	256,777	9.8	9.9	98
65–74	53.2	219,779	8.4	8.4	99
75+	65.2	184,431	7.0	7.4	95
Cost of Car (of only or most recently obtained car)				
Up to £2,999	511,195	24.6	22.9	107
£3,000– £4,999	259,482	12.5	13.5	92
£5,000– £6,999	200,938	9.7	11.1	87
£7,000– £9,999	174,876	8.4	11.1	75
£10,000–£19,999	203,227	9.8	12.8	77
£20,000+	13,338	0.6	1.1	57
Owner of a Company Car	116,561	5.6	7.7	73
Income Level of Households[1]				
Up to £4,999	142,595	13.8	10.9	126
£5,000– £9,999	199,368	19.2	16.3	118
£10,000–£14,999	205,251	19.8	18.1	109
£15,000–£19,999	163,197	15.7	15.7	100
£20,000–£24,999	114,088	11.0	12.0	92
£25,000–£29,999	75,017	7.2	8.5	85
£30,000–£34,999	48,097	4.6	5.9	79
£35,000–£39,999	30,657	3.0	4.0	74
£40,000–£44,999	19,631	1.9	2.7	71
£45,000–£49,999	12,696	1.2	1.8	67
£50,000+	26,407	2.5	4.3	60
Use of Multiple Stores in Last Year				
Dept. stores (not groceries)	1,570,032	75.5	78.5	96
Ladies' outfitters	1,155,009	55.5	53.5	104
Gentlemen's outfitters	1,363,862	65.6	64.0	103
DIY	1,239,065	59.6	60.5	98
Furniture, appliances, durables	1,352,514	65.0	64.6	101
Shoes	1,477,342	71.0	70.1	101

Data refers to **adults** except where indicated

Base: All GB	Total for Area	As a Percentage of:		Index (GB av.=100)
		Area	GB Base	
Visits to Licensed Premises (at least weekly)				
Pubs	606,943	29.2	26.3	111
Licensed clubs	265,370	12.8	11.6	110
Wine bars	29,769	1.4	1.4	102

Annual Personal Expenditure		Data refers to **adults** except where indicated		
Base: All GB	Total Spend in Area (£m)	Spend per Person in:		Index (GB av.=100)
		Area (£)	GB Base (£)	
Convenience Goods				
Cigarettes, tobacco	473	179.5	184.1	98
Food	2,069	786.2	806.4	97
Household goods	455	173.1	174.1	99
Newspaper, magazines, etc.	177	67.4	67.0	101
Alcohol (off-licence)	341	129.5	122.5	106
Total	**3,515**	**1,335.7**	**1,354.2**	**99**
Comparison Goods				
Personal				
Children's, infantswear	129	49.1	52.4	94
Footwear	159	60.5	63.6	95
Menswear	240	91.4	97.5	94
Womenswear	411	156.3	171.2	91
Total	**940**	**357.2**	**384.8**	**93**
Home				
Brown goods	171	65.0	65.0	100
White goods	208	79.2	74.7	106
Furniture, floorcoverings	372	141.2	137.8	102
H'hold textiles, soft furnishings	133	50.5	50.6	100
Total	**884**	**335.8**	**328.0**	**102**
Leisure				
Books	75	28.6	29.3	98
DIY, gardening	384	145.7	143.8	101
Eating out	439	166.9	181.0	92
Photographic	56	21.2	26.2	81
Records, tapes, CDs, videos	118	44.9	41.9	107
Sports equipment	121	46.1	47.8	97
Toys, games, cycles, prams	81	30.8	30.9	100
Total	**1,275**	**484.2**	**500.9**	**97**

© CACI Limited, 1998.   Tel: 0171 602-6000 (London) / 0131 557-0123 (Edinburgh).
Note: [1] PayCheck data. Please see Chapter 3 for details.
Sources: © BMRB International Limited, 1997.
              Buying potential information modelled using data from TGI 4/96–3/97.
              © Verdict Research Limited, 1997.
              Buying potential information modelled using data from Verdict Research.

7. WEST YORKSHIRE

Derived using **CACI's Population Projections for 1998**   Data refers to **adults** except where indicated

Base: All GB		Total for Area	As a Percentage of: Area	As a Percentage of: GB Base	Index (GB av.=100)
Total Resident Population		2,121,515	100.0	100.0	100
of whom female		1,074,089	50.6	50.8	100
By age	*of whom female (%)*				
0– 4	48.8	144,004	6.8	6.5	105
5– 9	49.1	146,740	6.9	6.6	106
10–14	48.7	140,434	6.6	6.3	104
15–19	48.6	139,042	6.6	6.2	106
20–24	48.5	128,632	6.1	5.9	103
25–34	48.2	335,441	15.8	15.4	102
35–44	49.0	302,383	14.3	14.3	100
45–54	49.7	269,104	12.7	13.1	97
55–64	50.8	201,340	9.5	9.9	95
65–74	54.3	168,141	7.9	8.4	94
75+	65.6	146,254	6.9	7.4	93
Cost of Car (of only or most recently obtained car)					
Up to £2,999		347,794	20.6	22.9	90
£3,000– £4,999		186,015	11.0	13.5	81
£5,000– £6,999		203,060	12.0	11.1	108
£7,000– £9,999		170,245	10.1	11.1	90
£10,000–£19,999		187,614	11.1	12.8	87
£20,000+		10,328	0.6	1.1	54
Owner of a Company Car		107,272	6.3	7.7	83
Income Level of Households[1]					
Up to £4,999		108,023	12.5	10.9	115
£5,000– £9,999		155,616	18.1	16.3	111
£10,000–£14,999		165,367	19.2	18.1	106
£15,000–£19,999		136,521	15.8	15.7	101
£20,000–£24,999		99,136	11.5	12.0	96
£25,000–£29,999		67,410	7.8	8.5	92
£30,000–£34,999		44,399	5.2	5.9	88
£35,000–£39,999		28,877	3.4	4.0	84
£40,000–£44,999		18,758	2.2	2.7	81
£45,000–£49,999		12,249	1.4	1.8	78
£50,000+		25,650	3.0	4.3	70
Use of Multiple Stores in Last Year					
Dept. stores (not groceries)		1,254,261	74.2	78.5	94
Ladies' outfitters		915,005	54.1	53.5	101
Gentlemen's outfitters		1,105,932	65.4	64.0	102
DIY		1,034,801	61.2	60.5	101
Furniture, appliances, durables		1,070,087	63.3	64.6	98
Shoes		1,194,543	70.7	70.1	101

Data refers to **adults** except where indicated

Base: All GB	Total for Area	As a Percentage of:		Index (GB av.=100)
		Area	GB Base	
Visits to Licensed Premises (at least weekly)				
Pubs	535,822	31.7	26.3	120
Licensed clubs	229,991	13.6	11.6	117
Wine bars	21,153	1.3	1.4	90

Annual Personal Expenditure		Data refers to **adults** except where indicated		
Base: All GB	Total Spend in Area (£m)	Spend per Person in:		Index (GB av.=100)
		Area (£)	GB Base (£)	
Convenience Goods				
Cigarettes, tobacco	400	188.5	184.1	102
Food	1,694	798.7	806.4	99
Household goods	366	172.6	174.1	99
Newspaper, magazines, etc.	136	64.3	67.0	96
Alcohol (off-licence)	260	122.6	122.5	100
Total	**2,857**	**1,346.6**	**1,354.2**	**99**
Comparison Goods				
Personal				
Children's, infantswear	98	46.2	52.4	88
Footwear	130	61.2	63.6	96
Menswear	207	97.7	97.5	100
Womenswear	349	164.6	171.2	96
Total	**784**	**369.7**	**384.8**	**96**
Home				
Brown goods	144	68.0	65.0	105
White goods	179	84.2	74.7	113
Furniture, floorcoverings	367	173.0	137.8	126
H'hold textiles, soft furnishings	120	56.6	50.6	112
Total	**810**	**381.7**	**328.0**	**116**
Leisure				
Books	57	26.8	29.3	91
DIY, gardening	310	146.0	143.8	102
Eating out	370	174.4	181.0	96
Photographic	62	29.2	26.2	111
Records, tapes, CDs, videos	89	41.9	41.9	100
Sports equipment	98	46.2	47.8	97
Toys, games, cycles, prams	68	31.8	30.9	103
Total	**1,053**	**496.4**	**500.9**	**99**

© CACI Limited, 1998.   Tel: 0171 602-6000 (London) / 0131 557-0123 (Edinburgh).
Note: [1] PayCheck data. Please see Chapter 3 for details.
Sources: © BMRB International Limited, 1997.
Buying potential information modelled using data from TGI 4/96–3/97.
© Verdict Research Limited, 1997.
Buying potential information modelled using data from Verdict Research.

8. CENTRAL CLYDESIDE

Derived using **CACI's Population Projections for 1998**   Data refers to **adults** except where indicated

Base: All GB	Total for Area	As a Percentage of: Area	As a Percentage of: GB Base	Index (GB av.=100)
Total Resident Population	1,602,552	100.0	100.0	100
of whom female	830,108	51.8	50.8	102
By age *of whom female (%)*				
0– 4	48.8	104,199	6.5	6.5	101
5– 9	48.8	102,975	6.4	6.6	98
10–14	49.0	102,503	6.4	6.3	101
15–19	49.1	104,666	6.5	6.2	106
20–24	49.9	99,839	6.2	5.9	106
25–34	50.0	259,266	16.2	15.4	105
35–44	50.5	239,036	14.9	14.3	104
45–54	50.9	192,146	12.0	13.1	91
55–64	52.8	163,431	10.2	9.9	103
65–74	56.4	136,068	8.5	8.4	101
75+	67.4	98,423	6.1	7.4	83
Cost of Car (of only or most recently obtained car)				
Up to £2,999	180,843	14.0	22.9	61
£3,000– £4,999	129,659	10.0	13.5	74
£5,000– £6,999	124,190	9.6	11.1	87
£7,000– £9,999	165,501	12.8	11.1	115
£10,000–£19,999	136,602	10.6	12.8	83
£20,000+	11,760	0.9	1.1	81
Owner of a Company Car	77,008	6.0	7.7	78
Income Level of Households[1]				
Up to £4,999	92,367	14.0	10.9	129
£5,000– £9,999	128,106	19.4	16.3	120
£10,000–£14,999	127,816	19.4	18.1	107
£15,000–£19,999	100,281	15.2	15.7	97
£20,000–£24,999	70,717	10.7	12.0	90
£25,000–£29,999	47,514	7.2	8.5	85
£30,000–£34,999	31,233	4.7	5.9	81
£35,000–£39,999	20,370	3.1	4.0	78
£40,000–£44,999	13,292	2.0	2.7	75
£45,000–£49,999	8,724	1.3	1.8	73
£50,000+	18,539	2.8	4.3	66
Use of Multiple Stores in Last Year				
Dept. stores (not groceries)	1,004,059	77.7	78.5	99
Ladies' outfitters	667,540	51.6	53.5	97
Gentlemen's outfitters	770,930	59.6	64.0	93
DIY	762,408	59.0	60.5	97
Furniture, appliances, durables	831,867	64.3	64.6	100
Shoes	946,847	73.2	70.1	104

Data refers to **adults** except where indicated

Base: All GB	Total for Area	As a Percentage of:		Index (GB av.=100)
		Area	GB Base	
Visits to Licensed Premises (at least weekly)				
Pubs	294,258	22.8	26.3	86
Licensed clubs	171,831	13.3	11.6	114
Wine bars	12,105	0.9	1.4	67

Annual Personal Expenditure		Data refers to **adults** except where indicated		
Base: All GB	Total Spend in Area (£m)	Spend per Person in:		Index (GB av.=100)
		Area (£)	GB Base (£)	
Convenience Goods				
Cigarettes, tobacco	393	245.4	184.1	133
Food	1,396	871.4	806.4	108
Household goods	262	163.3	174.1	94
Newspaper, magazines, etc.	113	70.3	67.0	105
Alcohol (off-licence)	193	120.3	122.5	98
Total	**2,357**	**1,470.6**	**1,354.2**	**109**
Comparison Goods				
Personal				
Children's, infantswear	94	58.5	52.4	112
Footwear	111	69.1	63.6	109
Menswear	173	107.9	97.5	111
Womenswear	286	178.1	171.2	104
Total	**663**	**413.5**	**384.8**	**107**
Home				
Brown goods	105	65.3	65.0	100
White goods	150	93.4	74.7	125
Furniture, floorcoverings	279	173.9	137.8	126
H'hold textiles, soft furnishings	88	54.6	50.6	108
Total	**620**	**387.1**	**328.0**	**118**
Leisure				
Books	45	28.1	29.3	96
DIY, gardening	242	151.3	143.8	105
Eating out	307	191.2	181.0	106
Photographic	41	25.4	26.2	97
Records, tapes, CDs, videos	77	48.3	41.9	115
Sports equipment	83	52.0	47.8	109
Toys, games, cycles, prams	47	29.0	30.9	94
Total	**842**	**525.4**	**500.9**	**105**

© CACI Limited, 1998.   Tel: 0171 602-6000 (London) / 0131 557-0123 (Edinburgh).
Note: ¹ PayCheck data. Please see Chapter 3 for details.
Sources: © BMRB International Limited, 1997.
             Buying potential information modelled using data from TGI 4/96–3/97.
             © Verdict Research Limited, 1997.
             Buying potential information modelled using data from Verdict Research.

9. EDINBURGH

Derived using **CACI's Population Projections for 1998** | Data refers to **adults** except where indicated

Base: All GB		Total for Area	As a Percentage of: Area	GB Base	Index (GB av.=100)
Total Resident Population		449,713	100.0	100.0	100
of whom female		232,134	51.6	50.8	102
By age	*of whom female (%)*				
0– 4	48.9	26,891	6.0	6.5	93
5– 9	49.2	25,395	5.6	6.6	86
10–14	49.0	23,666	5.3	6.3	83
15–19	49.2	25,431	5.7	6.2	92
20–24	50.3	33,815	7.5	5.9	128
25–34	48.7	83,403	18.5	15.4	120
35–44	49.5	67,596	15.0	14.3	105
45–54	51.3	53,496	11.9	13.1	91
55–64	52.3	41,228	9.2	9.9	92
65–74	56.6	37,144	8.3	8.4	98
75+	67.2	31,648	7.0	7.4	95
Cost of Car (of only or most recently obtained car)					
Up to £2,999		46,810	12.5	22.9	55
£3,000– £4,999		42,749	11.4	13.5	84
£5,000– £6,999		43,224	11.6	11.1	104
£7,000– £9,999		58,935	15.8	11.1	142
£10,000–£19,999		50,579	13.5	12.8	106
£20,000+		6,472	1.7	1.1	154
Owner of a Company Car		30,032	8.0	7.7	105
Income Level of Households[1]					
Up to £4,999		20,557	10.4	10.9	96
£5,000– £9,999		31,717	16.0	16.3	99
£10,000–£14,999		35,185	17.8	18.1	98
£15,000–£19,999		30,454	15.4	15.7	98
£20,000–£24,999		23,407	11.8	12.0	99
£25,000–£29,999		16,959	8.6	8.5	101
£30,000–£34,999		11,925	6.0	5.9	103
£35,000–£39,999		8,269	4.2	4.0	105
£40,000–£44,999		5,706	2.9	2.7	108
£45,000–£49,999		3,941	2.0	1.8	110
£50,000+		9,556	4.8	4.3	113
Use of Multiple Stores in Last Year					
Dept. stores (not groceries)		307,648	82.3	78.5	105
Ladies' outfitters		187,857	50.3	53.5	94
Gentlemen's outfitters		214,587	57.4	64.0	90
DIY		220,252	58.9	60.5	97
Furniture, appliances, durables		237,366	63.5	64.6	98
Shoes		278,111	74.4	70.1	106

Data refers to **adults** except where indicated

Base: All GB	Total for Area	As a Percentage of:		Index (GB av.=100)
		Area	GB Base	
Visits to Licensed Premises (at least weekly)				
Pubs	95,384	25.5	26.3	97
Licensed clubs	42,292	11.3	11.6	97
Wine bars	6,230	1.7	1.4	119

Annual Personal Expenditure		Data refers to **adults** except where indicated		
Base: All GB	Total Spend in Area (£m)	Spend per Person in:		Index (GB av.=100)
		Area (£)	GB Base (£)	
Convenience Goods				
Cigarettes, tobacco	92	203.8	184.1	111
Food	405	901.4	806.4	112
Household goods	76	167.8	174.1	96
Newspaper, magazines, etc.	33	72.5	67.0	108
Alcohol (off-licence)	61	135.2	122.5	110
Total	666	1,480.7	1,354.2	109
Comparison Goods				
Personal				
Children's, infantswear	25	55.4	52.4	106
Footwear	33	73.5	63.6	115
Menswear	54	120.3	97.5	123
Womenswear	86	190.9	171.2	111
Total	198	440.0	384.8	114
Home				
Brown goods	31	69.0	65.0	106
White goods	46	101.8	74.7	136
Furniture, floorcoverings	75	166.0	137.8	120
H'hold textiles, soft furnishings	25	55.7	50.6	110
Total	177	392.5	328.0	120
Leisure				
Books	16	34.6	29.3	118
DIY, gardening	67	148.6	143.8	103
Eating out	106	235.9	181.0	130
Photographic	13	28.7	26.2	109
Records, tapes, CDs, videos	21	47.5	41.9	113
Sports equipment	25	54.4	47.8	114
Toys, games, cycles, prams	11	25.0	30.9	81
Total	259	574.8	500.9	115

© CACI Limited, 1998.   Tel: 0171 602-6000 (London) / 0131 557-0123 (Edinburgh).
Note: [1] PayCheck data. Please see Chapter 3 for details.
Sources: © BMRB International Limited, 1997.
             Buying potential information modelled using data from TGI 4/96–3/97.
             © Verdict Research Limited, 1997.
             Buying potential information modelled using data from Verdict Research.

10. BRISTOL

Derived using **CACI's Population Projections for 1998**   Data refers to **adults** except where indicated

Base: All GB	Total for Area	As a Percentage of: Area	As a Percentage of: GB Base	Index (GB av.=100)
Total Resident Population	400,806	100.0	100.0	100
of whom female	201,081	50.2	50.8	99
By age *of whom female (%)*				
0– 4 49.0	26,527	6.6	6.5	102
5– 9 48.1	25,824	6.4	6.6	98
10–14 48.9	23,393	5.8	6.3	92
15–19 48.9	25,169	6.3	6.2	102
20–24 47.0	27,361	6.8	5.9	116
25–34 46.9	72,364	18.1	15.4	117
35–44 48.4	57,366	14.3	14.3	100
45–54 49.7	45,418	11.3	13.1	86
55–64 50.2	34,458	8.6	9.9	86
65–74 54.3	32,085	8.0	8.4	95
75+ 64.8	30,841	7.7	7.4	104
Cost of Car (of only or most recently obtained car)				
Up to £2,999	88,371	27.2	22.9	119
£3,000– £4,999	49,113	15.1	13.5	112
£5,000– £6,999	31,610	9.7	11.1	88
£7,000– £9,999	30,944	9.5	11.1	85
£10,000–£19,999	27,264	8.4	12.8	66
£20,000+	2,757	0.8	1.1	75
Owner of a Company Car	20,512	6.3	7.7	82
Income Level of Households[1]				
Up to £4,999	20,777	12.3	10.9	113
£5,000– £9,999	30,645	18.2	16.3	112
£10,000–£14,999	32,700	19.4	18.1	107
£15,000–£19,999	26,740	15.9	15.7	101
£20,000–£24,999	19,156	11.4	12.0	95
£25,000–£29,999	12,895	7.7	8.5	90
£30,000–£34,999	8,468	5.0	5.9	86
£35,000–£39,999	5,534	3.3	4.0	83
£40,000–£44,999	3,636	2.2	2.7	80
£45,000–£49,999	2,415	1.4	1.8	79
£50,000+	5,493	3.3	4.3	76
Use of Multiple Stores in Last Year				
Dept. stores (not groceries)	238,585	73.4	78.5	93
Ladies' outfitters	172,921	53.2	53.5	100
Gentlemen's outfitters	198,742	61.1	64.0	96
DIY	184,589	56.8	60.5	94
Furniture, appliances, durables	198,214	61.0	64.6	94
Shoes	221,626	68.2	70.1	97

Data refers to **adults** except where indicated

Base: All GB	Total for Area	As a Percentage of: Area	GB Base	Index (GB av.=100)
Visits to Licensed Premises (at least weekly)				
Pubs	93,786	28.9	26.3	110
Licensed clubs	46,917	14.4	11.6	124
Wine bars	3,644	1.1	1.4	80

Annual Personal Expenditure Data refers to **adults** except where indicated

Base: All GB	Total Spend in Area (£m)	Spend per Person in: Area (£)	GB Base (£)	Index (GB av.=100)
Convenience Goods				
Cigarettes, tobacco	66	164.1	184.1	89
Food	339	846.7	806.4	105
Household goods	69	173.2	174.1	99
Newspaper, magazines, etc.	27	66.5	67.0	99
Alcohol (off-licence)	45	112.1	122.5	91
Total	**546**	**1,362.7**	**1,354.2**	**101**
Comparison Goods				
Personal				
Children's, infantswear	19	47.4	52.4	90
Footwear	26	63.6	63.6	100
Menswear	39	97.0	97.5	99
Womenswear	74	185.0	171.2	108
Total	**158**	**392.9**	**384.8**	**102**
Home				
Brown goods	25	63.2	65.0	97
White goods	27	66.8	74.7	89
Furniture, floorcoverings	51	126.4	137.8	92
H'hold textiles, soft furnishings	17	41.7	50.6	82
Total	**120**	**298.1**	**328.0**	**91**
Leisure				
Books	13	31.3	29.3	107
DIY, gardening	57	143.0	143.8	99
Eating out	70	175.7	181.0	97
Photographic	10	24.5	26.2	94
Records, tapes, CDs, videos	17	41.4	41.9	99
Sports equipment	20	50.4	47.8	105
Toys, games, cycles, prams	12	29.5	30.9	95
Total	**199**	**495.7**	**500.9**	**99**

© CACI Limited, 1998. Tel: 0171 602-6000 (London) / 0131 557-0123 (Edinburgh).
Note: ¹ PayCheck data. Please see Chapter 3 for details.
Sources: © BMRB International Limited, 1997.
           Buying potential information modelled using data from TGI 4/96–3/97.
           © Verdict Research Limited, 1997.
           Buying potential information modelled using data from Verdict Research.

11. CARDIFF

Derived using **CACI's Population Projections** for 1998   Data refers to **adults** except where indicated

Base: All GB	Total for Area	As a Percentage of: Area	As a Percentage of: GB Base	Index (GB av.=100)
Total Resident Population	309,548	100.0	100.0	100
of whom female	157,327	50.8	50.8	100
By age *of whom female (%)*				
0– 4 48.7	21,569	7.0	6.5	108
5– 9 48.6	21,311	6.9	6.6	105
10–14 48.9	20,073	6.5	6.3	102
15–19 50.4	22,161	7.2	6.2	116
20–24 48.4	18,530	6.0	5.9	102
25–34 48.8	54,234	17.5	15.4	114
35–44 49.1	43,987	14.2	14.3	99
45–54 49.8	34,634	11.2	13.1	85
55–64 51.6	26,724	8.6	9.9	87
65–74 53.9	24,556	7.9	8.4	94
75+ 65.1	21,769	7.0	7.4	95
Cost of Car (of only or most recently obtained car)				
Up to £2,999	62,179	25.2	22.9	110
£3,000– £4,999	36,856	14.9	13.5	110
£5,000– £6,999	23,926	9.7	11.1	87
£7,000– £9,999	26,760	10.9	11.1	97
£10,000–£19,999	23,705	9.6	12.8	75
£20,000+	2,807	1.1	1.1	101
Owner of a Company Car	17,077	6.9	7.7	90
Income Level of Households[1]				
Up to £4,999	14,576	11.6	10.9	107
£5,000– £9,999	21,730	17.3	16.3	106
£10,000–£14,999	23,763	18.9	18.1	104
£15,000–£19,999	20,038	15.9	15.7	102
£20,000–£24,999	14,789	11.8	12.0	98
£25,000–£29,999	10,206	8.1	8.5	96
£30,000–£34,999	6,825	5.4	5.9	93
£35,000–£39,999	4,511	3.6	4.0	90
£40,000–£44,999	2,977	2.4	2.7	88
£45,000–£49,999	1,974	1.6	1.8	86
£50,000+	4,291	3.4	4.3	80
Use of Multiple Stores in Last Year				
Dept. stores (not groceries)	183,059	74.2	78.5	95
Ladies' outfitters	131,049	53.1	53.5	99
Gentlemen's outfitters	150,946	61.2	64.0	96
DIY	142,724	57.9	60.5	96
Furniture, appliances, durables	151,234	61.3	64.6	95
Shoes	168,491	68.3	70.1	97

Data refers to **adults** except where indicated

Base: All GB	Total for Area	As a Percentage of:		Index (GB av.=100)
		Area	GB Base	
Visits to Licensed Premises (at least weekly)				
Pubs	71,749	29.1	26.3	111
Licensed clubs	34,637	14.0	11.6	121
Wine bars	2,291	0.9	1.4	67

Annual Personal Expenditure　　　　Data refers to **adults** except where indicated

Base: All GB	Total Spend in Area (£m)	Spend per Person in:		Index (GB av.=100)
		Area (£)	GB Base (£)	
Convenience Goods				
Cigarettes, tobacco	47	153.0	184.1	83
Food	242	781.1	806.4	97
Household goods	51	165.9	174.1	95
Newspaper, magazines, etc.	20	63.6	67.0	95
Alcohol (off-licence)	34	109.0	122.5	89
Total	**394**	**1,272.5**	**1,354.2**	**94**
Comparison Goods				
Personal				
Children's, infantswear	14	46.0	52.4	88
Footwear	19	61.8	63.6	97
Menswear	29	93.4	97.5	96
Womenswear	56	181.2	171.2	106
Total	**118**	**382.4**	**384.8**	**99**
Home				
Brown goods	19	61.1	65.0	94
White goods	20	65.0	74.7	87
Furniture, floorcoverings	37	120.1	137.8	87
H'hold textiles, soft furnishings	12	38.6	50.6	76
Total	**88**	**284.8**	**328.0**	**87**
Leisure				
Books	9	29.2	29.3	99
DIY, gardening	43	138.7	143.8	96
Eating out	50	163.0	181.0	90
Photographic	7	23.4	26.2	89
Records, tapes, CDs, videos	12	39.4	41.9	94
Sports equipment	15	49.3	47.8	103
Toys, games, cycles, prams	9	28.3	30.9	92
Total	**146**	**471.2**	**500.9**	**94**

© CACI Limited, 1998.　Tel: 0171 602-6000 (London) / 0131 557-0123 (Edinburgh).
Note:　　¹ PayCheck data. Please see Chapter 3 for details.
Sources:　© BMRB International Limited, 1997.
　　　　　Buying potential information modelled using data from TGI 4/96–3/97.
　　　　　© Verdict Research Limited, 1997.
　　　　　Buying potential information modelled using data from Verdict Research.

12. LEICESTER

Derived using **CACI's Population Projections for 1998**   Data refers to **adults** except where indicated

Base: All GB		Total for Area	As a Percentage of: Area	As a Percentage of: GB Base	Index (GB av.=100)
Total Resident Population		299,718	100.0	100.0	100
of whom female		151,221	50.5	50.8	99
By age	*of whom female (%)*				
0– 4	48.4	23,318	7.8	6.5	120
5– 9	48.4	22,632	7.6	6.6	115
10–14	48.6	20,608	6.9	6.3	108
15–19	50.0	21,494	7.2	6.2	117
20–24	49.1	23,684	7.9	5.9	134
25–34	48.7	52,098	17.4	15.4	113
35–44	48.9	39,997	13.3	14.3	93
45–54	49.5	29,394	9.8	13.1	75
55–64	50.8	23,859	8.0	9.9	80
65–74	53.2	22,324	7.4	8.4	89
75+	64.7	20,310	6.8	7.4	92
Cost of Car (of only or most recently obtained car)					
Up to £2,999		58,562	25.1	22.9	110
£3,000– £4,999		28,596	12.3	13.5	91
£5,000– £6,999		19,472	8.4	11.1	75
£7,000– £9,999		14,697	6.3	11.1	57
£10,000–£19,999		15,421	6.6	12.8	52
£20,000+		943	0.4	1.1	36
Owner of a Company Car		8,596	3.7	7.7	48
Income Level of Households[1]					
Up to £4,999		18,657	16.2	10.9	149
£5,000– £9,999		24,608	21.3	16.3	131
£10,000–£14,999		23,790	20.6	18.1	114
£15,000–£19,999		17,788	15.4	15.7	98
£20,000–£24,999		11,732	10.2	12.0	85
£25,000–£29,999		7,291	6.3	8.5	74
£30,000–£34,999		4,421	3.8	5.9	66
£35,000–£39,999		2,666	2.3	4.0	58
£40,000–£44,999		1,617	1.4	2.7	52
£45,000–£49,999		993	0.9	1.8	47
£50,000+		1,798	1.6	4.3	37
Use of Multiple Stores in Last Year					
Dept. stores (not groceries)		171,819	73.7	78.5	94
Ladies' outfitters		132,108	56.7	53.5	106
Gentlemen's outfitters		152,290	65.3	64.0	102
DIY		135,778	58.2	60.5	96
Furniture, appliances, durables		150,691	64.6	64.6	100
Shoes		167,949	72.0	70.1	103

Data refers to **adults** except where indicated

Base: All GB	Total for Area	As a Percentage of: Area	GB Base	Index (GB av.=100)
Visits to Licensed Premises (at least weekly)				
Pubs	71,812	30.8	26.3	117
Licensed clubs	31,796	13.6	11.6	117
Wine bars	2,793	1.2	1.4	86

Annual Personal Expenditure		Data refers to **adults** except where indicated		
Base: All GB	Total Spend in Area (£m)	Spend per Person in: Area (£)	GB Base (£)	Index (GB av.=100)
Convenience Goods				
Cigarettes, tobacco	55	184.8	184.1	100
Food	222	739.1	806.4	92
Household goods	51	169.4	174.1	97
Newspaper, magazines, etc.	20	65.6	67.0	98
Alcohol (off-licence)	40	131.8	122.5	108
Total	**387**	**1,290.7**	**1,354.2**	**95**
Comparison Goods				
Personal				
Children's, infantswear	15	48.2	52.4	92
Footwear	17	57.4	63.6	90
Menswear	27	91.0	97.5	93
Womenswear	43	142.9	171.2	83
Total	**102**	**339.6**	**384.8**	**88**
Home				
Brown goods	19	63.7	65.0	98
White goods	22	74.5	74.7	100
Furniture, floorcoverings	40	132.7	137.8	96
H'hold textiles, soft furnishings	14	45.4	50.6	90
Total	**95**	**316.3**	**328.0**	**96**
Leisure				
Books	8	27.5	29.3	94
DIY, gardening	42	141.2	143.8	98
Eating out	48	159.7	181.0	88
Photographic	6	20.1	26.2	77
Records, tapes, CDs, videos	13	44.4	41.9	106
Sports equipment	14	44.9	47.8	94
Toys, games, cycles, prams	9	29.9	30.9	97
Total	**140**	**467.6**	**500.9**	**93**

© CACI Limited, 1998.   Tel: 0171 602-6000 (London) / 0131 557-0123 (Edinburgh).
Note: [1] PayCheck data. Please see Chapter 3 for details.
Sources: © BMRB International Limited, 1997.
Buying potential information modelled using data from TGI 4/96–3/97.
© Verdict Research Limited, 1997.
Buying potential information modelled using data from Verdict Research.

13. NOTTINGHAM

Derived using **CACI's Population Projections for 1998**   Data refers to **adults** except where indicated

Base: All GB	Total for Area	As a Percentage of: Area	As a Percentage of: GB Base	Index (GB av.=100)
Total Resident Population	284,026	100.0	100.0	100
of whom female	143,840	50.6	50.8	100
By age *of whom female (%)*				
0– 4 47.8	20,924	7.4	6.5	114
5– 9 49.4	20,471	7.2	6.6	110
10–14 48.8	17,781	6.3	6.3	99
15–19 49.2	19,274	6.8	6.2	110
20–24 48.3	23,700	8.3	5.9	142
25–34 49.1	50,074	17.6	15.4	114
35–44 49.9	35,645	12.5	14.3	88
45–54 49.3	28,624	10.1	13.1	77
55–64 50.8	24,394	8.6	9.9	86
65–74 53.6	23,344	8.2	8.4	98
75+ 64.2	19,795	7.0	7.4	94
Cost of Car (of only or most recently obtained car)				
Up to £2,999	57,213	25.4	22.9	111
£3,000– £4,999	27,121	12.1	13.5	89
£5,000– £6,999	19,075	8.5	11.1	76
£7,000– £9,999	17,375	7.7	11.1	69
£10,000–£19,999	18,532	8.2	12.8	65
£20,000+	1,245	0.6	1.1	49
Owner of a Company Car	10,838	4.8	7.7	63
Income Level of Households[1]				
Up to £4,999	19,454	16.6	10.9	153
£5,000– £9,999	25,366	21.7	16.3	133
£10,000–£14,999	24,039	20.5	18.1	113
£15,000–£19,999	17,619	15.0	15.7	96
£20,000–£24,999	11,477	9.8	12.0	82
£25,000–£29,999	7,129	6.1	8.5	72
£30,000–£34,999	4,374	3.7	5.9	64
£35,000–£39,999	2,698	2.3	4.0	58
£40,000–£44,999	1,687	1.4	2.7	54
£45,000–£49,999	1,073	0.9	1.8	50
£50,000+	2,190	1.9	4.3	44
Use of Multiple Stores in Last Year				
Dept. stores (not groceries)	165,925	73.8	78.5	94
Ladies' outfitters	125,597	55.9	53.5	104
Gentlemen's outfitters	146,642	65.2	64.0	102
DIY	130,952	58.2	60.5	96
Furniture, appliances, durables	143,932	64.0	64.6	99
Shoes	158,532	70.5	70.1	101

Data refers to **adults** except where indicated

Base: All GB	Total for Area	As a Percentage of:		Index (GB av.=100)
		Area	GB Base	
Visits to Licensed Premises (at least weekly)				
Pubs	69,367	30.9	26.3	117
Licensed clubs	29,903	13.3	11.6	115
Wine bars	3,348	1.5	1.4	107

Base: All GB	Total Spend in Area (£m)	Spend per Person in:		Index (GB av.=100)
Annual Personal Expenditure		Area (£)	GB Base (£)	Data refers to **adults** except where indicated
Convenience Goods				
Cigarettes, tobacco	55	192.5	184.1	105
Food	227	800.5	806.4	99
Household goods	50	175.8	174.1	101
Newspaper, magazines, etc.	19	67.2	67.0	100
Alcohol (off-licence)	37	130.2	122.5	106
Total	**388**	**1,366.2**	**1,354.2**	**101**
Comparison Goods				
Personal				
Children's, infantswear	14	48.9	52.4	93
Footwear	17	59.2	63.6	93
Menswear	26	89.8	97.5	92
Womenswear	42	148.7	171.2	87
Total	**98**	**346.6**	**384.8**	**90**
Home				
Brown goods	18	62.1	65.0	96
White goods	23	80.6	74.7	108
Furniture, floorcoverings	38	134.1	137.8	97
H'hold textiles, soft furnishings	14	49.4	50.6	98
Total	**93**	**326.3**	**328.0**	**99**
Leisure				
Books	8	29.4	29.3	100
DIY, gardening	39	137.1	143.8	95
Eating out	49	173.3	181.0	96
Photographic	6	22.7	26.2	87
Records, tapes, CDs, videos	12	43.6	41.9	104
Sports equipment	13	45.9	47.8	96
Toys, games, cycles, prams	9	30.1	30.9	97
Total	**137**	**482.1**	**500.9**	**96**

© CACI Limited, 1998.   Tel: 0171 602-6000 (London) / 0131 557-0123 (Edinburgh).
Note: [1] PayCheck data. Please see Chapter 3 for details.
Sources: © BMRB International Limited, 1997.
             Buying potential information modelled using data from TGI 4/96–3/97.
             © Verdict Research Limited, 1997.
             Buying potential information modelled using data from Verdict Research.

14. KINGSTON UPON HULL

Derived using CACI's Population Projections for 1998   Data refers to **adults** except where indicated

Base: All GB	Total for Area	As a Percentage of: Area	As a Percentage of: GB Base	Index (GB av.=100)
Total Resident Population	267,461	100.0	100.0	100
of whom female	134,791	50.4	50.8	99
By age *of whom female (%)*				
0– 4 49.0	18,861	7.1	6.5	109
5– 9 49.4	19,496	7.3	6.6	111
10–14 47.7	17,819	6.7	6.3	105
15–19 48.3	18,169	6.8	6.2	110
20–24 48.3	21,526	8.0	5.9	137
25–34 46.4	43,445	16.2	15.4	105
35–44 49.8	34,280	12.8	14.3	90
45–54 49.8	28,859	10.8	13.1	82
55–64 51.2	23,961	9.0	9.9	90
65–74 54.8	22,175	8.3	8.4	99
75+ 64.6	18,870	7.1	7.4	96
Cost of Car (of only or most recently obtained car)				
Up to £2,999	46,317	21.9	22.9	96
£3,000– £4,999	21,255	10.1	13.5	74
£5,000– £6,999	21,806	10.3	11.1	93
£7,000– £9,999	17,882	8.5	11.1	76
£10,000–£19,999	15,294	7.2	12.8	57
£20,000+	729	0.3	1.1	31
Owner of a Company Car	9,042	4.3	7.7	56
Income Level of Households[1]				
Up to £4,999	20,083	17.5	10.9	161
£5,000– £9,999	27,531	24.1	16.3	148
£10,000–£14,999	24,902	21.8	18.1	120
£15,000–£19,999	17,141	15.0	15.7	95
£20,000–£24,999	10,460	9.1	12.0	76
£25,000–£29,999	6,059	5.3	8.5	62
£30,000–£34,999	3,446	3.0	5.9	51
£35,000–£39,999	1,961	1.7	4.0	43
£40,000–£44,999	1,128	1.0	2.7	37
£45,000–£49,999	661	0.6	1.8	32
£50,000+	1,081	0.9	4.3	22
Use of Multiple Stores in Last Year				
Dept. stores (not groceries)	149,567	70.8	78.5	90
Ladies' outfitters	116,469	55.1	53.5	103
Gentlemen's outfitters	139,594	66.1	64.0	103
DIY	126,110	59.7	60.5	99
Furniture, appliances, durables	132,667	62.8	64.6	97
Shoes	147,606	69.9	70.1	100

Data refers to **adults** except where indicated

Base: All GB	Total for Area	As a Percentage of:		Index (GB av.=100)
		Area	GB Base	
Visits to Licensed Premises (at least weekly)				
Pubs	66,625	31.5	26.3	120
Licensed clubs	32,971	15.6	11.6	134
Wine bars	2,075	1.0	1.4	70

Annual Personal Expenditure		Data refers to **adults** except where indicated		
Base: All GB	Total Spend in Area (£m)	Spend per Person in:		Index (GB av.=100)
		Area (£)	GB Base (£)	
Convenience Goods				
Cigarettes, tobacco	61	227.3	184.1	124
Food	216	808.5	806.4	100
Household goods	47	175.8	174.1	101
Newspaper, magazines, etc.	17	64.0	67.0	96
Alcohol (off-licence)	32	119.4	122.5	97
Total	**373**	**1,395.1**	**1,354.2**	**103**
Comparison Goods				
Personal				
Children's, infantswear	13	48.2	52.4	92
Footwear	16	59.3	63.6	93
Menswear	25	93.6	97.5	96
Womenswear	41	154.4	171.2	90
Total	**95**	**355.5**	**384.8**	**92**
Home				
Brown goods	18	66.5	65.0	102
White goods	23	87.5	74.7	117
Furniture, floorcoverings	44	164.7	137.8	120
H'hold textiles, soft furnishings	15	54.5	50.6	108
Total	**100**	**373.3**	**328.0**	**114**
Leisure				
Books	7	25.7	29.3	88
DIY, gardening	38	141.6	143.8	99
Eating out	46	170.2	181.0	94
Photographic	7	27.0	26.2	103
Records, tapes, CDs, videos	11	41.9	41.9	100
Sports equipment	12	46.3	47.8	97
Toys, games, cycles, prams	9	33.8	30.9	109
Total	**130**	**486.5**	**500.9**	**97**

© CACI Limited, 1998.   Tel: 0171 602-6000 (London) / 0131 557-0123 (Edinburgh).
Note: [1] PayCheck data. Please see Chapter 3 for details.
Sources: © BMRB International Limited, 1997.
             Buying potential information modelled using data from TGI 4/96–3/97.
             © Verdict Research Limited, 1997.
             Buying potential information modelled using data from Verdict Research.

15. STOKE ON TRENT

Derived using **CACI's Population Projections for 1998**   Data refers to **adults** except where indicated

Base: All GB	Total for Area	As a Percentage of Area	GB Base	Index (GB av.=100)
Total Resident Population	255,037	100.0	100.0	100
of whom female	128,434	50.4	50.8	99
By age *of whom female (%)*				
0– 4	48.7	16,814	6.6	6.5	102
5– 9	49.1	17,030	6.7	6.6	102
10–14	48.2	15,999	6.3	6.3	99
15–19	48.6	15,812	6.2	6.2	101
20–24	49.0	16,319	6.4	5.9	109
25–34	47.3	42,661	16.7	15.4	108
35–44	48.2	33,664	13.2	14.3	92
45–54	49.2	30,937	12.1	13.1	92
55–64	50.7	25,177	9.9	9.9	99
65–74	53.7	22,767	8.9	8.4	106
75+	66.4	17,875	7.0	7.4	95
Cost of Car (of only or most recently obtained car)				
Up to £2,999	56,559	27.6	22.9	120
£3,000– £4,999	29,401	14.3	13.5	106
£5,000– £6,999	19,280	9.4	11.1	85
£7,000– £9,999	17,917	8.7	11.1	78
£10,000–£19,999	18,348	8.9	12.8	70
£20,000+	813	0.4	1.1	35
Owner of a Company Car	10,965	5.3	7.7	70
Income Level of Households[1]				
Up to £4,999	15,402	14.9	10.9	137
£5,000– £9,999	22,780	22.0	16.3	135
£10,000–£14,999	22,676	21.9	18.1	121
£15,000–£19,999	16,799	16.2	15.7	103
£20,000–£24,999	10,710	10.4	12.0	87
£25,000–£29,999	6,343	6.1	8.5	72
£30,000–£34,999	3,640	3.5	5.9	60
£35,000–£39,999	2,073	2.0	4.0	51
£40,000–£44,999	1,187	1.1	2.7	43
£45,000–£49,999	690	0.7	1.8	37
£50,000+	1,086	1.1	4.3	25
Use of Multiple Stores in Last Year				
Dept. stores (not groceries)	150,867	73.5	78.5	94
Ladies' outfitters	118,120	57.6	53.5	108
Gentlemen's outfitters	139,436	68.0	64.0	106
DIY	125,747	61.3	60.5	101
Furniture, appliances, durables	135,054	65.8	64.6	102
Shoes	147,128	71.7	70.1	102

Data refers to **adults** except where indicated

Base: All GB	Total for Area	As a Percentage of:		Index
		Area	GB Base	(GB av.=100)
Visits to Licensed Premises (at least weekly)				
Pubs	59,983	29.2	26.3	111
Licensed clubs	29,659	14.5	11.6	125
Wine bars	3,953	1.9	1.4	138

Annual Personal Expenditure		Data refers to **adults** except where indicated		
Base: All GB	Total Spend in Area (£m)	Spend per Person in:		Index
		Area (£)	GB Base (£)	(GB av.=100)
Convenience Goods				
Cigarettes, tobacco	49	192.4	184.1	105
Food	201	787.8	806.4	98
Household goods	47	182.7	174.1	105
Newspaper, magazines, etc.	17	67.7	67.0	101
Alcohol (off-licence)	34	133.4	122.5	109
Total	**348**	**1,363.9**	**1,354.2**	**101**
Comparison Goods				
Personal				
Children's, infantswear	13	52.3	52.4	100
Footwear	15	58.9	63.6	93
Menswear	24	92.4	97.5	95
Womenswear	39	153.6	171.2	90
Total	**91**	**357.2**	**384.8**	**93**
Home				
Brown goods	16	64.3	65.0	99
White goods	20	77.9	74.7	104
Furniture, floorcoverings	35	137.5	137.8	100
H'hold textiles, soft furnishings	13	49.9	50.6	99
Total	**84**	**329.6**	**328.0**	**101**
Leisure				
Books	7	27.3	29.3	93
DIY, gardening	38	147.6	143.8	103
Eating out	42	165.7	181.0	92
Photographic	5	20.1	26.2	77
Records, tapes, CDs, videos	11	43.7	41.9	104
Sports equipment	12	46.5	47.8	97
Toys, games, cycles, prams	9	33.5	30.9	108
Total	**124**	**484.3**	**500.9**	**97**

© CACI Limited, 1998.   Tel: 0171 602-6000 (London) / 0131 557- 0123 (Edinburgh).
Note: ¹ PayCheck data. Please see Chapter 3 for details.
Sources: © BMRB International Limited, 1997.
　　　　Buying potential information modelled using data from TGI 4/96–3/97.
　　　　© Verdict Research Limited, 1997.
　　　　Buying potential information modelled using data from Verdict Research.

16. PLYMOUTH

Derived using **CACI's Population Projections for 1998**   Data refers to **adults** except where indicated

Base: All GB	Total for Area	As a Percentage of Area	GB Base	Index (GB av.=100)
Total Resident Population	258,764	100.0	100.0	100
of whom female	130,114	50.3	50.8	99
By age *of whom female (%)*				
0– 4	47.8	16,075	6.2	6.5	96
5– 9	49.2	16,883	6.5	6.6	100
10–14	48.0	16,243	6.3	6.3	99
15–19	48.1	17,593	6.8	6.2	110
20–24	47.5	18,005	7.0	5.9	118
25–34	46.6	43,301	16.7	15.4	108
35–44	49.5	34,674	13.4	14.3	94
45–54	50.6	31,845	12.3	13.1	94
55–64	50.7	24,421	9.4	9.9	95
65–74	54.1	20,627	8.0	8.4	95
75+	64.6	19,097	7.4	7.4	100
Cost of Car (of only or most recently obtained car)				
Up to £2,999	75,977	36.3	22.9	158
£3,000– £4,999	31,875	15.2	13.5	112
£5,000– £6,999	20,113	9.6	11.1	86
£7,000– £9,999	11,523	5.5	11.1	49
£10,000–£19,999	14,248	6.8	12.8	53
£20,000+	1,192	0.6	1.1	51
Owner of a Company Car	9,976	4.8	7.7	62
Income Level of Households[1]				
Up to £4,999	13,855	13.2	10.9	121
£5,000– £9,999	21,317	20.3	16.3	125
£10,000–£14,999	22,326	21.3	18.1	118
£15,000–£19,999	17,463	16.7	15.7	106
£20,000–£24,999	11,716	11.2	12.0	94
£25,000–£29,999	7,262	6.9	8.5	81
£30,000–£34,999	4,342	4.1	5.9	71
£35,000–£39,999	2,568	2.4	4.0	62
£40,000–£44,999	1,524	1.5	2.7	54
£45,000–£49,999	915	0.9	1.8	48
£50,000+	1,552	1.5	4.3	35
Use of Multiple Stores in Last Year				
Dept. stores (not groceries)	158,067	75.4	78.5	96
Ladies' outfitters	119,366	57.0	53.5	107
Gentlemen's outfitters	138,108	65.9	64.0	103
DIY	129,724	61.9	60.5	102
Furniture, appliances, durables	141,137	67.3	64.6	104
Shoes	144,768	69.1	70.1	99

Data refers to **adults** except where indicated

Base: All GB	Total for Area	As a Percentage of:		Index (GB av.=100)
		Area	GB Base	
Visits to Licensed Premises (at least weekly)				
Pubs	56,117	26.8	26.3	102
Licensed clubs	32,141	15.3	11.6	132
Wine bars	2,844	1.4	1.4	97

Annual Personal Expenditure Data refers to **adults** except where indicated

Base: All GB	Total Spend in Area (£m)	Spend per Person in:		Index (GB av.=100)
		Area (£)	GB Base (£)	
Convenience Goods				
Cigarettes, tobacco	49	187.9	184.1	102
Food	195	754.5	806.4	94
Household goods	44	169.3	174.1	97
Newspaper, magazines, etc.	16	61.1	67.0	91
Alcohol (off-licence)	29	111.1	122.5	91
Total	**332**	**1,283.8**	**1,354.2**	**95**
Comparison Goods				
Personal				
Children's, infantswear	13	51.9	52.4	99
Footwear	15	57.6	63.6	91
Menswear	21	82.5	97.5	85
Womenswear	41	160.1	171.2	94
Total	**91**	**352.2**	**384.8**	**92**
Home				
Brown goods	16	61.9	65.0	95
White goods	18	69.9	74.7	94
Furniture, floorcoverings	33	128.9	137.8	94
H'hold textiles, soft furnishings	12	46.8	50.6	93
Total	**80**	**307.5**	**328.0**	**94**
Leisure				
Books	8	29.7	29.3	101
DIY, gardening	37	141.8	143.8	99
Eating out	40	152.9	181.0	84
Photographic	6	21.5	26.2	82
Records, tapes, CDs, videos	12	44.9	41.9	107
Sports equipment	13	48.4	47.8	101
Toys, games, cycles, prams	8	31.1	30.9	101
Total	**122**	**470.4**	**500.9**	**94**

Note: [1] PayCheck data. Please see Chapter 3 for details.
Sources: © BMRB International Limited, 1997.
Buying potential information modelled using data from TGI 4/96–3/97.
© Verdict Research Limited, 1997.
Buying potential information modelled using data from Verdict Research.

CHAPTER 5

A PORTRAIT OF BRITAIN'S COUNTIES

INNER LONDON

Derived using **CACI's Population Projections for 1998**   Data refers to **adults** except where indicated

Base: All GB	Total for Area	As a Percentage of: Area	GB Base	Index (GB av. = 100)
Total Resident Population	2,735,892	100.0	100.0	100
of whom female	1,397,107	51.1	50.8	100
By age: *of whom female (%)*				
0– 4 48.8	214,473	7.8	6.5	121
5– 9 49.4	179,485	6.6	6.6	100
10–14 49.4	153,739	5.6	6.3	89
15–19 50.5	165,061	6.0	6.2	98
20–24 51.8	188,921	6.9	5.9	117
25–34 50.0	573,366	21.0	15.4	136
35–44 49.2	451,250	16.5	14.3	115
45–54 51.4	283,913	10.4	13.1	79
55–64 51.1	211,995	7.7	9.9	78
65–74 52.7	166,791	6.1	8.4	73
75+ 65.2	146,898	5.4	7.4	73
Cost of Car (of only or most recently obtained car)				
Up to £2,999	453,021	20.7	22.9	90
£3,000– £4,999	197,282	9.0	13.5	67
£5,000– £6,999	163,505	7.5	11.1	67
£7,000– £9,999	129,559	5.9	11.1	53
£10,000–£19,999	171,299	7.8	12.8	61
£20,000+	22,372	1.0	1.1	91
Owner of a Company Car	130,183	5.9	7.7	78
Income Level of Households[1]				
Up to £4,999	112,664	9.4	10.9	86
£5,000– £9,999	154,650	12.9	16.3	79
£10,000–£14,999	180,089	15.0	18.1	83
£15,000–£19,999	169,049	14.1	15.7	90
£20,000–£24,999	141,408	11.8	12.0	98
£25,000–£29,999	111,165	9.2	8.5	109
£30,000–£34,999	84,523	7.0	5.9	120
£35,000–£39,999	63,156	5.3	4.0	132
£40,000–£44,999	46,802	3.9	2.7	145
£45,000–£49,999	34,583	2.9	1.8	158
£50,000+	104,198	8.7	4.3	203
Use of Multiple Stores in Last Year				
Dept. stores (not groceries)	1,746,700	79.8	78.5	102
Ladies' outfitters	1,107,279	50.6	53.5	95
Gentlemen's outfitters	1,265,979	57.9	64.0	90
DIY	1,184,424	54.1	60.5	89
Furniture, appliances, durables	1,311,631	59.9	64.6	93
Shoes	1,434,524	65.6	70.1	94
Visits to Licensed Premises (at least weekly)				
Pubs	557,306	25.5	26.3	97
Licensed clubs	111,275	5.1	11.6	44
Wine bars	42,222	1.9	1.4	138

© CACI Limited, 1998.   Tel: 0171 602-6000 (London) / 0131 557-0123 (Edinburgh).
Note: [1] PayCheck data. Please see Chapter 3 for details.
Source: © BMRB International Limited, 1997. Buying potential info. modelled using data from TGI 4/96-3/97.

OUTER LONDON

Derived using **CACI's Population Projections for 1998**   Data refers to **adults** except where indicated

Base: All GB		Total for Area	As a Percentage of:		Index (GB av. = 100)
			Area	GB Base	
Total Resident Population		4,370,876	100.0	100.0	100
of whom female		2,219,403	50.8	50.8	100
By age:	*of whom female (%)*				
0– 4	48.7	305,728	7.0	6.5	108
5– 9	48.8	291,437	6.7	6.6	102
10–14	48.4	268,892	6.2	6.3	97
15–19	48.4	271,749	6.2	6.2	101
20–24	49.0	275,053	6.3	5.9	107
25–34	49.4	744,939	17.0	15.4	110
35–44	49.2	662,846	15.2	14.3	106
45–54	50.3	548,603	12.6	13.1	96
55–64	50.9	393,754	9.0	9.9	91
65–74	53.9	314,168	7.2	8.4	86
75+	65.5	293,707	6.7	7.4	91
Cost of Car (of only or most recently obtained car)					
Up to £2,999		739,252	21.1	22.9	92
£3,000– £4,999		462,854	13.2	13.5	97
£5,000– £6,999		400,347	11.4	11.1	103
£7,000– £9,999		370,360	10.6	11.1	95
£10,000–£19,999		546,532	15.6	12.8	122
£20,000+		61,552	1.8	1.1	156
Owner of a Company Car		341,268	9.7	7.7	127
Income Level of Households[1]					
Up to £4,999		130,011	7.4	10.9	68
£5,000– £9,999		205,905	11.7	16.3	72
£10,000–£14,999		262,060	14.8	18.1	82
£15,000–£19,999		261,881	14.8	15.7	94
£20,000–£24,999		227,125	12.9	12.0	108
£25,000–£29,999		180,895	10.2	8.5	120
£30,000–£34,999		136,869	7.7	5.9	132
£35,000–£39,999		100,486	5.7	4.0	143
£40,000–£44,999		72,561	4.1	2.7	153
£45,000–£49,999		51,991	2.9	1.8	162
£50,000+		137,406	7.8	4.3	182
Use of Multiple Stores in Last Year					
Dept. stores (not groceries)		2,942,791	84.0	78.5	107
Ladies' outfitters		1,736,777	49.6	53.5	93
Gentlemen's outfitters		2,105,524	60.1	64.0	94
DIY		2,109,032	60.2	60.5	99
Furniture, appliances, durables		2,209,319	63.0	64.6	98
Shoes		2,331,013	66.5	70.1	95
Visits to Licensed Premises (at least weekly)					
Pubs		784,458	22.4	26.3	85
Licensed clubs		269,403	7.7	11.6	66
Wine bars		55,973	1.6	1.4	114

© CACI Limited, 1998.   Tel: 0171 602-6000 (London) / 0131 557-0123 (Edinburgh).
Note: [1] PayCheck data. Please see Chapter 3 for details.
Source: © BMRB International Limited, 1997. Buying potential info. modelled using data from TGI 4/96-3/97.

GREATER MANCHESTER

Derived using **CACI's Population Projections for 1998**   Data refers to **adults** except where indicated

Base: All GB	Total for Area	As a Percentage of: Area	GB Base	Index (GB av. = 100)
Total Resident Population	2,590,672	100.0	100.0	100
of whom female	1,313,261	50.7	50.8	100

By age: *of whom female (%)*

		Total for Area	Area	GB Base	Index
0– 4	48.7	176,997	6.8	6.5	106
5– 9	48.7	184,230	7.1	6.6	109
10–14	48.7	177,013	6.8	6.3	108
15–19	48.8	166,876	6.4	6.2	105
20–24	48.7	157,339	6.1	5.9	103
25–34	48.7	407,412	15.7	15.4	102
35–44	49.4	365,126	14.1	14.3	99
45–54	49.6	327,941	12.7	13.1	96
55–64	50.3	250,700	9.7	9.9	97
65–74	54.2	202,092	7.8	8.4	93
75+	66.3	174,946	6.8	7.4	91

Cost of Car (of only or most recently obtained car)

	Total for Area	Area	GB Base	Index
Up to £2,999	513,274	25.0	22.9	109
£3,000– £4,999	248,523	12.1	13.5	89
£5,000– £6,999	194,677	9.5	11.1	85
£7,000– £9,999	224,572	10.9	11.1	98
£10,000–£19,999	185,145	9.0	12.8	71
£20,000+	15,343	0.7	1.1	66
Owner of a Company Car	130,260	6.3	7.7	83

Income Level of Households[1]

	Total for Area	Area	GB Base	Index
Up to £4,999	133,154	12.7	10.9	117
£5,000– £9,999	190,651	18.2	16.3	112
£10,000–£14,999	200,900	19.2	18.1	106
£15,000–£19,999	164,662	15.7	15.7	100
£20,000–£24,999	119,104	11.4	12.0	95
£25,000–£29,999	80,935	7.7	8.5	91
£30,000–£34,999	53,382	5.1	5.9	87
£35,000–£39,999	34,797	3.3	4.0	84
£40,000–£44,999	22,655	2.2	2.7	81
£45,000–£49,999	14,822	1.4	1.8	78
£50,000+	31,133	3.0	4.3	70

Use of Multiple Stores in Last Year

	Total for Area	Area	GB Base	Index
Dept. stores (not groceries)	1,550,959	75.6	78.5	96
Ladies' outfitters	1,140,532	55.6	53.5	104
Gentlemen's outfitters	1,408,315	68.6	64.0	107
DIY	1,232,277	60.0	60.5	99
Furniture, appliances, durables	1,372,568	66.9	64.6	104
Shoes	1,479,661	72.1	70.1	103

Visits to Licensed Premises (at least weekly)

	Total for Area	Area	GB Base	Index
Pubs	584,464	28.5	26.3	108
Licensed clubs	276,179	13.5	11.6	116
Wine bars	37,261	1.8	1.4	130

© CACI Limited, 1998.   Tel: 0171 602-6000 (London) / 0131 557-0123 (Edinburgh).
Note: [1] PayCheck data. Please see Chapter 3 for details.
Source: © BMRB International Limited, 1997. Buying potential info. modelled using data from TGI 4/96-3/97.

MERSEYSIDE

Derived using **CACI's Population Projections for 1998**   Data refers to **adults** except where indicated

Base: All GB		Total for Area	As a Percentage of: Area	As a Percentage of: GB Base	Index (GB av. = 100)
Total Resident Population		1,421,001	100.0	100.0	100
of whom female		732,458	51.5	50.8	101
By age:	*of whom female (%)*				
0– 4	48.6	91,504	6.4	6.5	100
5– 9	48.7	96,100	6.8	6.6	103
10–14	48.9	96,453	6.8	6.3	107
15–19	48.9	91,322	6.4	6.2	104
20–24	48.8	83,637	5.9	5.9	100
25–34	49.6	210,238	14.8	15.4	96
35–44	50.6	201,797	14.2	14.3	99
45–54	50.6	176,054	12.4	13.1	94
55–64	51.7	144,315	10.2	9.9	102
65–74	54.8	125,623	8.8	8.4	105
75+	66.9	103,958	7.3	7.4	99
Cost of Car (of only or most recently obtained car)					
Up to £2,999		267,735	23.5	22.9	103
£3,000– £4,999		128,859	11.3	13.5	84
£5,000– £6,999		103,924	9.1	11.1	82
£7,000– £9,999		125,606	11.0	11.1	99
£10,000–£19,999		91,178	8.0	12.8	63
£20,000+		8,754	0.8	1.1	68
Owner of a Company Car		71,604	6.3	7.7	82
Income Level of Households[1]					
Up to £4,999		81,776	14.4	10.9	132
£5,000– £9,999		110,433	19.4	16.3	119
£10,000–£14,999		110,987	19.5	18.1	108
£15,000–£19,999		87,513	15.4	15.7	98
£20,000–£24,999		61,408	10.8	12.0	90
£25,000–£29,999		40,749	7.2	8.5	84
£30,000–£34,999		26,377	4.6	5.9	79
£35,000–£39,999		16,941	3.0	4.0	75
£40,000–£44,999		10,900	1.9	2.7	71
£45,000–£49,999		7,065	1.2	1.8	68
£50,000+		14,575	2.6	4.3	60
Use of Multiple Stores in Last Year					
Dept. stores (not groceries)		851,645	74.9	78.5	95
Ladies' outfitters		614,773	54.1	53.5	101
Gentlemen's outfitters		771,449	67.9	64.0	106
DIY		671,000	59.0	60.5	97
Furniture, appliances, durables		759,238	66.8	64.6	103
Shoes		806,079	70.9	70.1	101
Visits to Licensed Premises (at least weekly)					
Pubs		318,630	28.0	26.3	106
Licensed clubs		165,358	14.5	11.6	125
Wine bars		17,100	1.5	1.4	108

© CACI Limited, 1998.   Tel: 0171 602-6000 (London) / 0131 557-0123 (Edinburgh).
Note: [1] PayCheck data. Please see Chapter 3 for details.
Source: © BMRB International Limited, 1997. Buying potential info. modelled using data from TGI 4/96-3/97.

SOUTH YORKSHIRE

Derived using **CACI's Population Projections for 1998**   Data refers to **adults** except where indicated

Base: All GB	Total for Area	As a Percentage of: Area	GB Base	Index (GB av. = 100)
Total Resident Population	1,304,796	100.0	100.0	100
of whom female	658,794	50.5	50.8	99
By age: *of whom female (%)*				
0– 4 48.8	83,214	6.4	6.5	99
5– 9 48.6	86,395	6.6	6.6	101
10–14 48.8	81,874	6.3	6.3	99
15–19 48.3	77,773	6.0	6.2	97
20–24 48.1	75,543	5.8	5.9	99
25–34 47.7	207,186	15.9	15.4	103
35–44 48.7	186,469	14.3	14.3	100
45–54 49.7	167,063	12.8	13.1	97
55–64 50.8	131,061	10.0	9.9	101
65–74 53.9	111,321	8.5	8.4	102
75+ 65.1	96,897	7.4	7.4	101
Cost of Car (of only or most recently obtained car)				
Up to £2,999	226,781	21.5	22.9	94
£3,000– £4,999	121,777	11.6	13.5	85
£5,000– £6,999	122,780	11.7	11.1	105
£7,000– £9,999	102,859	9.8	11.1	88
£10,000–£19,999	108,851	10.3	12.8	81
£20,000+	5,633	0.5	1.1	48
Owner of a Company Car	62,325	5.9	7.7	77
Income Level of Households[1]				
Up to £4,999	82,754	15.4	10.9	142
£5,000– £9,999	112,654	21.0	16.3	129
£10,000–£14,999	109,330	20.4	18.1	113
£15,000–£19,999	82,157	15.3	15.7	98
£20,000–£24,999	54,859	10.2	12.0	86
£25,000–£29,999	34,772	6.5	8.5	76
£30,000–£34,999	21,625	4.0	5.9	69
£35,000–£39,999	13,425	2.5	4.0	63
£40,000–£44,999	8,398	1.6	2.7	58
£45,000–£49,999	5,319	1.0	1.8	55
£50,000+	10,523	2.0	4.3	46
Use of Multiple Stores in Last Year				
Dept. stores (not groceries)	768,825	73.0	78.5	93
Ladies' outfitters	577,360	54.8	53.5	103
Gentlemen's outfitters	693,619	65.9	64.0	103
DIY	644,071	61.1	60.5	101
Furniture, appliances, durables	665,646	63.2	64.6	98
Shoes	742,516	70.5	70.1	101
Visits to Licensed Premises (at least weekly)				
Pubs	332,597	31.6	26.3	120
Licensed clubs	159,208	15.1	11.6	130
Wine bars	12,989	1.2	1.4	88

© CACI Limited, 1998. Tel: 0171 602-6000 (London) / 0131 557-0123 (Edinburgh).
Note: [1] PayCheck data. Please see Chapter 3 for details.
Source: © BMRB International Limited, 1997. Buying potential info. modelled using data from TGI 4/96-3/97.

TYNE AND WEAR

Derived using **CACI's Population Projections** for 1998   Data refers to **adults** except where indicated

Base: All GB	Total for Area	As a Percentage of: Area	As a Percentage of: GB Base	Index (GB av. = 100)
Total Resident Population	1,128,971	100.0	100.0	100
of whom female	577,607	51.2	50.8	101
By age: *of whom female (%)*				
0– 4 48.7	69,812	6.2	6.5	96
5– 9 48.6	73,010	6.5	6.6	99
10–14 49.0	72,336	6.4	6.3	101
15–19 48.9	73,719	6.5	6.2	106
20–24 48.6	67,771	6.0	5.9	102
25–34 49.1	170,484	15.1	15.4	98
35–44 49.6	164,798	14.6	14.3	102
45–54 49.9	141,702	12.6	13.1	96
55–64 51.4	111,304	9.9	9.9	99
65–74 54.9	102,568	9.1	8.4	108
75+ 66.0	81,467	7.2	7.4	98
Cost of Car (of only or most recently obtained car)				
Up to £2,999	187,297	20.5	22.9	89
£3,000– £4,999	94,787	10.4	13.5	77
£5,000– £6,999	90,155	9.9	11.1	89
£7,000– £9,999	88,342	9.7	11.1	87
£10,000–£19,999	94,535	10.3	12.8	81
£20,000+	1,673	0.2	1.1	16
Owner of a Company Car	44,869	4.9	7.7	64
Income Level of Households[1]				
Up to £4,999	75,877	16.0	10.9	147
£5,000– £9,999	102,088	21.6	16.3	133
£10,000–£14,999	96,599	20.4	18.1	113
£15,000–£19,999	70,990	15.0	15.7	96
£20,000–£24,999	46,741	9.9	12.0	83
£25,000–£29,999	29,452	6.2	8.5	73
£30,000–£34,999	18,326	3.9	5.9	66
£35,000–£39,999	11,437	2.4	4.0	61
£40,000–£44,999	7,216	1.5	2.7	57
£45,000–£49,999	4,621	1.0	1.8	54
£50,000+	9,548	2.0	4.3	47
Use of Multiple Stores in Last Year				
Dept. stores (not groceries)	701,378	76.8	78.5	98
Ladies' outfitters	508,380	55.6	53.5	104
Gentlemen's outfitters	604,885	66.2	64.0	103
DIY	466,401	51.0	60.5	84
Furniture, appliances, durables	590,790	64.7	64.6	100
Shoes	645,878	70.7	70.1	101
Visits to Licensed Premises (at least weekly)				
Pubs	303,238	33.2	26.3	126
Licensed clubs	185,977	20.4	11.6	175
Wine bars	19,185	2.1	1.4	150

© CACI Limited, 1998.   Tel: 0171 602-6000 (London) / 0131 557-0123 (Edinburgh).
Note: [1] PayCheck data. Please see Chapter 3 for details.
Source: © BMRB International Limited, 1997. Buying potential info. modelled using data from TGI 4/96-3/97.

WEST MIDLANDS

Derived using **CACI's Population Projections for 1998**   Data refers to **adults** except where indicated

Base: All GB	Total for Area	As a Percentage of: Area	As a Percentage of: GB Base	Index (GB av. = 100)
Total Resident Population	2,631,931	100.0	100.0	100
of whom female	1,333,338	50.7	50.8	100
By age: *of whom female (%)*				
0– 4 48.9	185,793	7.1	6.5	109
5– 9 48.9	187,416	7.1	6.6	109
10–14 48.8	178,703	6.8	6.3	107
15–19 49.0	174,989	6.6	6.2	108
20–24 48.6	158,786	6.0	5.9	103
25–34 49.0	409,930	15.6	15.4	101
35–44 49.2	361,011	13.7	14.3	96
45–54 49.7	314,316	11.9	13.1	91
55–64 50.3	256,777	9.8	9.9	98
65–74 53.2	219,779	8.4	8.4	99
75+ 65.2	184,431	7.0	7.4	95
Cost of Car (of only or most recently obtained car)				
Up to £2,999	511,195	24.6	22.9	107
£3,000– £4,999	259,482	12.5	13.5	92
£5,000– £6,999	200,938	9.7	11.1	87
£7,000– £9,999	174,876	8.4	11.1	75
£10,000–£19,999	203,227	9.8	12.8	77
£20,000+	13,338	0.6	1.1	57
Owner of a Company Car	116,561	5.6	7.7	73
Income Level of Households[1]				
Up to £4,999	142,595	13.8	10.9	126
£5,000– £9,999	199,368	19.2	16.3	118
£10,000–£14,999	205,251	19.8	18.1	109
£15,000–£19,999	163,197	15.7	15.7	100
£20,000–£24,999	114,088	11.0	12.0	92
£25,000–£29,999	75,017	7.2	8.5	85
£30,000–£34,999	48,097	4.6	5.9	79
£35,000–£39,999	30,657	3.0	4.0	74
£40,000–£44,999	19,631	1.9	2.7	71
£45,000–£49,999	12,696	1.2	1.8	67
£50,000+	26,407	2.5	4.3	60
Use of Multiple Stores in Last Year				
Dept. stores (not groceries)	1,570,032	75.5	78.5	96
Ladies' outfitters	1,155,009	55.5	53.5	104
Gentlemen's outfitters	1,363,862	65.6	64.0	103
DIY	1,239,065	59.6	60.5	98
Furniture, appliances, durables	1,352,514	65.0	64.6	101
Shoes	1,477,342	71.0	70.1	101
Visits to Licensed Premises (at least weekly)				
Pubs	606,943	29.2	26.3	111
Licensed clubs	265,370	12.8	11.6	110
Wine bars	29,769	1.4	1.4	102

© CACI Limited, 1998. Tel: 0171 602-6000 (London) / 0131 557-0123 (Edinburgh).
Note: [1] PayCheck data. Please see Chapter 3 for details.
Source: © BMRB International Limited, 1997. Buying potential info. modelled using data from TGI 4/96-3/97.

WEST YORKSHIRE

Derived using **CACI's Population Projections for 1998**   Data refers to **adults** except where indicated

Base: All GB	Total for Area	As a Percentage of: Area	As a Percentage of: GB Base	Index (GB av. = 100)
Total Resident Population	2,121,515	100.0	100.0	100
of whom female	1,074,089	50.6	50.8	100
By age: *of whom female (%)*				
0– 4 48.8	144,004	6.8	6.5	105
5– 9 49.1	146,740	6.9	6.6	106
10–14 48.7	140,434	6.6	6.3	104
15–19 48.6	139,042	6.6	6.2	106
20–24 48.5	128,632	6.1	5.9	103
25–34 48.2	335,441	15.8	15.4	102
35–44 49.0	302,383	14.3	14.3	100
45–54 49.7	269,104	12.7	13.1	97
55–64 50.8	201,340	9.5	9.9	95
65–74 54.3	168,141	7.9	8.4	94
75+ 65.6	146,254	6.9	7.4	93
Cost of Car (of only or most recently obtained car)				
Up to £2,999	347,794	20.6	22.9	90
£3,000– £4,999	186,015	11.0	13.5	81
£5,000– £6,999	203,060	12.0	11.1	108
£7,000– £9,999	170,245	10.1	11.1	90
£10,000–£19,999	187,614	11.1	12.8	87
£20,000+	10,328	0.6	1.1	54
Owner of a Company Car	107,272	6.3	7.7	83
Income Level of Households[1]				
Up to £4,999	108,023	12.5	10.9	115
£5,000– £9,999	155,616	18.1	16.3	111
£10,000–£14,999	165,367	19.2	18.1	106
£15,000–£19,999	136,521	15.8	15.7	101
£20,000–£24,999	99,136	11.5	12.0	96
£25,000–£29,999	67,410	7.8	8.5	92
£30,000–£34,999	44,399	5.2	5.9	88
£35,000–£39,999	28,877	3.4	4.0	84
£40,000–£44,999	18,758	2.2	2.7	81
£45,000–£49,999	12,249	1.4	1.8	78
£50,000+	25,650	3.0	4.3	70
Use of Multiple Stores in Last Year				
Dept. stores (not groceries)	1,254,261	74.2	78.5	94
Ladies' outfitters	915,005	54.1	53.5	101
Gentlemen's outfitters	1,105,932	65.4	64.0	102
DIY	1,034,801	61.2	60.5	101
Furniture, appliances, durables	1,070,087	63.3	64.6	98
Shoes	1,194,543	70.7	70.1	101
Visits to Licensed Premises (at least weekly)				
Pubs	535,822	31.7	26.3	120
Licensed clubs	229,991	13.6	11.6	117
Wine bars	21,153	1.3	1.4	90

© CACI Limited, 1998.   Tel: 0171 602-6000 (London) / 0131 557-0123 (Edinburgh).
Note: [1] PayCheck data. Please see Chapter 3 for details.
Source: © BMRB International Limited, 1997. Buying potential info. modelled using data from TGI 4/96-3/97.

AVON

Derived using **CACI's Population Projections for 1998**   Data refers to **adults** except where indicated

Base: All GB	Total for Area	As a Percentage of: Area	GB Base	Index (GB av. = 100)
Total Resident Population	991,979	100.0	100.0	100
of whom female	499,824	50.4	50.8	99
By age: *of whom female (%)*				
0– 4 49.1	62,383	6.3	6.5	97
5– 9 48.3	62,518	6.3	6.6	96
10–14 48.4	59,505	6.0	6.3	94
15–19 48.1	59,637	6.0	6.2	98
20–24 47.0	58,234	5.9	5.9	100
25–34 47.4	160,538	16.2	15.4	105
35–44 49.2	143,059	14.4	14.3	101
45–54 49.9	129,627	13.1	13.1	100
55–64 50.5	95,919	9.7	9.9	97
65–74 53.6	82,489	8.3	8.4	99
75+ 64.5	78,070	7.9	7.4	107
Cost of Car (of only or most recently obtained car)				
Up to £2,999	202,041	25.0	22.9	109
£3,000– £4,999	131,822	16.3	13.5	120
£5,000– £6,999	89,151	11.0	11.1	99
£7,000– £9,999	95,873	11.9	11.1	107
£10,000–£19,999	90,623	11.2	12.8	88
£20,000+	10,293	1.3	1.1	113
Owner of a Company Car	65,028	8.1	7.7	105
Income Level of Households[1]				
Up to £4,999	41,920	10.3	10.9	94
£5,000– £9,999	65,386	16.0	16.3	98
£10,000–£14,999	75,237	18.4	18.1	102
£15,000–£19,999	66,307	16.2	15.7	103
£20,000–£24,999	50,550	12.4	12.0	104
£25,000–£29,999	35,634	8.7	8.5	103
£30,000–£34,999	24,132	5.9	5.9	101
£35,000–£39,999	16,056	3.9	4.0	99
£40,000–£44,999	10,634	2.6	2.7	97
£45,000–£49,999	7,067	1.7	1.8	95
£50,000+	15,628	3.8	4.3	90
Use of Multiple Stores in Last Year				
Dept. stores (not groceries)	611,740	75.8	78.5	96
Ladies' outfitters	429,360	53.2	53.5	99
Gentlemen's outfitters	500,136	61.9	64.0	97
DIY	476,858	59.0	60.5	98
Furniture, appliances, durables	503,095	62.3	64.6	96
Shoes	557,529	69.0	70.1	98
Visits to Licensed Premises (at least weekly)				
Pubs	229,926	28.5	26.3	108
Licensed clubs	108,797	13.5	11.6	116
Wine bars	8,475	1.0	1.4	75

© CACI Limited, 1998.   Tel: 0171 602-6000 (London) / 0131 557-0123 (Edinburgh).

Note: [1] PayCheck data. Please see Chapter 3 for details.
Source: © BMRB International Limited, 1997. Buying potential info. modelled using data from TGI 4/96-3/97.

BEDFORDSHIRE

Derived using **CACI's Population Projections for 1998**   Data refers to **adults** except where indicated

Base: All GB	Total for Area	As a Percentage of: Area	As a Percentage of: GB Base	Index (GB av. = 100)
Total Resident Population	555,081	100.0	100.0	100
of whom female	277,455	50.0	50.8	98
By age: *of whom female (%)*				
0– 4 48.8	39,006	7.0	6.5	109
5– 9 48.2	40,394	7.3	6.6	111
10–14 49.4	38,157	6.9	6.3	108
15–19 48.8	35,175	6.3	6.2	103
20–24 48.7	33,045	6.0	5.9	101
25–34 48.7	86,314	15.5	15.4	101
35–44 48.8	82,898	14.9	14.3	104
45–54 49.6	73,581	13.3	13.1	101
55–64 49.6	53,943	9.7	9.9	98
65–74 51.4	40,502	7.3	8.4	87
75+ 63.4	32,066	5.8	7.4	78
Cost of Car (of only or most recently obtained car)				
Up to £2,999	112,299	25.7	22.9	112
£3,000– £4,999	64,877	14.8	13.5	109
£5,000– £6,999	48,146	11.0	11.1	99
£7,000– £9,999	53,290	12.2	11.1	109
£10,000–£19,999	53,346	12.2	12.8	95
£20,000+	6,180	1.4	1.1	126
Owner of a Company Car	34,177	7.8	7.7	102
Income Level of Households[1]				
Up to £4,999	17,443	8.0	10.9	74
£5,000– £9,999	28,406	13.1	16.3	80
£10,000–£14,999	35,821	16.5	18.1	91
£15,000–£19,999	34,750	16.0	15.7	102
£20,000–£24,999	28,830	13.3	12.0	111
£25,000–£29,999	21,780	10.0	8.5	118
£30,000–£34,999	15,584	7.2	5.9	122
£35,000–£39,999	10,825	5.0	4.0	125
£40,000–£44,999	7,414	3.4	2.7	127
£45,000–£49,999	5,055	2.3	1.8	128
£50,000+	11,608	5.3	4.3	125
Use of Multiple Stores in Last Year				
Dept. stores (not groceries)	352,368	80.5	78.5	103
Ladies' outfitters	237,179	54.2	53.5	101
Gentlemen's outfitters	287,494	65.7	64.0	103
DIY	262,981	60.1	60.5	99
Furniture, appliances, durables	283,211	64.7	64.6	100
Shoes	299,937	68.6	70.1	98
Visits to Licensed Premises (at least weekly)				
Pubs	98,077	22.4	26.3	85
Licensed clubs	41,084	9.4	11.6	81
Wine bars	2,625	0.6	1.4	43

© CACI Limited, 1998.   Tel: 0171 602-6000 (London) / 0131 557-0123 (Edinburgh).
Note: [1] PayCheck data. Please see Chapter 3 for details.
Source: © BMRB International Limited, 1997. Buying potential info. modelled using data from TGI 4/96-3/97.

BERKSHIRE

Derived using **CACI's Population Projections for 1998**   Data refers to **adults** except where indicated

Base: All GB	Total for Area	As a Percentage of: Area	As a Percentage of: GB Base	Index (GB av. = 100)
Total Resident Population	799,563	100.0	100.0	100
of whom female	397,482	49.7	50.8	98
By age: *of whom female (%)*				
0– 4 48.3	55,551	6.9	6.5	108
5– 9 48.2	53,704	6.7	6.6	102
10–14 47.6	52,089	6.5	6.3	103
15–19 48.6	48,866	6.1	6.2	99
20–24 49.7	45,831	5.7	5.9	98
25–34 47.9	138,940	17.4	15.4	113
35–44 48.1	125,167	15.7	14.3	109
45–54 49.6	106,723	13.3	13.1	102
55–64 49.7	73,420	9.2	9.9	92
65–74 52.5	54,350	6.8	8.4	81
75+ 64.0	44,922	5.6	7.4	76
Cost of Car (of only or most recently obtained car)				
Up to £2,999	142,795	22.4	22.9	98
£3,000– £4,999	92,793	14.5	13.5	107
£5,000– £6,999	76,079	11.9	11.1	107
£7,000– £9,999	80,456	12.6	11.1	113
£10,000–£19,999	120,122	18.8	12.8	147
£20,000+	13,009	2.0	1.1	181
Owner of a Company Car	71,644	11.2	7.7	146
Income Level of Households[1]				
Up to £4,999	19,122	6.1	10.9	56
£5,000– £9,999	32,455	10.3	16.3	63
£10,000–£14,999	43,899	13.9	18.1	77
£15,000–£19,999	46,239	14.7	15.7	93
£20,000–£24,999	41,780	13.3	12.0	111
£25,000–£29,999	34,264	10.9	8.5	128
£30,000–£34,999	26,433	8.4	5.9	143
£35,000–£39,999	19,636	6.2	4.0	157
£40,000–£44,999	14,267	4.5	2.7	169
£45,000–£49,999	10,246	3.3	1.8	179
£50,000+	26,742	8.5	4.3	199
Use of Multiple Stores in Last Year				
Dept. stores (not groceries)	545,547	85.5	78.5	109
Ladies' outfitters	329,586	51.6	53.5	97
Gentlemen's outfitters	401,736	62.9	64.0	98
DIY	416,199	65.2	60.5	108
Furniture, appliances, durables	425,882	66.7	64.6	103
Shoes	441,001	69.1	70.1	99
Visits to Licensed Premises (at least weekly)				
Pubs	140,113	22.0	26.3	83
Licensed clubs	52,947	8.3	11.6	71
Wine bars	6,972	1.1	1.4	78

© CACI Limited, 1998.   Tel: 0171 602-6000 (London) / 0131 557-0123 (Edinburgh).
Note: [1] PayCheck data. Please see Chapter 3 for details.
Source: © BMRB International Limited, 1997. Buying potential info. modelled using data from TGI 4/96-3/97.

BUCKINGHAMSHIRE

Derived using **CACI's Population Projections for 1998**   Data refers to **adults** except where indicated

Base: All GB	Total for Area	As a Percentage of: Area	As a Percentage of: GB Base	Index (GB av. = 100)
Total Resident Population	687,826	100.0	100.0	100
of whom female	346,375	50.4	50.8	99
By age: *of whom female (%)*				
0– 4	48.4	47,231	6.9	6.5	106
5– 9	48.7	47,859	7.0	6.6	106
10–14	48.9	46,055	6.7	6.3	105
15–19	48.8	42,328	6.2	6.2	100
20–24	50.0	40,754	5.9	5.9	101
25–34	49.4	108,684	15.8	15.4	102
35–44	49.7	103,833	15.1	14.3	106
45–54	49.8	98,640	14.3	13.1	109
55–64	49.6	66,606	9.7	9.9	97
65–74	52.2	47,239	6.9	8.4	82
75+	63.8	38,597	5.6	7.4	76
Cost of Car (of only or most recently obtained car)				
Up to £2,999	116,212	21.3	22.9	93
£3,000– £4,999	80,462	14.7	13.5	109
£5,000– £6,999	67,807	12.4	11.1	112
£7,000– £9,999	77,905	14.3	11.1	128
£10,000–£19,999	103,917	19.0	12.8	149
£20,000+	12,977	2.4	1.1	211
Owner of a Company Car	60,728	11.1	7.7	145
Income Level of Households[1]				
Up to £4,999	15,988	6.0	10.9	55
£5,000– £9,999	27,721	10.3	16.3	64
£10,000–£14,999	37,445	14.0	18.1	77
£15,000–£19,999	39,245	14.6	15.7	93
£20,000–£24,999	35,282	13.1	12.0	110
£25,000–£29,999	28,845	10.7	8.5	126
£30,000–£34,999	22,263	8.3	5.9	142
£35,000–£39,999	16,613	6.2	4.0	156
£40,000–£44,999	12,165	4.5	2.7	169
£45,000–£49,999	8,823	3.3	1.8	181
£50,000+	23,987	8.9	4.3	210
Use of Multiple Stores in Last Year				
Dept. stores (not groceries)	459,964	84.1	78.5	107
Ladies' outfitters	285,328	52.2	53.5	98
Gentlemen's outfitters	356,251	65.2	64.0	102
DIY	349,292	63.9	60.5	106
Furniture, appliances, durables	361,711	66.2	64.6	102
Shoes	381,834	69.8	70.1	100
Visits to Licensed Premises (at least weekly)				
Pubs	128,807	23.6	26.3	90
Licensed clubs	46,510	8.5	11.6	73
Wine bars	6,061	1.1	1.4	79

© CACI Limited, 1998.   Tel: 0171 602-6000 (London) / 0131 557-0123 (Edinburgh).
Note: [1] PayCheck data. Please see Chapter 3 for details.
Source: © BMRB International Limited, 1997. Buying potential info. modelled using data from TGI 4/96-3/97.

CAMBRIDGESHIRE

Derived using **CACI's** Population Projections for 1998   Data refers to **adults** except where indicated

Base: All GB		Total for Area	As a Percentage of:		Index (GB av. = 100)
			Area	GB Base	
Total Resident Population		719,447	100.0	100.0	100
of whom female		361,612	50.3	50.8	99
By age:	*of whom female (%)*				
0– 4	48.8	48,119	6.7	6.5	104
5– 9	48.9	47,390	6.6	6.6	101
10–14	49.4	44,404	6.2	6.3	97
15–19	49.0	43,664	6.1	6.2	99
20–24	47.9	45,700	6.4	5.9	108
25–34	48.9	120,697	16.8	15.4	109
35–44	48.9	105,587	14.7	14.3	103
45–54	49.6	96,724	13.4	13.1	102
55–64	50.0	66,311	9.2	9.9	93
65–74	52.9	53,421	7.4	8.4	88
75+	62.8	47,430	6.6	7.4	89
Cost of Car (of only or most recently obtained car)					
Up to £2,999		145,057	25.0	22.9	109
£3,000– £4,999		89,164	15.4	13.5	114
£5,000– £6,999		65,569	11.3	11.1	102
£7,000– £9,999		75,521	13.0	11.1	117
£10,000–£19,999		76,284	13.2	12.8	103
£20,000+		9,728	1.7	1.1	149
Owner of a Company Car		49,346	8.5	7.7	111
Income Level of Households[1]					
Up to £4,999		25,274	8.8	10.9	80
£5,000– £9,999		41,121	14.2	16.3	88
£10,000–£14,999		50,208	17.4	18.1	96
£15,000–£19,999		46,847	16.2	15.7	103
£20,000–£24,999		37,497	13.0	12.0	109
£25,000–£29,999		27,493	9.5	8.5	112
£30,000–£34,999		19,198	6.6	5.9	114
£35,000–£39,999		13,073	4.5	4.0	114
£40,000–£44,999		8,808	3.1	2.7	114
£45,000–£49,999		5,925	2.1	1.8	113
£50,000+		13,259	4.6	4.3	108
Use of Multiple Stores in Last Year					
Dept. stores (not groceries)		467,798	80.7	78.5	103
Ladies' outfitters		310,376	53.6	53.5	100
Gentlemen's outfitters		375,440	64.8	64.0	101
DIY		345,324	59.6	60.5	98
Furniture, appliances, durables		372,131	64.2	64.6	99
Shoes		396,496	68.4	70.1	98
Visits to Licensed Premises (at least weekly)					
Pubs		130,361	22.5	26.3	85
Licensed clubs		51,550	8.9	11.6	77
Wine bars		3,606	0.6	1.4	45

© CACI Limited, 1998. Tel: 0171 602-6000 (London) / 0131 557-0123 (Edinburgh).
Note: [1] PayCheck data. Please see Chapter 3 for details.
Source: © BMRB International Limited, 1997. Buying potential info. modelled using data from TGI 4/96-3/97.

CHESHIRE

Derived using **CACI's Population Projections for 1998**   Data refers to **adults** except where indicated

Base: All GB	Total for Area	As a Percentage of: Area	As a Percentage of: GB Base	Index (GB av. = 100)
Total Resident Population	990,168	100.0	100.0	100
of whom female	501,508	50.6	50.8	100
By age: *of whom female (%)*				
0– 4 48.7	62,275	6.3	6.5	97
5– 9 48.5	65,214	6.6	6.6	100
10–14 48.6	64,558	6.5	6.3	103
15–19 48.6	59,820	6.0	6.2	98
20–24 48.8	53,542	5.4	5.9	92
25–34 49.1	147,218	14.9	15.4	96
35–44 49.6	142,860	14.4	14.3	101
45–54 49.5	139,860	14.1	13.1	108
55–64 50.5	104,898	10.6	9.9	107
65–74 53.5	82,645	8.3	8.4	99
75+ 64.4	67,278	6.8	7.4	92
Cost of Car (of only or most recently obtained car)				
Up to £2,999	187,826	23.5	22.9	103
£3,000– £4,999	106,502	13.3	13.5	98
£5,000– £6,999	87,712	11.0	11.1	99
£7,000– £9,999	108,826	13.6	11.1	122
£10,000–£19,999	99,062	12.4	12.8	97
£20,000+	10,751	1.3	1.1	120
Owner of a Company Car	68,149	8.5	7.7	111
Income Level of Households[1]				
Up to £4,999	37,419	9.4	10.9	87
£5,000– £9,999	58,479	14.7	16.3	91
£10,000–£14,999	68,103	17.2	18.1	95
£15,000–£19,999	61,887	15.6	15.7	99
£20,000–£24,999	49,293	12.4	12.0	104
£25,000–£29,999	36,490	9.2	8.5	108
£30,000–£34,999	25,931	6.5	5.9	112
£35,000–£39,999	18,031	4.5	4.0	115
£40,000–£44,999	12,414	3.1	2.7	117
£45,000–£49,999	8,525	2.1	1.8	118
£50,000+	19,998	5.0	4.3	118
Use of Multiple Stores in Last Year				
Dept. stores (not groceries)	619,830	77.7	78.5	99
Ladies' outfitters	444,195	55.7	53.5	104
Gentlemen's outfitters	551,330	69.1	64.0	108
DIY	499,408	62.6	60.5	103
Furniture, appliances, durables	541,294	67.8	64.6	105
Shoes	583,141	73.1	70.1	104
Visits to Licensed Premises (at least weekly)				
Pubs	224,333	28.1	26.3	107
Licensed clubs	97,759	12.2	11.6	106
Wine bars	15,873	2.0	1.4	142

© CACI Limited, 1998.   Tel: 0171 602-6000 (London) / 0131 557-0123 (Edinburgh).
Note: [1] PayCheck data. Please see Chapter 3 for details.
Source: © BMRB International Limited, 1997. Buying potential info. modelled using data from TGI 4/96-3/97.

65

CLEVELAND

Derived using **CACI's Population Projections for 1998**   Data refers to **adults** except where indicated

Base: All GB		Total for Area	As a Percentage of: Area	As a Percentage of: GB Base	Index (GB av. = 100)
Total Resident Population		556,509	100.0	100.0	100
of whom female		283,385	50.9	50.8	100
By age:	*of whom female (%)*				
0– 4	48.8	35,692	6.4	6.5	99
5– 9	49.0	38,842	7.0	6.6	106
10–14	48.9	40,670	7.3	6.3	115
15–19	48.7	38,135	6.9	6.2	111
20–24	47.5	33,734	6.1	5.9	103
25–34	50.0	76,329	13.7	15.4	89
35–44	50.4	80,125	14.4	14.3	101
45–54	49.9	72,565	13.0	13.1	99
55–64	51.0	56,926	10.2	9.9	103
65–74	53.4	48,673	8.7	8.4	104
75+	65.1	34,818	6.3	7.4	85
Cost of Car (of only or most recently obtained car)					
Up to £2,999		89,193	20.2	22.9	88
£3,000– £4,999		47,956	10.9	13.5	80
£5,000– £6,999		45,758	10.4	11.1	93
£7,000– £9,999		47,108	10.7	11.1	96
£10,000–£19,999		52,158	11.8	12.8	93
£20,000+		977	0.2	1.1	20
Owner of a Company Car		23,750	5.4	7.7	70
Income Level of Households[1]					
Up to £4,999		33,275	14.9	10.9	137
£5,000– £9,999		45,349	20.3	16.3	125
£10,000–£14,999		44,416	19.9	18.1	110
£15,000–£19,999		34,197	15.3	15.7	97
£20,000–£24,999		23,615	10.6	12.0	88
£25,000–£29,999		15,480	6.9	8.5	81
£30,000–£34,999		9,891	4.4	5.9	76
£35,000–£39,999		6,250	2.8	4.0	70
£40,000–£44,999		3,942	1.8	2.7	66
£45,000–£49,999		2,496	1.1	1.8	61
£50,000+		4,734	2.1	4.3	50
Use of Multiple Stores in Last Year					
Dept. stores (not groceries)		338,520	76.7	78.5	98
Ladies' outfitters		249,876	56.6	53.5	106
Gentlemen's outfitters		296,104	67.1	64.0	105
DIY		231,487	52.5	60.5	87
Furniture, appliances, durables		290,978	65.9	64.6	102
Shoes		314,335	71.2	70.1	102
Visits to Licensed Premises (at least weekly)					
Pubs		139,945	31.7	26.3	121
Licensed clubs		88,495	20.1	11.6	173
Wine bars		8,734	2.0	1.4	142

© CACI Limited, 1998.   Tel: 0171 602-6000 (London) / 0131 557-0123 (Edinburgh).
Note: [1] PayCheck data. Please see Chapter 3 for details.
Source: © BMRB International Limited, 1997. Buying potential info. modelled using data from TGI 4/96-3/97.

CORNWALL AND THE ISLES OF SCILLY

Derived using **CACI's Population Projections for 1998**   Data refers to **adults** except where indicated

Base: All GB		Total for Area	As a Percentage of:		Index (GB av. = 100)
			Area	GB Base	
Total Resident Population		494,183	100.0	100.0	100
of whom female		253,219	51.2	50.8	101
By age:	*of whom female (%)*				
0– 4	48.6	27,463	5.6	6.5	86
5– 9	48.8	29,273	5.9	6.6	90
10–14	48.3	30,396	6.2	6.3	97
15–19	47.3	28,058	5.7	6.2	92
20–24	48.3	26,892	5.4	5.9	93
25–34	48.3	63,319	12.8	15.4	83
35–44	50.4	64,117	13.0	14.3	91
45–54	51.0	71,005	14.4	13.1	109
55–64	51.2	54,906	11.1	9.9	112
65–74	53.6	51,145	10.3	8.4	123
75+	63.2	47,609	9.6	7.4	130
Cost of Car (of only or most recently obtained car)					
Up to £2,999		142,473	35.0	22.9	153
£3,000– £4,999		66,113	16.2	13.5	120
£5,000– £6,999		45,069	11.1	11.1	100
£7,000– £9,999		27,824	6.8	11.1	61
£10,000–£19,999		37,060	9.1	12.8	71
£20,000+		2,828	0.7	1.1	62
Owner of a Company Car		23,120	5.7	7.7	74
Income Level of Households[1]					
Up to £4,999		27,148	13.6	10.9	125
£5,000– £9,999		40,014	20.0	16.3	123
£10,000–£14,999		42,025	21.0	18.1	116
£15,000–£19,999		33,104	16.5	15.7	105
£20,000–£24,999		22,371	11.2	12.0	94
£25,000–£29,999		13,984	7.0	8.5	82
£30,000–£34,999		8,441	4.2	5.9	72
£35,000–£39,999		5,043	2.5	4.0	63
£40,000–£44,999		3,023	1.5	2.7	56
£45,000–£49,999		1,833	0.9	1.8	50
£50,000+		3,202	1.6	4.3	38
Use of Multiple Stores in Last Year					
Dept. stores (not groceries)		309,273	76.0	78.5	97
Ladies' outfitters		227,575	55.9	53.5	105
Gentlemen's outfitters		263,394	64.7	64.0	101
DIY		248,399	61.0	60.5	101
Furniture, appliances, durables		265,708	65.3	64.6	101
Shoes		280,739	69.0	70.1	98
Visits to Licensed Premises (at least weekly)					
Pubs		103,918	25.5	26.3	97
Licensed clubs		52,041	12.8	11.6	110
Wine bars		5,227	1.3	1.4	92

© CACI Limited, 1998.   Tel: 0171 602-6000 (London) / 0131 557-0123 (Edinburgh).
Note: [1] PayCheck data. Please see Chapter 3 for details.
Source: © BMRB International Limited, 1997. Buying potential info. modelled using data from TGI 4/96-3/97.

CUMBRIA

Derived using **CACI's Population Projections for 1998**   Data refers to **adults** except where indicated

Base: All GB	Total for Area	As a Percentage of: Area	As a Percentage of: GB Base	Index (GB av. = 100)
Total Resident Population	492,921	100.0	100.0	100
of whom female	250,649	50.8	50.8	100
By age: *of whom female (%)*				
0– 4	48.3	28,175	5.7	6.5	89
5– 9	47.9	30,952	6.3	6.6	96
10–14	48.3	30,558	6.2	6.3	98
15–19	48.8	27,710	5.6	6.2	91
20–24	49.2	26,985	5.5	5.9	93
25–34	48.6	67,676	13.7	15.4	89
35–44	49.2	67,421	13.7	14.3	96
45–54	49.4	69,558	14.1	13.1	107
55–64	50.8	55,093	11.2	9.9	112
65–74	54.1	47,689	9.7	8.4	115
75+	64.3	41,104	8.3	7.4	113
Cost of Car (of only or most recently obtained car)				
Up to £2,999	80,957	20.1	22.9	88
£3,000– £4,999	60,266	14.9	13.5	110
£5,000– £6,999	51,927	12.9	11.1	116
£7,000– £9,999	45,966	11.4	11.1	102
£10,000–£19,999	45,149	11.2	12.8	88
£20,000+	3,801	0.9	1.1	84
Owner of a Company Car	19,812	4.9	7.7	64
Income Level of Households[1]				
Up to £4,999	21,662	10.7	10.9	98
£5,000– £9,999	35,222	17.3	16.3	107
£10,000–£14,999	40,087	19.7	18.1	109
£15,000–£19,999	34,194	16.8	15.7	107
£20,000–£24,999	24,984	12.3	12.0	103
£25,000–£29,999	16,814	8.3	8.5	97
£30,000–£34,999	10,853	5.3	5.9	91
£35,000–£39,999	6,878	3.4	4.0	85
£40,000–£44,999	4,340	2.1	2.7	80
£45,000–£49,999	2,748	1.4	1.8	74
£50,000+	5,235	2.6	4.3	60
Use of Multiple Stores in Last Year				
Dept. stores (not groceries)	295,735	73.3	78.5	93
Ladies' outfitters	217,448	53.9	53.5	101
Gentlemen's outfitters	268,375	66.6	64.0	104
DIY	237,811	59.0	60.5	97
Furniture, appliances, durables	259,464	64.3	64.6	100
Shoes	279,321	69.3	70.1	99
Visits to Licensed Premises (at least weekly)				
Pubs	120,116	29.8	26.3	113
Licensed clubs	51,444	12.8	11.6	110
Wine bars	7,883	2.0	1.4	140

© CACI Limited, 1998.   Tel: 0171 602-6000 (London) / 0131 557-0123 (Edinburgh).
Note: [1] PayCheck data. Please see Chapter 3 for details.
Source: © BMRB International Limited, 1997. Buying potential info. modelled using data from TGI 4/96-3/97.

DERBYSHIRE

Derived using **CACI's Population Projections for 1998**   Data refers to **adults** except where indicated

Base: All GB		Total for Area	As a Percentage of:		Index (GB av. = 100)
			Area	GB Base	
Total Resident Population		970,974	100.0	100.0	100
of whom female		489,501	50.4	50.8	99
By age:	*of whom female (%)*				
0– 4	48.8	61,367	6.3	6.5	98
5– 9	48.9	62,880	6.5	6.6	99
10–14	48.7	60,150	6.2	6.3	98
15–19	48.2	56,055	5.8	6.2	94
20–24	48.2	50,716	5.2	5.9	89
25–34	48.7	152,995	15.8	15.4	102
35–44	49.0	139,030	14.3	14.3	10
45–54	49.2	133,474	13.7	13.1	105
55–64	50.1	98,540	10.1	9.9	102
65–74	53.2	84,263	8.7	8.4	103
75+	63.6	71,504	7.4	7.4	100
Cost of Car (of only or most recently obtained car)					
Up to £2,999		187,471	23.8	22.9	104
£3,000– £4,999		114,374	14.5	13.5	107
£5,000– £6,999		91,351	11.6	11.1	105
£7,000– £9,999		85,450	10.9	11.1	98
£10,000–£19,999		97,303	12.4	12.8	97
£20,000+		6,317	0.8	1.1	71
Owner of a Company Car		56,574	7.2	7.7	94
Income Level of Households[1]					
Up to £4,999		45,731	11.6	10.9	106
£5,000– £9,999		69,111	17.5	16.3	108
£10,000–£14,999		76,265	19.3	18.1	107
£15,000–£19,999		64,398	16.3	15.7	104
£20,000–£24,999		47,189	11.9	12.0	100
£25,000–£29,999		32,087	8.1	8.5	96
£30,000–£34,999		21,015	5.3	5.9	91
£35,000–£39,999		13,547	3.4	4.0	86
£40,000–£44,999		8,706	2.2	2.7	82
£45,000–£49,999		5,620	1.4	1.8	78
£50,000+		11,413	2.9	4.3	68
Use of Multiple Stores in Last Year					
Dept. stores (not groceries)		597,458	76.0	78.5	97
Ladies' outfitters		438,623	55.8	53.5	104
Gentlemen's outfitters		525,052	66.8	64.0	104
DIY		489,697	62.3	60.5	103
Furniture, appliances, durables		514,220	65.4	64.6	101
Shoes		563,795	71.7	70.1	102
Visits to Licensed Premises (at least weekly)					
Pubs		231,730	29.5	26.3	112
Licensed clubs		101,647	12.9	11.6	111
Wine bars		13,428	1.7	1.4	122

© CACI Limited, 1998.   Tel: 0171 602-6000 (London) / 0131 557-0123 (Edinburgh).
Note: [1] PayCheck data. Please see Chapter 3 for details.
Source: © BMRB International Limited, 1997. Buying potential info. modelled using data from TGI 4/96-3/97.

DEVON

Derived using **CACI's Population Projections** for 1998   Data refers to **adults** except where indicated

Base: All GB		Total for Area	As a Percentage of: Area	As a Percentage of: GB Base	Index (GB av. = 100)
Total Resident Population		1,075,971	100.0	100.0	100
of whom female		553,707	51.5	50.8	101
By age:	*of whom female (%)*				
0– 4	48.9	60,547	5.6	6.5	87
5– 9	48.9	65,100	6.1	6.6	92
10–14	48.4	65,151	6.1	6.3	95
15–19	48.8	64,990	6.0	6.2	98
20–24	49.2	59,796	5.6	5.9	95
25–34	48.8	144,507	13.4	15.4	87
35–44	50.0	142,372	13.2	14.3	92
45–54	50.5	145,373	13.5	13.1	103
55–64	51.0	113,854	10.6	9.9	106
65–74	53.9	105,494	9.8	8.4	117
75+	64.2	108,787	10.1	7.4	137
Cost of Car (of only or most recently obtained car)					
Up to £2,999		303,610	34.3	22.9	150
£3,000– £4,999		139,158	15.7	13.5	116
£5,000– £6,999		97,223	11.0	11.1	99
£7,000– £9,999		57,119	6.5	11.1	58
£10,000–£19,999		79,104	8.9	12.8	70
£20,000+		6,873	0.8	1.1	69
Owner of a Company Car		50,687	5.7	7.7	75
Income Level of Households[1]					
Up to £4,999		53,731	12.1	10.9	111
£5,000– £9,999		83,651	18.9	16.3	116
£10,000–£14,999		91,324	20.6	18.1	114
£15,000–£19,999		74,436	16.8	15.7	107
£20,000–£24,999		51,880	11.7	12.0	98
£25,000–£29,999		33,350	7.5	8.5	89
£30,000–£34,999		20,654	4.7	5.9	80
£35,000–£39,999		12,635	2.9	4.0	72
£40,000–£44,999		7,744	1.7	2.7	65
£45,000–£49,999		4,794	1.1	1.8	59
£50,000+		8,834	2.0	4.3	47
Use of Multiple Stores in Last Year					
Dept. stores (not groceries)		680,794	76.9	78.5	98
Ladies' outfitters		493,882	55.8	53.5	104
Gentlemen's outfitters		570,805	64.5	64.0	101
DIY		547,619	61.9	60.5	102
Furniture, appliances, durables		583,785	66.0	64.6	102
Shoes		611,988	69.1	70.1	99
Visits to Licensed Premises (at least weekly)					
Pubs		234,473	26.5	26.3	101
Licensed clubs		118,776	13.4	11.6	116
Wine bars		12,833	1.4	1.4	104

© CACI Limited, 1998. Tel: 0171 602-6000 (London) / 0131 557-0123 (Edinburgh).
Note: [1] PayCheck data. Please see Chapter 3 for details.
Source: © BMRB International Limited, 1997. Buying potential info. modelled using data from TGI 4/96-3/97.

DORSET

Derived using **CACI's** Population Projections for 1998   Data refers to **adults** except where indicated

Base: All GB		Total for Area	As a Percentage of: Area	GB Base	Index (GB av. = 100)
Total Resident Population		695,042	100.0	100.0	100
of whom female		359,139	51.7	50.8	102
By age:	*of whom female (%)*				
0– 4	48.9	38,543	5.5	6.5	86
5– 9	49.1	39,487	5.7	6.6	87
10–14	48.4	40,147	5.8	6.3	91
15–19	48.4	38,125	5.5	6.2	89
20–24	48.3	38,206	5.5	5.9	94
25–34	48.3	96,580	13.9	15.4	90
35–44	49.7	89,286	12.8	14.3	90
45–54	50.5	91,559	13.2	13.1	100
55–64	51.5	70,533	10.1	9.9	102
65–74	55.0	72,360	10.4	8.4	124
75+	63.8	80,216	11.5	7.4	156
Cost of Car (of only or most recently obtained car)					
Up to £2,999		162,184	28.1	22.9	123
£3,000– £4,999		85,923	14.9	13.5	110
£5,000– £6,999		65,243	11.3	11.1	102
£7,000– £9,999		57,169	9.9	11.1	89
£10,000–£19,999		78,715	13.6	12.8	107
£20,000+		5,265	0.9	1.1	81
Owner of a Company Car		46,957	8.1	7.7	106
Income Level of Households[1]					
Up to £4,999		31,022	10.7	10.9	98
£5,000– £9,999		48,588	16.8	16.3	103
£10,000–£14,999		55,810	19.3	18.1	106
£15,000–£19,999		48,438	16.7	15.7	106
£20,000–£24,999		35,940	12.4	12.0	104
£25,000–£29,999		24,489	8.5	8.5	99
£30,000–£34,999		15,990	5.5	5.9	94
£35,000–£39,999		10,258	3.5	4.0	89
£40,000–£44,999		6,559	2.3	2.7	84
£45,000–£49,999		4,215	1.5	1.8	80
£50,000+		8,447	2.9	4.3	68
Use of Multiple Stores in Last Year					
Dept. stores (not groceries)		470,817	81.6	78.5	104
Ladies' outfitters		311,839	54.1	53.5	101
Gentlemen's outfitters		353,457	61.3	64.0	96
DIY		371,909	64.5	60.5	106
Furniture, appliances, durables		382,658	66.3	64.6	103
Shoes		403,879	70.0	70.1	100
Visits to Licensed Premises (at least weekly)					
Pubs		128,885	22.3	26.3	85
Licensed clubs		61,905	10.7	11.6	92
Wine bars		5,535	1.0	1.4	69

© CACI Limited, 1998.   Tel: 0171 602-6000 (London) / 0131 557-0123 (Edinburgh).
Note: [1] PayCheck data. Please see Chapter 3 for details.
Source: © BMRB International Limited, 1997. Buying potential info. modelled using data from TGI 4/96-3/97.

DURHAM

Derived using **CACI's Population Projections for 1998**   Data refers to **adults** except where indicated

Base: All GB		Total for Area	As a Percentage of: Area	GB Base	Index (GB av. = 100)
Total Resident Population		609,496	100.0	100.0	100
of whom female		310,108	50.9	50.8	100
By age:	*of whom female (%)*				
0– 4	48.8	35,981	5.9	6.5	91
5– 9	49.1	38,768	6.4	6.6	97
10–14	48.1	39,215	6.4	6.3	101
15–19	47.7	38,815	6.4	6.2	103
20–24	49.3	34,114	5.6	5.9	95
25–34	48.8	88,006	14.4	15.4	94
35–44	50.0	86,567	14.2	14.3	99
45–54	50.0	83,636	13.7	13.1	104
55–64	50.9	65,156	10.7	9.9	108
65–74	53.6	55,845	9.2	8.4	109
75+	64.9	43,393	7.1	7.4	96
Cost of Car (of only or most recently obtained car)					
Up to £2,999		106,000	21.4	22.9	93
£3,000– £4,999		57,267	11.6	13.5	85
£5,000– £6,999		51,889	10.5	11.1	94
£7,000– £9,999		52,320	10.6	11.1	95
£10,000–£19,999		56,197	11.3	12.8	89
£20,000+		1,024	0.2	1.1	18
Owner of a Company Car		27,932	5.6	7.7	74
Income Level of Households[1]					
Up to £4,999		35,802	14.3	10.9	131
£5,000– £9,999		50,943	20.3	16.3	125
£10,000–£14,999		50,870	20.3	18.1	112
£15,000–£19,999		39,059	15.6	15.7	99
£20,000–£24,999		26,556	10.6	12.0	89
£25,000–£29,999		17,108	6.8	8.5	80
£30,000–£34,999		10,796	4.3	5.9	74
£35,000–£39,999		6,786	2.7	4.0	68
£40,000–£44,999		4,287	1.7	2.7	64
£45,000–£49,999		2,736	1.1	1.8	60
£50,000+		5,450	2.2	4.3	51
Use of Multiple Stores in Last Year					
Dept. stores (not groceries)		379,515	76.6	78.5	98
Ladies' outfitters		279,385	56.4	53.5	105
Gentlemen's outfitters		331,932	67.0	64.0	105
DIY		259,059	52.3	60.5	86
Furniture, appliances, durables		324,375	65.5	64.6	101
Shoes		353,942	71.4	70.1	102
Visits to Licensed Premises (at least weekly)					
Pubs		160,480	32.4	26.3	123
Licensed clubs		101,920	20.6	11.6	177
Wine bars		12,809	2.6	1.4	185

© CACI Limited, 1998. Tel: 0171 602-6000 (London) / 0131 557-0123 (Edinburgh).
Note: [1] PayCheck data. Please see Chapter 3 for details.
Source: © BMRB International Limited, 1997. Buying potential info. modelled using data from TGI 4/96-3/97.

EAST SUSSEX

Derived using **CACI's** Population Projections for 1998   Data refers to **adults** except where indicated

Base: All GB	Total for Area	As a Percentage of: Area	As a Percentage of: GB Base	Index (GB av. = 100)
Total Resident Population	737,481	100.0	100.0	100
of whom female	386,397	52.4	50.8	103
By age: *of whom female (%)*				
0– 4 48.7	42,122	5.7	6.5	88
5– 9 49.1	43,500	5.9	6.6	90
10–14 49.9	41,927	5.7	6.3	90
15–19 49.0	40,804	5.5	6.2	90
20–24 50.1	40,726	5.5	5.9	94
25–34 49.5	101,894	13.8	15.4	90
35–44 50.4	98,531	13.4	14.3	93
45–54 50.3	97,272	13.2	13.1	100
55–64 51.6	72,986	9.9	9.9	100
65–74 55.9	72,055	9.8	8.4	116
75+ 65.8	85,664	11.6	7.4	157
Cost of Car (of only or most recently obtained car)				
Up to £2,999	164,640	27.0	22.9	118
£3,000– £4,999	84,167	13.8	13.5	102
£5,000– £6,999	65,816	10.8	11.1	97
£7,000– £9,999	61,436	10.1	11.1	90
£10,000–£19,999	83,872	13.8	12.8	108
£20,000+	5,642	0.9	1.1	82
Owner of a Company Car	52,898	8.7	7.7	113
Income Level of Households[1]				
Up to £4,999	35,377	11.1	10.9	102
£5,000– £9,999	51,750	16.2	16.3	99
£10,000–£14,999	58,090	18.2	18.1	100
£15,000–£19,999	50,549	15.8	15.7	101
£20,000–£24,999	38,418	12.0	12.0	101
£25,000–£29,999	27,212	8.5	8.5	100
£30,000–£34,999	18,618	5.8	5.9	99
£35,000–£39,999	12,556	3.9	4.0	99
£40,000–£44,999	8,442	2.6	2.7	98
£45,000–£49,999	5,697	1.8	1.8	98
£50,000+	13,150	4.1	4.3	96
Use of Multiple Stores in Last Year				
Dept. stores (not groceries)	501,855	82.3	78.5	105
Ladies' outfitters	325,086	53.3	53.5	100
Gentlemen's outfitters	365,634	59.9	64.0	94
DIY	391,583	64.2	60.5	106
Furniture, appliances, durables	400,434	65.7	64.6	102
Shoes	426,710	70.0	70.1	100
Visits to Licensed Premises (at least weekly)				
Pubs	134,428	22.0	26.3	84
Licensed clubs	60,469	9.9	11.6	85
Wine bars	5,550	0.9	1.4	65

© CACI Limited, 1998.   Tel: 0171 602-6000 (London) / 0131 557-0123 (Edinburgh).
Note: [1] PayCheck data. Please see Chapter 3 for details.
Source: © BMRB International Limited, 1997. Buying potential info. modelled using data from TGI 4/96-3/97.

ESSEX

Derived using **CACI's Population Projections for 1998**   Data refers to **adults** except where indicated

Base: All GB		Total for Area	As a Percentage of: Area	GB Base	Index (GB av. = 100)
Total Resident Population		1,595,977	100.0	100.0	100
of whom female		812,584	50.9	50.8	100
By age:	*of whom female (%)*				
0– 4	48.7	102,972	6.5	6.5	100
5– 9	48.8	102,153	6.4	6.6	98
10–14	48.9	97,727	6.1	6.3	96
15–19	48.7	92,311	5.8	6.2	94
20–24	48.6	90,571	5.7	5.9	97
25–34	48.9	246,705	15.5	15.4	100
35–44	49.7	221,366	13.9	14.3	97
45–54	50.4	222,898	14.0	13.1	106
55–64	50.8	160,481	10.1	9.9	101
65–74	53.6	136,453	8.5	8.4	102
75+	63.9	122,340	7.7	7.4	104
Cost of Car (of only or most recently obtained car)					
Up to £2,999		291,372	22.5	22.9	98
£3,000– £4,999		199,744	15.4	13.5	114
£5,000– £6,999		160,384	12.4	11.1	112
£7,000– £9,999		166,215	12.9	11.1	115
£10,000–£19,999		220,458	17.0	12.8	133
£20,000+		24,488	1.9	1.1	168
Owner of a Company Car		130,754	10.1	7.7	132
Income Level of Households[1]					
Up to £4,999		57,149	8.8	10.9	81
£5,000– £9,999		88,221	13.6	16.3	84
£10,000–£14,999		106,772	16.5	18.1	91
£15,000–£19,999		100,651	15.5	15.7	99
£20,000–£24,999		82,346	12.7	12.0	106
£25,000–£29,999		62,126	9.6	8.5	113
£30,000–£34,999		44,781	6.9	5.9	118
£35,000–£39,999		31,500	4.9	4.0	123
£40,000–£44,999		21,906	3.4	2.7	126
£45,000–£49,999		15,182	2.3	1.8	129
£50,000+		36,782	5.7	4.3	133
Use of Multiple Stores in Last Year					
Dept. stores (not groceries)		1,080,196	83.5	78.5	106
Ladies' outfitters		663,284	51.3	53.5	96
Gentlemen's outfitters		825,741	63.9	64.0	100
DIY		815,551	63.1	60.5	104
Furniture, appliances, durables		840,871	65.0	64.6	101
Shoes		882,363	68.2	70.1	97
Visits to Licensed Premises (at least weekly)					
Pubs		283,813	21.9	26.3	83
Licensed clubs		110,429	8.5	11.6	74
Wine bars		12,872	1.0	1.4	71

© CACI Limited, 1998.   Tel: 0171 602-6000 (London) / 0131 557-0123 (Edinburgh).
Note: [1] PayCheck data. Please see Chapter 3 for details.
Source: © BMRB International Limited, 1997. Buying potential info. modelled using data from TGI 4/96-3/97.

GLOUCESTERSHIRE

Derived using **CACI's Population Projections for 1998**   Data refers to **adults** except where indicated

Base: All GB		Total for Area	As a Percentage of: Area	As a Percentage of: GB Base	Index (GB av. = 100)
Total Resident Population		562,901	100.0	100.0	100
of whom female		284,637	50.6	50.8	99
By age:	*of whom female (%)*				
0– 4	48.2	34,235	6.1	6.5	94
5– 9	47.7	36,134	6.4	6.6	98
10–14	49.2	34,910	6.2	6.3	98
15–19	48.6	32,945	5.9	6.2	95
20–24	48.6	29,812	5.3	5.9	90
25–34	47.7	81,785	14.5	15.4	94
35–44	49.1	78,648	14.0	14.3	98
45–54	49.9	77,881	13.8	13.1	105
55–64	49.9	58,837	10.5	9.9	105
65–74	53.6	50,887	9.0	8.4	108
75+	64.3	46,827	8.3	7.4	113
Cost of Car (of only or most recently obtained car)					
Up to £2,999		106,878	23.4	22.9	102
£3,000– £4,999		72,068	15.7	13.5	116
£5,000– £6,999		55,652	12.2	11.1	110
£7,000– £9,999		56,113	12.3	11.1	110
£10,000–£19,999		67,482	14.7	12.8	115
£20,000+		6,538	1.4	1.1	127
Owner of a Company Car		39,738	8.7	7.7	113
Income Level of Households[1]					
Up to £4,999		21,784	9.4	10.9	86
£5,000– £9,999		35,126	15.2	16.3	93
£10,000–£14,999		41,973	18.1	18.1	100
£15,000–£19,999		38,127	16.4	15.7	105
£20,000–£24,999		29,684	12.8	12.0	107
£25,000–£29,999		21,207	9.1	8.5	108
£30,000–£34,999		14,471	6.2	5.9	107
£35,000–£39,999		9,659	4.2	4.0	105
£40,000–£44,999		6,397	2.8	2.7	103
£45,000–£49,999		4,240	1.8	1.8	100
£50,000+		9,179	4.0	4.3	93
Use of Multiple Stores in Last Year					
Dept. stores (not groceries)		356,716	78.0	78.5	99
Ladies' outfitters		249,577	54.5	53.5	102
Gentlemen's outfitters		296,525	64.8	64.0	101
DIY		282,730	61.8	60.5	102
Furniture, appliances, durables		295,164	64.5	64.6	100
Shoes		325,380	71.1	70.1	101
Visits to Licensed Premises (at least weekly)					
Pubs		132,648	29.0	26.3	110
Licensed clubs		51,359	11.2	11.6	97
Wine bars		7,188	1.6	1.4	112

© CACI Limited, 1998.   Tel: 0171 602-6000 (London) / 0131 557-0123 (Edinburgh).
Note: [1] PayCheck data. Please see Chapter 3 for details.
Source: © BMRB International Limited, 1997. Buying potential info. modelled using data from TGI 4/96-3/97.

HAMPSHIRE

Derived using **CACI's Population Projections for 1998**   Data refers to **adults** except where indicated

Base: All GB		Total for Area	As a Percentage of: Area	As a Percentage of: GB Base	Index (GB av. = 100)
Total Resident Population		1,634,056	100.0	100.0	100
of whom female		824,454	50.5	50.8	99
By age:	*of whom female (%)*				
0– 4	48.8	102,351	6.3	6.5	97
5– 9	48.9	105,507	6.5	6.6	99
10–14	48.7	103,758	6.3	6.3	100
15–19	48.7	100,722	6.2	6.2	100
20–24	48.5	93,924	5.7	5.9	98
25–34	47.3	251,448	15.4	15.4	100
35–44	48.9	236,343	14.5	14.3	101
45–54	50.1	221,467	13.6	13.1	103
55–64	50.5	162,273	9.9	9.9	100
65–74	53.4	133,935	8.2	8.4	98
75+	64.3	122,328	7.5	7.4	101
Cost of Car (of only or most recently obtained car)					
Up to £2,999		362,293	27.4	22.9	119
£3,000– £4,999		188,796	14.3	13.5	105
£5,000– £6,999		144,618	10.9	11.1	98
£7,000– £9,999		140,014	10.6	11.1	95
£10,000–£19,999		191,895	14.5	12.8	114
£20,000+		13,028	1.0	1.1	88
Owner of a Company Car		118,995	9.0	7.7	117
Income Level of Households[1]					
Up to £4,999		57,473	8.7	10.9	80
£5,000– £9,999		93,468	14.2	16.3	87
£10,000–£14,999		113,602	17.2	18.1	95
£15,000–£19,999		105,833	16.1	15.7	102
£20,000–£24,999		84,920	12.9	12.0	108
£25,000–£29,999		62,634	9.5	8.5	112
£30,000–£34,999		44,108	6.7	5.9	114
£35,000–£39,999		30,330	4.6	4.0	116
£40,000–£44,999		20,643	3.1	2.7	117
£45,000–£49,999		14,022	2.1	1.8	117
£50,000+		32,153	4.9	4.3	114
Use of Multiple Stores in Last Year					
Dept. stores (not groceries)		1,093,268	82.7	78.5	105
Ladies' outfitters		713,376	53.9	53.5	101
Gentlemen's outfitters		825,401	62.4	64.0	98
DIY		870,996	65.9	60.5	109
Furniture, appliances, durables		892,927	67.5	64.6	105
Shoes		930,187	70.3	70.1	100
Visits to Licensed Premises (at least weekly)					
Pubs		282,574	21.4	26.3	81
Licensed clubs		131,544	9.9	11.6	86
Wine bars		10,694	0.8	1.4	58

© CACI Limited, 1998.   Tel: 0171 602-6000 (London) / 0131 557-0123 (Edinburgh).
Note: [1] PayCheck data. Please see Chapter 3 for details.
Source: © BMRB International Limited, 1997. Buying potential info. modelled using data from TGI 4/96-3/97.

HEREFORD AND WORCESTER

Derived using **CACI's Population Projections for 1998**   Data refers to **adults** except where indicated

Base: All GB		Total for Area	As a Percentage of:		Index (GB av. = 100)
			Area	GB Base	
Total Resident Population		708,300	100.0	100.0	100
of whom female		359,206	50.7	50.8	100
By age:	*of whom female (%)*				
0– 4	49.0	43,563	6.2	6.5	95
5– 9	48.7	44,943	6.3	6.6	97
10–14	48.4	43,698	6.2	6.3	97
15–19	48.5	40,497	5.7	6.2	93
20–24	48.6	36,328	5.1	5.9	87
25–34	49.0	105,018	14.8	15.4	96
35–44	50.0	97,869	13.8	14.3	97
45–54	49.9	103,610	14.6	13.1	111
55–64	49.9	75,641	10.7	9.9	107
65–74	53.0	62,580	8.8	8.4	105
75+	63.4	54,553	7.7	7.4	104
Cost of Car (of only or most recently obtained car)					
Up to £2,999		134,863	23.4	22.9	102
£3,000– £4,999		85,499	14.8	13.5	110
£5,000– £6,999		71,619	12.4	11.1	112
£7,000– £9,999		68,965	12.0	11.1	107
£10,000–£19,999		92,815	16.1	12.8	126
£20,000+		7,812	1.4	1.1	121
Owner of a Company Car		50,512	8.8	7.7	114
Income Level of Households[1]					
Up to £4,999		28,253	10.0	10.9	92
£5,000– £9,999		44,235	15.6	16.3	96
£10,000–£14,999		51,447	18.2	18.1	100
£15,000–£19,999		45,832	16.2	15.7	103
£20,000–£24,999		35,316	12.5	12.0	104
£25,000–£29,999		25,156	8.9	8.5	104
£30,000–£34,999		17,203	6.1	5.9	104
£35,000–£39,999		11,543	4.1	4.0	103
£40,000–£44,999		7,699	2.7	2.7	101
£45,000–£49,999		5,143	1.8	1.8	100
£50,000+		11,388	4.0	4.3	94
Use of Multiple Stores in Last Year					
Dept. stores (not groceries)		453,020	78.6	78.5	100
Ladies' outfitters		319,625	55.5	53.5	104
Gentlemen's outfitters		385,239	66.9	64.0	105
DIY		363,291	63.1	60.5	104
Furniture, appliances, durables		377,750	65.6	64.6	102
Shoes		415,609	72.1	70.1	103
Visits to Licensed Premises (at least weekly)					
Pubs		167,880	29.1	26.3	111
Licensed clubs		59,753	10.4	11.6	89
Wine bars		9,722	1.7	1.4	121

© CACI Limited, 1998.   Tel: 0171 602-6000 (London) / 0131 557-0123 (Edinburgh).
Note: [1] PayCheck data. Please see Chapter 3 for details.
Source: © BMRB International Limited, 1997. Buying potential info. modelled using data from TGI 4/96-3/97.

HERTFORDSHIRE

Derived using **CACI's Population Projections for 1998**   Data refers to **adults** except where indicated

Base: All GB	Total for Area	As a Percentage of: Area	GB Base	Index (GB av. = 100)
Total Resident Population	1,023,216	100.0	100.0	100
of whom female	518,233	50.6	50.8	100
By age: *of whom female (%)*				
0– 4	48.8	68,686	6.7	6.5	104
5– 9	49.0	69,139	6.8	6.6	103
10–14	48.5	64,305	6.3	6.3	99
15–19	48.6	61,183	6.0	6.2	97
20–24	48.6	55,902	5.5	5.9	93
25–34	49.5	157,344	15.4	15.4	100
35–44	49.2	153,388	15.0	14.3	105
45–54	50.0	138,659	13.6	13.1	103
55–64	50.5	101,447	9.9	9.9	100
65–74	53.1	83,508	8.2	8.4	97
75+	63.6	69,655	6.8	7.4	92
Cost of Car (of only or most recently obtained car)				
Up to £2,999	171,327	20.9	22.9	91
£3,000– £4,999	124,368	15.1	13.5	112
£5,000– £6,999	102,825	12.5	11.1	113
£7,000– £9,999	110,048	13.4	11.1	120
£10,000–£19,999	159,983	19.5	12.8	153
£20,000+	19,288	2.3	1.1	209
Owner of a Company Car	94,129	11.5	7.7	150
Income Level of Households[1]				
Up to £4,999	27,742	6.8	10.9	63
£5,000– £9,999	45,431	11.1	16.3	69
£10,000–£14,999	59,052	14.5	18.1	80
£15,000–£19,999	59,969	14.7	15.7	94
£20,000–£24,999	52,703	12.9	12.0	108
£25,000–£29,999	42,464	10.4	8.5	123
£30,000–£34,999	32,462	8.0	5.9	136
£35,000–£39,999	24,049	5.9	4.0	149
£40,000–£44,999	17,498	4.3	2.7	160
£45,000–£49,999	12,614	3.1	1.8	170
£50,000+	33,480	8.2	4.3	193
Use of Multiple Stores in Last Year				
Dept. stores (not groceries)	702,509	85.6	78.5	109
Ladies' outfitters	410,709	50.0	53.5	94
Gentlemen's outfitters	517,935	63.1	64.0	99
DIY	525,257	64.0	60.5	106
Furniture, appliances, durables	536,782	65.4	64.6	101
Shoes	560,254	68.2	70.1	97
Visits to Licensed Premises (at least weekly)				
Pubs	181,048	22.0	26.3	84
Licensed clubs	65,658	8.0	11.6	69
Wine bars	10,059	1.2	1.4	88

© CACI Limited, 1998.   Tel: 0171 602-6000 (London) / 0131 557-0123 (Edinburgh).
Note: [1] PayCheck data. Please see Chapter 3 for details.
Source: © BMRB International Limited, 1997. Buying potential info. modelled using data from TGI 4/96-3/97.

HUMBERSIDE

Derived using **CACI's Population Projections for 1998**   Data refers to **adults** except where indicated

Base: All GB		Total for Area	As a Percentage of: Area	As a Percentage of: GB Base	Index (GB av. = 100)
Total Resident Population		897,958	100.0	100.0	100
of whom female		455,959	50.8	50.8	100
By age:	*of whom female (%)*				
0– 4	48.8	55,757	6.2	6.5	96
5– 9	48.7	60,269	6.7	6.6	102
10–14	48.7	60,304	6.7	6.3	106
15–19	48.7	56,730	6.3	6.2	103
20–24	47.5	53,965	6.0	5.9	102
25–34	48.8	126,542	14.1	15.4	91
35–44	49.7	124,357	13.8	14.3	97
45–54	50.0	119,323	13.3	13.1	101
55–64	50.8	92,391	10.3	9.9	103
65–74	53.5	80,529	9.0	8.4	107
75+	64.3	67,791	7.5	7.4	102
Cost of Car (of only or most recently obtained car)					
Up to £2,999		149,213	20.7	22.9	90
£3,000– £4,999		85,706	11.9	13.5	88
£5,000– £6,999		90,638	12.6	11.1	113
£7,000– £9,999		78,979	10.9	11.1	98
£10,000–£19,999		87,466	12.1	12.8	95
£20,000+		5,240	0.7	1.1	65
Owner of a Company Car		48,047	6.7	7.7	87
Income Level of Households[1]					
Up to £4,999		47,049	13.0	10.9	119
£5,000– £9,999		70,379	19.4	16.3	119
£10,000–£14,999		73,132	20.2	18.1	111
£15,000–£19,999		58,209	16.1	15.7	102
£20,000–£24,999		40,612	11.2	12.0	94
£25,000–£29,999		26,542	7.3	8.5	86
£30,000–£34,999		16,838	4.6	5.9	79
£35,000–£39,999		10,584	2.9	4.0	74
£40,000–£44,999		6,669	1.8	2.7	69
£45,000–£49,999		4,241	1.2	1.8	64
£50,000+		8,392	2.3	4.3	54
Use of Multiple Stores in Last Year					
Dept. stores (not groceries)		531,432	73.6	78.5	94
Ladies' outfitters		394,787	54.7	53.5	102
Gentlemen's outfitters		476,536	66.0	64.0	103
DIY		447,107	62.0	60.5	102
Furniture, appliances, durables		458,405	63.5	64.6	98
Shoes		510,340	70.7	70.1	101
Visits to Licensed Premises (at least weekly)					
Pubs		222,928	30.9	26.3	117
Licensed clubs		100,009	13.9	11.6	119
Wine bars		8,821	1.2	1.4	88

© CACI Limited, 1998.   Tel: 0171 602-6000 (London) / 0131 557-0123 (Edinburgh).
Note: [1] PayCheck data. Please see Chapter 3 for details.
Source: © BMRB International Limited, 1997. Buying potential info. modelled using data from TGI 4/96-3/97.

ISLE OF WIGHT

Derived using **CACI's Population Projections for 1998** Data refers to **adults** except where indicated

Base: All GB		Total for Area	As a Percentage of: Area	GB Base	Index (GB av. = 100)
Total Resident Population		125,846	100.0	100.0	100
of whom female		65,112	51.7	50.8	102
By age:	*of whom female (%)*				
0– 4	48.3	6,611	5.3	6.5	81
5– 9	48.2	6,840	5.4	6.6	83
10–14	47.6	7,424	5.9	6.3	93
15–19	47.3	6,875	5.5	6.2	89
20–24	48.4	6,833	5.4	5.9	92
25–34	47.7	15,500	12.3	15.4	80
35–44	51.0	14,661	11.6	14.3	81
45–54	50.0	17,906	14.2	13.1	108
55–64	51.5	14,206	11.3	9.9	114
65–74	55.4	13,904	11.0	8.4	132
75+	64.2	15,086	12.0	7.4	162
Cost of Car (of only or most recently obtained car)					
Up to £2,999		29,804	28.4	22.9	124
£3,000– £4,999		15,353	14.6	13.5	108
£5,000– £6,999		11,160	10.6	11.1	96
£7,000– £9,999		10,514	10.0	11.1	90
£10,000–£19,999		14,029	13.4	12.8	105
£20,000+		764	0.7	1.1	65
Owner of a Company Car		7,795	7.4	7.7	97
Income Level of Households[1]					
Up to £4,999		7,317	13.8	10.9	127
£5,000– £9,999		10,558	19.9	16.3	122
£10,000–£14,999		11,011	20.8	18.1	115
£15,000–£19,999		8,672	16.4	15.7	104
£20,000–£24,999		5,889	11.1	12.0	93
£25,000–£29,999		3,711	7.0	8.5	82
£30,000–£34,999		2,262	4.3	5.9	73
£35,000–£39,999		1,366	2.6	4.0	65
£40,000–£44,999		828	1.6	2.7	58
£45,000–£49,999		507	1.0	1.8	53
£50,000+		914	1.7	4.3	40
Use of Multiple Stores in Last Year					
Dept. stores (not groceries)		84,499	80.5	78.5	103
Ladies' outfitters		56,766	54.1	53.5	101
Gentlemen's outfitters		63,697	60.7	64.0	95
DIY		67,661	64.5	60.5	106
Furniture, appliances, durables		68,749	65.5	64.6	101
Shoes		73,054	69.6	70.1	99
Visits to Licensed Premises (at least weekly)					
Pubs		21,799	20.8	26.3	79
Licensed clubs		11,488	10.9	11.6	94
Wine bars		878	0.8	1.4	60

© CACI Limited, 1998. Tel: 0171 602-6000 (London) / 0131 557-0123 (Edinburgh).
Note: [1] PayCheck data. Please see Chapter 3 for details.
Source: © BMRB International Limited, 1997. Buying potential info. modelled using data from TGI 4/96-3/97.

KENT

Derived using **CACI's Population Projections** for 1998   Data refers to **adults** except where indicated

Base: All GB		Total for Area	As a Percentage of:		Index (GB av. = 100)
			Area	GB Base	
Total Resident Population		1,566,487	100.0	100.0	100
of whom female		798,714	51.0	50.8	100
By age:	*of whom female (%)*				
0– 4	48.8	98,362	6.3	6.5	97
5– 9	48.6	102,076	6.5	6.6	99
10–14	48.6	100,045	6.4	6.3	101
15–19	48.7	92,077	5.9	6.2	95
20–24	48.9	90,140	5.8	5.9	98
25–34	48.6	228,518	14.6	15.4	95
35–44	49.9	214,126	13.7	14.3	96
45–54	50.2	218,470	13.9	13.1	106
55–64	50.4	161,553	10.3	9.9	104
65–74	54.1	134,911	8.6	8.4	103
75+	64.6	126,209	8.1	7.4	109
Cost of Car (of only or most recently obtained car)					
Up to £2,999		345,671	27.3	22.9	119
£3,000– £4,999		184,479	14.6	13.5	108
£5,000– £6,999		140,304	11.1	11.1	100
£7,000– £9,999		130,700	10.3	11.1	93
£10,000–£19,999		180,212	14.2	12.8	111
£20,000+		13,285	1.0	1.1	93
Owner of a Company Car		111,015	8.8	7.7	114
Income Level of Households[1]					
Up to £4,999		59,763	9.5	10.9	87
£5,000– £9,999		93,105	14.8	16.3	91
£10,000–£14,999		110,381	17.5	18.1	97
£15,000–£19,999		100,982	16.0	15.7	102
£20,000–£24,999		79,906	12.7	12.0	106
£25,000–£29,999		58,255	9.2	8.5	109
£30,000–£34,999		40,597	6.4	5.9	110
£35,000–£39,999		27,656	4.4	4.0	111
£40,000–£44,999		18,672	3.0	2.7	110
£45,000–£49,999		12,601	2.0	1.8	110
£50,000+		28,722	4.6	4.3	107
Use of Multiple Stores in Last Year					
Dept. stores (not groceries)		1,039,451	82.1	78.5	105
Ladies' outfitters		677,421	53.5	53.5	100
Gentlemen's outfitters		788,749	62.3	64.0	97
DIY		826,052	65.2	60.5	108
Furniture, appliances, durables		844,795	66.7	64.6	103
Shoes		883,522	69.8	70.1	100
Visits to Licensed Premises (at least weekly)					
Pubs		269,868	21.3	26.3	81
Licensed clubs		126,868	10.0	11.6	86
Wine bars		11,171	0.9	1.4	63

© CACI Limited, 1998.   Tel: 0171 602-6000 (London) / 0131 557-0123 (Edinburgh).
Note: [1] PayCheck data. Please see Chapter 3 for details.
Source: © BMRB International Limited, 1997. Buying potential info. modelled using data from TGI 4/96-3/97.

LANCASHIRE

Derived using **CACI's Population Projections for 1998**   Data refers to **adults** except where indicated

Base: All GB	Total for Area	As a Percentage of: Area	GB Base	Index (GB av. = 100)
Total Resident Population	1,435,630	100.0	100.0	100
of whom female	731,292	50.9	50.8	100
By age: *of whom female (%)*				
0– 4	48.7	91,538	6.4	6.5	99
5– 9	48.7	96,077	6.7	6.6	102
10–14	48.4	95,539	6.7	6.3	105
15–19	48.4	89,873	6.3	6.2	102
20–24	48.1	85,605	6.0	5.9	101
25–34	48.6	203,827	14.2	15.4	92
35–44	50.0	194,409	13.5	14.3	95
45–54	49.7	192,206	13.4	13.1	102
55–64	50.5	147,922	10.3	9.9	104
65–74	54.2	126,185	8.8	8.4	105
75+	65.7	112,449	7.8	7.4	106
Cost of Car (of only or most recently obtained car)				
Up to £2,999	280,419	24.3	22.9	106
£3,000– £4,999	152,893	13.3	13.5	98
£5,000– £6,999	119,920	10.4	11.1	94
£7,000– £9,999	138,408	12.0	11.1	108
£10,000–£19,999	120,015	10.4	12.8	82
£20,000+	11,499	1.0	1.1	89
Owner of a Company Car	81,684	7.1	7.7	92
Income Level of Households[1]				
Up to £4,999	65,917	11.5	10.9	106
£5,000– £9,999	100,517	17.5	16.3	108
£10,000–£14,999	110,583	19.3	18.1	107
£15,000–£19,999	93,079	16.2	15.7	103
£20,000–£24,999	68,116	11.9	12.0	100
£25,000–£29,999	46,355	8.1	8.5	95
£30,000–£34,999	30,445	5.3	5.9	91
£35,000–£39,999	19,711	3.4	4.0	87
£40,000–£44,999	12,734	2.2	2.7	83
£45,000–£49,999	8,269	1.4	1.8	79
£50,000+	17,077	3.0	4.3	70
Use of Multiple Stores in Last Year				
Dept. stores (not groceries)	881,402	76.5	78.5	97
Ladies' outfitters	643,737	55.9	53.5	104
Gentlemen's outfitters	791,622	68.7	64.0	107
DIY	706,859	61.3	60.5	101
Furniture, appliances, durables	776,102	67.3	64.6	104
Shoes	842,234	73.1	70.1	104
Visits to Licensed Premises (at least weekly)				
Pubs	329,185	28.6	26.3	109
Licensed clubs	147,827	12.8	11.6	110
Wine bars	22,543	2.0	1.4	140

© CACI Limited, 1998. Tel: 0171 602-6000 (London) / 0131 557-0123 (Edinburgh).
Note: [1] PayCheck data. Please see Chapter 3 for details.
Source: © BMRB International Limited, 1997. Buying potential info. modelled using data from TGI 4/96-3/97.

LEICESTERSHIRE

Derived using **CACI's Population Projections** for 1998   Data refers to **adults** except where indicated

Base: All GB	Total for Area	As a Percentage of:		Index (GB av. = 100)
		Area	GB Base	
Total Resident Population	939,705	100.0	100.0	100
of whom female	472,348	50.3	50.8	99
By age: *of whom female (%)*				
0– 4 48.8	62,317	6.6	6.5	103
5– 9 48.4	63,321	6.7	6.6	103
10–14 48.2	61,834	6.6	6.3	104
15–19 48.0	61,977	6.6	6.2	107
20–24 48.4	59,613	6.3	5.9	108
25–34 49.1	145,008	15.4	15.4	100
35–44 49.3	135,711	14.4	14.3	101
45–54 49.6	123,780	13.2	13.1	100
55–64 49.8	88,767	9.4	9.9	95
65–74 52.8	73,779	7.9	8.4	93
75+ 63.0	63,598	6.8	7.4	92
Cost of Car (of only or most recently obtained car)				
Up to £2,999	175,925	23.4	22.9	102
£3,000– £4,999	109,938	14.6	13.5	108
£5,000– £6,999	85,188	11.3	11.1	102
£7,000– £9,999	80,499	10.7	11.1	96
£10,000–£19,999	100,138	13.3	12.8	104
£20,000+	7,506	1.0	1.1	89
Owner of a Company Car	55,532	7.4	7.7	96
Income Level of Households[1]				
Up to £4,999	39,679	10.8	10.9	99
£5,000– £9,999	60,488	16.4	16.3	101
£10,000–£14,999	68,558	18.6	18.1	103
£15,000–£19,999	59,821	16.2	15.7	103
£20,000–£24,999	45,234	12.3	12.0	103
£25,000–£29,999	31,611	8.6	8.5	101
£30,000–£34,999	21,197	5.8	5.9	98
£35,000–£39,999	13,951	3.8	4.0	95
£40,000–£44,999	9,135	2.5	2.7	92
£45,000–£49,999	6,000	1.6	1.8	89
£50,000+	12,757	3.5	4.3	81
Use of Multiple Stores in Last Year				
Dept. stores (not groceries)	584,942	77.8	78.5	99
Ladies' outfitters	423,257	56.3	53.5	105
Gentlemen's outfitters	500,464	66.5	64.0	104
DIY	468,219	62.2	60.5	103
Furniture, appliances, durables	495,989	65.9	64.6	102
Shoes	544,346	72.4	70.1	103
Visits to Licensed Premises (at least weekly)				
Pubs	223,595	29.7	26.3	113
Licensed clubs	89,285	11.9	11.6	102
Wine bars	12,201	1.6	1.4	116

© CACI Limited, 1998.   Tel: 0171 602-6000 (London) / 0131 557-0123 (Edinburgh).
Note: [1] PayCheck data. Please see Chapter 3 for details.
Source: © BMRB International Limited, 1997. Buying potential info. modelled using data from TGI 4/96-3/97.

LINCOLNSHIRE

Derived using **CACI's Population Projections for 1998**   Data refers to **adults** except where indicated

Base: All GB	Total for Area	As a Percentage of: Area	GB Base	Index (GB av. = 100)
Total Resident Population	626,475	100.0	100.0	100
of whom female	319,409	51.0	50.8	100
By age: *of whom female (%)*				
0– 4 48.8	36,152	5.8	6.5	89
5– 9 49.0	38,152	6.1	6.6	93
10–14 49.0	37,826	6.0	6.3	95
15–19 48.7	35,124	5.6	6.2	91
20–24 49.6	33,420	5.3	5.9	91
25–34 48.7	87,746	14.0	15.4	91
35–44 49.8	83,048	13.3	14.3	93
45–54 50.6	87,333	13.9	13.1	106
55–64 50.7	69,490	11.1	9.9	112
65–74 53.0	63,915	10.2	8.4	121
75+ 61.8	54,269	8.7	7.4	117
Cost of Car (of only or most recently obtained car)				
Up to £2,999	107,845	21.0	22.9	91
£3,000– £4,999	69,235	13.5	13.5	99
£5,000– £6,999	69,939	13.6	11.1	122
£7,000– £9,999	63,602	12.4	11.1	111
£10,000–£19,999	78,863	15.3	12.8	120
£20,000+	5,194	1.0	1.1	90
Owner of a Company Car	41,672	8.1	7.7	106
Income Level of Households[1]				
Up to £4,999	39,679	10.8	10.9	99
£5,000– £9,999	60,488	16.4	16.3	101
£10,000–£14,999	68,558	18.6	18.1	103
£15,000–£19,999	59,821	16.2	15.7	103
£20,000–£24,999	45,234	12.3	12.0	103
£25,000–£29,999	31,611	8.6	8.5	101
£30,000–£34,999	21,197	5.8	5.9	98
£35,000–£39,999	13,951	3.8	4.0	95
£40,000–£44,999	9,135	2.5	2.7	92
£45,000–£49,999	6,000	1.6	1.8	89
£50,000+	12,757	3.5	4.3	81
Use of Multiple Stores in Last Year				
Dept. stores (not groceries)	387,302	75.3	78.5	96
Ladies' outfitters	280,070	54.5	53.5	102
Gentlemen's outfitters	338,799	65.9	64.0	103
DIY	321,046	62.4	60.5	103
Furniture, appliances, durables	327,971	63.8	64.6	99
Shoes	365,194	71.0	70.1	101
Visits to Licensed Premises (at least weekly)				
Pubs	154,943	30.1	26.3	114
Licensed clubs	59,504	11.6	11.6	100
Wine bars	6,907	1.3	1.4	96

© CACI Limited, 1998. Tel: 0171 602-6000 (London) / 0131 557-0123 (Edinburgh).
Note: [1] PayCheck data. Please see Chapter 3 for details.
Source: © BMRB International Limited, 1997. Buying potential info. modelled using data from TGI 4/96-3/97.

NORFOLK

Derived using CACI's Population Projections for 1998   Data refers to **adults** except where indicated

Base: All GB	Total for Area	As a Percentage of: Area	As a Percentage of: GB Base	Index (GB av. = 100)
Total Resident Population	787,920	100.0	100.0	100
of whom female	400,787	50.9	50.8	100
By age: *of whom female (%)*				
0– 4 49.0	45,200	5.7	6.5	89
5– 9 49.1	47,215	6.0	6.6	91
10–14 48.6	45,952	5.8	6.3	92
15–19 48.8	44,422	5.6	6.2	92
20–24 48.6	42,205	5.4	5.9	91
25–34 48.3	111,115	14.1	15.4	91
35–44 49.7	103,052	13.1	14.3	91
45–54 50.2	109,342	13.9	13.1	106
55–64 50.4	85,384	10.8	9.9	109
65–74 53.2	79,303	10.1	8.4	120
75+ 61.6	74,730	9.5	7.4	128
Cost of Car (of only or most recently obtained car)				
Up to £2,999	168,667	26.0	22.9	113
£3,000– £4,999	101,375	15.6	13.5	115
£5,000– £6,999	73,697	11.3	11.1	102
£7,000– £9,999	81,957	12.6	11.1	113
£10,000–£19,999	83,042	12.8	12.8	100
£20,000+	9,121	1.4	1.1	125
Owner of a Company Car	49,697	7.7	7.7	100
Income Level of Households[1]				
Up to £4,999	38,207	11.7	10.9	107
£5,000– £9,999	58,126	17.8	16.3	109
£10,000–£14,999	64,559	19.7	18.1	109
£15,000–£19,999	54,347	16.6	15.7	106
£20,000–£24,999	39,303	12.0	12.0	101
£25,000–£29,999	26,198	8.0	8.5	94
£30,000–£34,999	16,771	5.1	5.9	88
£35,000–£39,999	10,562	3.2	4.0	81
£40,000–£44,999	6,636	2.0	2.7	76
£45,000–£49,999	4,194	1.3	1.8	70
£50,000+	8,033	2.5	4.3	58
Use of Multiple Stores in Last Year				
Dept. stores (not groceries)	512,119	78.8	78.5	100
Ladies' outfitters	349,793	53.9	53.5	101
Gentlemen's outfitters	417,591	64.3	64.0	101
DIY	382,402	58.9	60.5	97
Furniture, appliances, durables	412,138	63.4	64.6	98
Shoes	440,429	67.8	70.1	97
Visits to Licensed Premises (at least weekly)				
Pubs	139,937	21.5	26.3	82
Licensed clubs	60,893	9.4	11.6	81
Wine bars	3,832	0.6	1.4	42

© CACI Limited, 1998.   Tel: 0171 602-6000 (London) / 0131 557-0123 (Edinburgh).
Note: [1] PayCheck data. Please see Chapter 3 for details.
Source: © BMRB International Limited, 1997. Buying potential info. modelled using data from TGI 4/96-3/97.

NORTHAMPTONSHIRE

Derived using **CACI's Population Projections for 1998**   Data refers to **adults** except where indicated

Base: All GB	Total for Area	As a Percentage of: Area	As a Percentage of: GB Base	Index (GB av. = 100)
Total Resident Population	615,413	100.0	100.0	100
of whom female	310,085	50.4	50.8	99
By age: of whom female (%)				
0– 4	49.0	41,041	6.7	6.5	103
5– 9	48.2	43,423	7.1	6.6	108
10–14	47.7	42,095	6.8	6.3	108
15–19	48.9	39,839	6.5	6.2	105
20–24	49.1	35,495	5.8	5.9	98
25–34	49.1	93,871	15.3	15.4	99
35–44	49.8	88,980	14.5	14.3	101
45–54	49.8	86,828	14.1	13.1	107
55–64	49.4	57,521	9.3	9.9	94
65–74	53.1	45,768	7.4	8.4	89
75+	63.2	40,552	6.6	7.4	89
Cost of Car (of only or most recently obtained car)				
Up to £2,999	127,402	26.1	22.9	114
£3,000– £4,999	74,228	15.2	13.5	112
£5,000– £6,999	54,680	11.2	11.1	101
£7,000– £9,999	59,125	12.1	11.1	109
£10,000–£19,999	62,589	12.8	12.8	100
£20,000+	6,478	1.3	1.1	118
Owner of a Company Car	38,527	7.9	7.7	103
Income Level of Households[1]				
Up to £4,999	21,909	9.0	10.9	83
£5,000– £9,999	35,951	14.8	16.3	91
£10,000–£14,999	43,264	17.8	18.1	98
£15,000–£19,999	39,614	16.3	15.7	104
£20,000–£24,999	31,177	12.8	12.0	107
£25,000–£29,999	22,557	9.3	8.5	109
£30,000–£34,999	15,597	6.4	5.9	110
£35,000–£39,999	10,551	4.3	4.0	109
£40,000–£44,999	7,081	2.9	2.7	108
£45,000–£49,999	4,757	2.0	1.8	107
£50,000+	10,792	4.4	4.3	104
Use of Multiple Stores in Last Year				
Dept. stores (not groceries)	386,622	79.1	78.5	101
Ladies' outfitters	268,954	55.0	53.5	103
Gentlemen's outfitters	325,856	66.7	64.0	104
DIY	298,661	61.1	60.5	101
Furniture, appliances, durables	318,216	65.1	64.6	101
Shoes	339,131	69.4	70.1	99
Visits to Licensed Premises (at least weekly)				
Pubs	115,591	23.6	26.3	90
Licensed clubs	50,146	10.3	11.6	88
Wine bars	4,223	0.9	1.4	62

© CACI Limited, 1998. Tel: 0171 602-6000 (London) / 0131 557-0123 (Edinburgh).
Note: [1] PayCheck data. Please see Chapter 3 for details.
Source: © BMRB International Limited, 1997. Buying potential info. modelled using data from TGI 4/96-3/97.

NORTHUMBERLAND

Derived using **CACI's Population Projections for 1998**   Data refers to **adults** except where indicated

Base: All GB		Total for Area	As a Percentage of: Area	As a Percentage of: GB Base	Index (GB av. = 100)
Total Resident Population		310,540	100.0	100.0	100
of whom female		158,771	51.1	50.8	101
By age:	*of whom female (%)*				
0– 4	48.7	17,299	5.6	6.5	86
5– 9	48.8	18,370	5.9	6.6	90
10–14	49.4	19,363	6.2	6.3	98
15–19	48.2	18,921	6.1	6.2	99
20–24	46.5	18,100	5.8	5.9	99
25–34	50.1	39,736	12.8	15.4	83
35–44	50.5	44,560	14.3	14.3	100
45–54	50.3	46,297	14.9	13.1	114
55–64	51.0	34,322	11.1	9.9	111
65–74	53.4	29,904	9.6	8.4	115
75+	63.9	23,668	7.6	7.4	103
Cost of Car (of only or most recently obtained car)					
Up to £2,999		50,848	19.9	22.9	87
£3,000– £4,999		30,592	12.0	13.5	88
£5,000– £6,999		30,674	12.0	11.1	108
£7,000– £9,999		30,674	12.0	11.1	108
£10,000–£19,999		36,493	14.3	12.8	112
£20,000+		922	0.4	1.1	32
Owner of a Company Car		16,363	6.4	7.7	84
Income Level of Households[1]					
Up to £4,999		15,911	12.5	10.9	115
£5,000– £9,999		23,325	18.4	16.3	113
£10,000–£14,999		24,610	19.4	18.1	107
£15,000–£19,999		20,092	15.8	15.7	101
£20,000–£24,999		14,459	11.4	12.0	95
£25,000–£29,999		9,772	7.7	8.5	91
£30,000–£34,999		6,412	5.0	5.9	86
£35,000–£39,999		4,163	3.3	4.0	83
£40,000–£44,999		2,704	2.1	2.7	79
£45,000–£49,999		1,768	1.4	1.8	77
£50,000+		3,756	3.0	4.3	69
Use of Multiple Stores in Last Year					
Dept. stores (not groceries)		198,765	77.8	78.5	99
Ladies' outfitters		141,847	55.5	53.5	104
Gentlemen's outfitters		170,144	66.6	64.0	104
DIY		135,551	53.1	60.5	88
Furniture, appliances, durables		165,814	64.9	64.6	100
Shoes		182,595	71.5	70.1	102
Visits to Licensed Premises (at least weekly)					
Pubs		81,421	31.9	26.3	121
Licensed clubs		44,973	17.6	11.6	152
Wine bars		6,179	2.4	1.4	173

© CACI Limited, 1998. Tel: 0171 602-6000 (London) / 0131 557-0123 (Edinburgh).
Note: [1] PayCheck data. Please see Chapter 3 for details.
Source: © BMRB International Limited, 1997. Buying potential info. modelled using data from TGI 4/96-3/97.

NORTH YORKSHIRE

Derived using CACI's **Population Projections** for 1998   Data refers to **adults** except where indicated

Base: All GB	Total for Area	As a Percentage of: Area	GB Base	Index (GB av. = 100)
Total Resident Population	745,166	100.0	100.0	100
of whom female	379,462	50.9	50.8	100
By age: *of whom female (%)*				
0– 4 48.8	42,351	5.7	6.5	88
5– 9 48.4	45,491	6.1	6.6	93
10–14 48.9	44,670	6.0	6.3	94
15–19 47.2	43,737	5.9	6.2	95
20–24 49.4	41,313	5.5	5.9	94
25–34 48.1	104,135	14.0	15.4	91
35–44 49.5	104,381	14.0	14.3	98
45–54 50.2	105,245	14.1	13.1	108
55–64 51.0	80,859	10.9	9.9	109
65–74 53.8	69,600	9.3	8.4	111
75+ 64.1	63,384	8.5	7.4	115
Cost of Car (of only or most recently obtained car)				
Up to £2,999	114,805	18.7	22.9	82
£3,000– £4,999	76,411	12.5	13.5	92
£5,000– £6,999	84,043	13.7	11.1	124
£7,000– £9,999	81,779	13.3	11.1	120
£10,000–£19,999	101,053	16.5	12.8	129
£20,000+	4,994	0.8	1.1	72
Owner of a Company Car	49,251	8.0	7.7	105
Income Level of Households[1]				
Up to £4,999	30,042	9.9	10.9	91
£5,000– £9,999	48,479	15.9	16.3	98
£10,000–£14,999	56,888	18.7	18.1	103
£15,000–£19,999	50,433	16.5	15.7	105
£20,000–£24,999	38,295	12.6	12.0	105
£25,000–£29,999	26,763	8.8	8.5	103
£30,000–£34,999	17,953	5.9	5.9	101
£35,000–£39,999	11,841	3.9	4.0	98
£40,000–£44,999	7,785	2.6	2.7	95
£45,000–£49,999	5,142	1.7	1.8	93
£50,000+	11,193	3.7	4.3	86
Use of Multiple Stores in Last Year				
Dept. stores (not groceries)	478,701	78.1	78.5	99
Ladies' outfitters	334,776	54.6	53.5	102
Gentlemen's outfitters	403,698	65.9	64.0	103
DIY	353,841	57.8	60.5	95
Furniture, appliances, durables	394,393	64.4	64.6	100
Shoes	440,953	72.0	70.1	103
Visits to Licensed Premises (at least weekly)				
Pubs	196,296	32.0	26.3	122
Licensed clubs	83,565	13.6	11.6	117
Wine bars	11,692	1.9	1.4	137

© CACI Limited, 1998. Tel: 0171 602-6000 (London) / 0131 557-0123 (Edinburgh).
Note: [1] PayCheck data. Please see Chapter 3 for details.
Source: © BMRB International Limited, 1997. Buying potential info. modelled using data from TGI 4/96-3/97.

NOTTINGHAMSHIRE

Derived using CACI's **Population Projections** for 1998   Data refers to **adults** except where indicated

Base: All GB	Total for Area	As a Percentage of: Area	As a Percentage of: GB Base	Index (GB av. = 100)
Total Resident Population	1,042,900	100.0	100.0	100
of whom female	527,863	50.6	50.8	100
By age: *of whom female (%)*				
0– 4 48.7	66,569	6.4	6.5	99
5– 9 48.7	68,192	6.5	6.6	100
10–14 48.6	65,694	6.3	6.3	99
15–19 48.4	64,130	6.1	6.2	100
20–24 47.9	60,884	5.8	5.9	99
25–34 49.2	165,962	15.9	15.4	103
35–44 49.9	148,549	14.2	14.3	100
45–54 49.6	136,866	13.1	13.1	100
55–64 50.5	103,361	9.9	9.9	100
65–74 53.1	88,568	8.5	8.4	101
75+ 63.6	74,125	7.1	7.4	96
Cost of Car (of only or most recently obtained car)				
Up to £2,999	197,956	23.5	22.9	102
£3,000– £4,999	116,319	13.8	13.5	102
£5,000– £6,999	94,208	11.2	11.1	101
£7,000– £9,999	88,854	10.5	11.1	95
£10,000–£19,999	105,502	12.5	12.8	98
£20,000+	7,701	0.9	1.1	81
Owner of a Company Car	60,403	7.2	7.7	94
Income Level of Households[1]				
Up to £4,999	55,565	13.1	10.9	120
£5,000– £9,999	79,704	18.8	16.3	115
£10,000–£14,999	83,303	19.6	18.1	108
£15,000–£19,999	67,244	15.8	15.7	101
£20,000–£24,999	47,731	11.2	12.0	94
£25,000–£29,999	31,831	7.5	8.5	88
£30,000–£34,999	20,649	4.9	5.9	83
£35,000–£39,999	13,280	3.1	4.0	79
£40,000–£44,999	8,557	2.0	2.7	75
£45,000–£49,999	5,555	1.3	1.8	72
£50,000+	11,570	2.7	4.3	64
Use of Multiple Stores in Last Year				
Dept. stores (not groceries)	642,133	76.2	78.5	97
Ladies' outfitters	467,115	55.4	53.5	104
Gentlemen's outfitters	555,729	66.0	64.0	103
DIY	518,711	61.6	60.5	102
Furniture, appliances, durables	547,233	65.0	64.6	101
Shoes	601,411	71.4	70.1	102
Visits to Licensed Premises (at least weekly)				
Pubs	252,764	30.0	26.3	114
Licensed clubs	106,261	12.6	11.6	109
Wine bars	14,378	1.7	1.4	122

© CACI Limited, 1998.   Tel: 0171 602-6000 (London) / 0131 557-0123 (Edinburgh).
Note: [1] PayCheck data. Please see Chapter 3 for details.
Source: © BMRB International Limited, 1997. Buying potential info. modelled using data from TGI 4/96-3/97.

OXFORDSHIRE

Derived using CACI's **Population Projections for 1998**   Data refers to **adults** except where indicated

Base: All GB	Total for Area	As a Percentage of: Area	GB Base	Index (GB av. = 100)
Total Resident Population	613,891	100.0	100.0	100
of whom female	306,611	49.9	50.8	98
By age: *of whom female (%)*				
0– 4 49.0	41,554	6.8	6.5	105
5– 9 48.9	42,478	6.9	6.6	106
10–14 48.6	38,968	6.3	6.3	100
15–19 47.6	40,026	6.5	6.2	106
20–24 48.1	37,213	6.1	5.9	103
25–34 48.1	102,837	16.8	15.4	109
35–44 48.1	90,900	14.8	14.3	103
45–54 49.9	79,672	13.0	13.1	99
55–64 50.2	56,584	9.2	9.9	93
65–74 52.5	44,263	7.2	8.4	86
75+ 63.4	39,396	6.4	7.4	87
Cost of Car (of only or most recently obtained car)				
Up to £2,999	105,201	21.4	22.9	93
£3,000– £4,999	72,050	14.7	13.5	108
£5,000– £6,999	61,887	12.6	11.1	114
£7,000– £9,999	64,546	13.1	11.1	118
£10,000–£19,999	83,929	17.1	12.8	134
£20,000+	8,182	1.7	1.1	148
Owner of a Company Car	47,400	9.7	7.7	126
Income Level of Households[1]				
Up to £4,999	16,721	7.0	10.9	64
£5,000– £9,999	28,567	12.0	16.3	74
£10,000–£14,999	37,405	15.7	18.1	87
£15,000–£19,999	37,469	15.7	15.7	100
£20,000–£24,999	31,959	13.4	12.0	112
£25,000–£29,999	24,740	10.4	8.5	122
£30,000–£34,999	18,097	7.6	5.9	130
£35,000–£39,999	12,832	5.4	4.0	136
£40,000–£44,999	8,963	3.8	2.7	140
£45,000–£49,999	6,229	2.6	1.8	144
£50,000+	15,276	6.4	4.3	150
Use of Multiple Stores in Last Year				
Dept. stores (not groceries)	395,995	80.7	78.5	103
Ladies' outfitters	268,866	54.8	53.5	102
Gentlemen's outfitters	323,486	65.9	64.0	103
DIY	309,827	63.1	60.5	104
Furniture, appliances, durables	322,265	65.6	64.6	102
Shoes	356,040	72.5	70.1	103
Visits to Licensed Premises (at least weekly)				
Pubs	152,300	31.0	26.3	118
Licensed clubs	48,617	9.9	11.6	85
Wine bars	9,509	1.9	1.4	139

© CACI Limited, 1998.   Tel: 0171 602-6000 (London) / 0131 557-0123 (Edinburgh).
Note: [1] PayCheck data. Please see Chapter 3 for details.
Source: © BMRB International Limited, 1997. Buying potential info. modelled using data from TGI 4/96-3/97.

SHROPSHIRE

Derived using **CACI's Population Projections for 1998**   Data refers to **adults** except where indicated

Base: All GB	Total for Area	As a Percentage of: Area	As a Percentage of: GB Base	Index (GB av. = 100)
Total Resident Population	430,039	100.0	100.0	100
of whom female	217,279	50.5	50.8	99
By age: *of whom female (%)*				
0– 4 48.6	27,099	6.3	6.5	98
5– 9 48.7	27,888	6.5	6.6	99
10–14 47.9	28,419	6.6	6.3	104
15–19 48.0	25,315	5.9	6.2	96
20–24 49.2	24,730	5.8	5.9	98
25–34 48.6	61,899	14.4	15.4	93
35–44 49.5	58,662	13.6	14.3	95
45–54 49.9	60,935	14.2	13.1	108
55–64 50.0	46,319	10.8	9.9	108
65–74 52.9	37,127	8.6	8.4	103
75+ 64.0	31,646	7.4	7.4	100
Cost of Car (of only or most recently obtained car)				
Up to £2,999	86,164	24.9	22.9	108
£3,000– £4,999	51,627	14.9	13.5	110
£5,000– £6,999	41,535	12.0	11.1	108
£7,000– £9,999	38,481	11.1	11.1	100
£10,000–£19,999	51,374	14.8	12.8	116
£20,000+	3,707	1.1	1.1	95
Owner of a Company Car	27,453	7.9	7.7	103
Income Level of Households[1]				
Up to £4,999	18,597	11.0	10.9	101
£5,000– £9,999	28,935	17.0	16.3	105
£10,000–£14,999	32,620	19.2	18.1	106
£15,000–£19,999	27,920	16.4	15.7	105
£20,000–£24,999	20,634	12.2	12.0	102
£25,000–£29,999	14,118	8.3	8.5	98
£30,000–£34,999	9,300	5.5	5.9	94
£35,000–£39,999	6,031	3.6	4.0	89
£40,000–£44,999	3,900	2.3	2.7	86
£45,000–£49,999	2,534	1.5	1.8	82
£50,000+	5,235	3.1	4.3	72
Use of Multiple Stores in Last Year				
Dept. stores (not groceries)	267,585	77.2	78.5	98
Ladies' outfitters	192,503	55.5	53.5	104
Gentlemen's outfitters	231,952	66.9	64.0	105
DIY	215,975	62.3	60.5	103
Furniture, appliances, durables	226,092	65.2	64.6	101
Shoes	248,680	71.7	70.1	102
Visits to Licensed Premises (at least weekly)				
Pubs	99,897	28.8	26.3	110
Licensed clubs	37,175	10.7	11.6	92
Wine bars	5,630	1.6	1.4	116

© CACI Limited, 1998.   Tel: 0171 602-6000 (London) / 0131 557-0123 (Edinburgh).
Note: [1] PayCheck data. Please see Chapter 3 for details.
Source: © BMRB International Limited, 1997. Buying potential info. modelled using data from TGI 4/96-3/97.

SOMERSET

Derived using **CACI's Population Projections for 1998**   Data refers to **adults** except where indicated

Base: All GB		Total for Area	As a Percentage of: Area	GB Base	Index (GB av. = 100)
Total Resident Population		491,678	100.0	100.0	100
of whom female		251,997	51.3	50.8	101
By age:	*of whom female (%)*				
0– 4	48.7	29,053	5.9	6.5	92
5– 9	49.5	30,581	6.2	6.6	95
10–14	47.7	31,130	6.3	6.3	100
15–19	48.7	28,229	5.7	6.2	93
20–24	48.4	27,510	5.6	5.9	95
25–34	48.6	65,064	13.2	15.4	86
35–44	50.5	64,644	13.1	14.3	92
45–54	50.6	68,474	13.9	13.1	106
55–64	50.7	52,069	10.6	9.9	107
65–74	54.0	48,449	9.9	8.4	117
75+	63.3	46,475	9.5	7.4	128
Cost of Car (of only or most recently obtained car)					
Up to £2,999		106,140	26.5	22.9	115
£3,000– £4,999		70,995	17.7	13.5	131
£5,000– £6,999		45,137	11.3	11.1	101
£7,000– £9,999		48,517	12.1	11.1	109
£10,000–£19,999		47,398	11.8	12.8	93
£20,000+		5,424	1.4	1.1	120
Owner of a Company Car		32,072	8.0	7.7	104
Income Level of Households[1]					
Up to £4,999		21,362	10.7	10.9	98
£5,000– £9,999		34,282	17.2	16.3	106
£10,000–£14,999		39,315	19.7	18.1	109
£15,000–£19,999		33,703	16.9	15.7	108
£20,000–£24,999		24,619	12.3	12.0	103
£25,000–£29,999		16,523	8.3	8.5	97
£30,000–£34,999		10,645	5.3	5.9	91
£35,000–£39,999		6,751	3.4	4.0	85
£40,000–£44,999		4,274	2.1	2.7	80
£45,000–£49,999		2,724	1.4	1.8	75
£50,000+		5,372	2.7	4.3	63
Use of Multiple Stores in Last Year					
Dept. stores (not groceries)		297,341	74.2	78.5	94
Ladies' outfitters		216,993	54.1	53.5	101
Gentlemen's outfitters		251,629	62.8	64.0	98
DIY		237,415	59.2	60.5	98
Furniture, appliances, durables		249,339	62.2	64.6	96
Shoes		275,728	68.8	70.1	98
Visits to Licensed Premises (at least weekly)					
Pubs		111,327	27.8	26.3	106
Licensed clubs		51,768	12.9	11.6	111
Wine bars		3,791	0.9	1.4	68

© CACI Limited, 1998. Tel: 0171 602-6000 (London) / 0131 557-0123 (Edinburgh).

Note: [1] PayCheck data. Please see Chapter 3 for details.
Source: © BMRB International Limited, 1997. Buying potential info. modelled using data from TGI 4/96-3/97.

STAFFORDSHIRE

Derived using CACI's **Population Projections for 1998**   Data refers to **adults** except where indicated

Base: All GB	Total for Area	As a Percentage of: Area	As a Percentage of: GB Base	Index (GB av. = 100)
Total Resident Population	1,066,956	100.0	100.0	100
of whom female	536,886	50.3	50.8	99
By age: *of whom female (%)*				
0– 4 48.8	65,374	6.1	6.5	95
5– 9 48.8	69,187	6.5	6.6	99
10–14 48.3	68,939	6.5	6.3	102
15–19 47.9	66,010	6.2	6.2	101
20–24 47.2	60,263	5.6	5.9	96
25–34 48.8	160,714	15.1	15.4	98
35–44 49.3	152,210	14.3	14.3	100
45–54 49.5	151,024	14.2	13.1	108
55–64 49.7	113,080	10.6	9.9	107
65–74 53.2	89,869	8.4	8.4	100
75+ 64.8	70,286	6.6	7.4	89
Cost of Car (of only or most recently obtained car)				
Up to £2,999	213,349	24.7	22.9	108
£3,000– £4,999	129,734	15.0	13.5	111
£5,000– £6,999	97,897	11.3	11.1	102
£7,000– £9,999	95,583	11.1	11.1	99
£10,000–£19,999	116,667	13.5	12.8	106
£20,000+	8,267	1.0	1.1	85
Owner of a Company Car	65,604	7.6	7.7	99
Income Level of Households[1]				
Up to £4,999	47,181	11.2	10.9	103
£5,000– £9,999	73,346	17.4	16.3	107
£10,000–£14,999	81,354	19.3	18.1	107
£15,000–£19,999	68,810	16.3	15.7	104
£20,000–£24,999	50,521	12.0	12.0	100
£25,000–£29,999	34,453	8.2	8.5	96
£30,000–£34,999	22,654	5.4	5.9	92
£35,000–£39,999	14,678	3.5	4.0	88
£40,000–£44,999	9,492	2.3	2.7	84
£45,000–£49,999	6,173	1.5	1.8	80
£50,000+	12,839	3.0	4.3	71
Use of Multiple Stores in Last Year				
Dept. stores (not groceries)	666,174	77.2	78.5	98
Ladies' outfitters	487,745	56.5	53.5	106
Gentlemen's outfitters	583,212	67.5	64.0	106
DIY	544,337	63.0	60.5	104
Furniture, appliances, durables	571,397	66.2	64.6	102
Shoes	623,331	72.2	70.1	103
Visits to Licensed Premises (at least weekly)				
Pubs	251,452	29.1	26.3	111
Licensed clubs	105,341	12.2	11.6	105
Wine bars	15,439	1.8	1.4	128

© CACI Limited, 1998.   Tel: 0171 602-6000 (London) / 0131 557-0123 (Edinburgh).
Note: [1] PayCheck data. Please see Chapter 3 for details.
Source: © BMRB International Limited, 1997. Buying potential info. modelled using data from TGI 4/96-3/97.

SUFFOLK

Derived using CACI's Population Projections for 1998		Data refers to **adults** except where indicated			
Base: All GB		Total for Area	As a Percentage of:		Index (GB av. = 100)
			Area	GB Base	
Total Resident Population		670,965	100.0	100.0	100
of whom female		339,538	50.6	50.8	100
By age:	of whom female (%)				
0– 4	48.7	41,459	6.2	6.5	96
5– 9	49.4	44,950	6.7	6.6	102
10–14	48.4	42,212	6.3	6.3	99
15–19	47.9	38,912	5.8	6.2	94
20–24	48.1	39,280	5.9	5.9	100
25–34	48.3	97,420	14.5	15.4	94
35–44	49.5	89,481	13.3	14.3	93
45–54	50.0	91,583	13.6	13.1	104
55–64	50.1	67,541	10.1	9.9	101
65–74	53.2	60,328	9.0	8.4	107
75+	62.5	57,799	8.6	7.4	117
Cost of Car (of only or most recently obtained car)					
Up to £2,999		140,859	26.0	22.9	113
£3,000– £4,999		84,650	15.6	13.5	115
£5,000– £6,999		62,626	11.5	11.1	104
£7,000– £9,999		69,146	12.7	11.1	114
£10,000–£19,999		69,722	12.9	12.8	101
£20,000+		8,200	1.5	1.1	134
Owner of a Company Car		43,309	8.0	7.7	104
Income Level of Households[1]					
Up to £4,999		27,857	10.2	10.9	94
£5,000– £9,999		44,062	16.2	16.3	100
£10,000–£14,999		51,340	18.9	18.1	104
£15,000–£19,999		45,341	16.7	15.7	106
£20,000–£24,999		34,265	12.6	12.0	105
£25,000–£29,999		23,744	8.7	8.5	103
£30,000–£34,999		15,721	5.8	5.9	99
£35,000–£39,999		10,196	3.7	4.0	94
£40,000–£44,999		6,575	2.4	2.7	90
£45,000–£49,999		4,254	1.6	1.8	86
£50,000+		8,678	3.2	4.3	75
Use of Multiple Stores in Last Year					
Dept. stores (not groceries)		430,563	79.4	78.5	101
Ladies' outfitters		294,468	54.3	53.5	102
Gentlemen's outfitters		353,331	65.1	64.0	102
DIY		322,476	59.5	60.5	98
Furniture, appliances, durables		347,852	64.1	64.6	99
Shoes		370,223	68.3	70.1	97
Visits to Licensed Premises (at least weekly)					
Pubs		119,103	22.0	26.3	83
Licensed clubs		50,564	9.3	11.6	80
Wine bars		3,377	0.6	1.4	45

© CACI Limited, 1998.   Tel: 0171 602-6000 (London) / 0131 557-0123 (Edinburgh).
Note: [1] PayCheck data. Please see Chapter 3 for details.
Source: © BMRB International Limited, 1997. Buying potential info. modelled using data from TGI 4/96-3/97.

SURREY

Derived using **CACI's Population Projections for 1998**   Data refers to **adults** except where indicated

Base: All GB		Total for Area	As a Percentage of:		Index (GB av. = 100)
			Area	GB Base	
Total Resident Population		1,054,093	100.0	100.0	100
of whom female		534,785	50.7	50.8	100
By age:	*of whom female (%)*				
0– 4	48.9	65,003	6.2	6.5	95
5– 9	48.9	67,047	6.4	6.6	97
10–14	48.2	64,714	6.1	6.3	97
15–19	48.5	62,354	5.9	6.2	96
20–24	49.4	53,659	5.1	5.9	87
25–34	48.8	152,026	14.4	15.4	93
35–44	49.0	155,870	14.8	14.3	103
45–54	50.0	152,823	14.5	13.1	110
55–64	50.5	110,197	10.5	9.9	105
65–74	52.8	88,546	8.4	8.4	100
75+	64.5	81,854	7.8	7.4	105
Cost of Car (of only or most recently obtained car)					
Up to £2,999		153,685	17.9	22.9	78
£3,000– £4,999		128,996	15.0	13.5	111
£5,000– £6,999		114,453	13.3	11.1	120
£7,000– £9,999		129,415	15.1	11.1	136
£10,000–£19,999		202,719	23.6	12.8	185
£20,000+		28,451	3.3	1.1	295
Owner of a Company Car		117,405	13.7	7.7	179
Income Level of Households[1]					
Up to £4,999		23,078	5.5	10.9	50
£5,000– £9,999		39,194	9.3	16.3	57
£10,000–£14,999		54,047	12.8	18.1	71
£15,000–£19,999		58,432	13.8	15.7	88
£20,000–£24,999		54,424	12.9	12.0	108
£25,000–£29,999		46,149	10.9	8.5	128
£30,000–£34,999		36,865	8.7	5.9	149
£35,000–£39,999		28,359	6.7	4.0	169
£40,000–£44,999		21,311	5.0	2.7	188
£45,000–£49,999		15,795	3.7	1.8	205
£50,000+		44,938	10.6	4.3	249
Use of Multiple Stores in Last Year					
Dept. stores (not groceries)		753,327	87.9	78.5	112
Ladies' outfitters		422,687	49.3	53.5	92
Gentlemen's outfitters		532,297	62.1	64.0	97
DIY		556,888	65.0	60.5	107
Furniture, appliances, durables		566,769	66.1	64.6	102
Shoes		591,158	69.0	70.1	98
Visits to Licensed Premises (at least weekly)					
Pubs		188,331	22.0	26.3	83
Licensed clubs		62,831	7.3	11.6	63
Wine bars		11,220	1.3	1.4	94

© CACI Limited, 1998.   Tel: 0171 602-6000 (London) / 0131 557-0123 (Edinburgh).
Note: [1] PayCheck data. Please see Chapter 3 for details.
Source: © BMRB International Limited, 1997. Buying potential info. modelled using data from TGI 4/96-3/97.

WARWICKSHIRE

Derived using **CACI's Population Projections for 1998**   Data refers to **adults** except where indicated

Base: All GB	Total for Area	As a Percentage of: Area	GB Base	Index (GB av. = 100)
Total Resident Population	504,183	100.0	100.0	100
of whom female	254,475	50.5	50.8	99
By age: *of whom female (%)*				
0– 4 48.5	30,593	6.1	6.5	94
5– 9 49.1	31,438	6.2	6.6	95
10–14 48.8	31,246	6.2	6.3	98
15–19 48.8	29,212	5.8	6.2	94
20–24 47.9	28,029	5.6	5.9	95
25–34 49.2	73,850	14.6	15.4	95
35–44 49.0	71,442	14.2	14.3	99
45–54 49.8	74,282	14.7	13.1	112
55–64 50.0	54,399	10.8	9.9	109
65–74 52.8	43,231	8.6	8.4	102
75+ 62.9	36,461	7.2	7.4	98
Cost of Car (of only or most recently obtained car)				
Up to £2,999	93,964	22.9	22.9	100
£3,000– £4,999	60,888	14.8	13.5	109
£5,000– £6,999	50,243	12.2	11.1	110
£7,000– £9,999	49,597	12.1	11.1	108
£10,000–£19,999	64,292	15.6	12.8	123
£20,000+	5,460	1.3	1.1	118
Owner of a Company Car	36,290	8.8	7.7	115
Income Level of Households[1]				
Up to £4,999	19,318	9.5	10.9	87
£5,000– £9,999	30,402	14.9	16.3	92
£10,000–£14,999	35,872	17.6	18.1	97
£15,000–£19,999	32,502	16.0	15.7	102
£20,000–£24,999	25,496	12.5	12.0	105
£25,000–£29,999	18,499	9.1	8.5	107
£30,000–£34,999	12,892	6.3	5.9	108
£35,000–£39,999	8,821	4.3	4.0	109
£40,000–£44,999	6,002	2.9	2.7	110
£45,000–£49,999	4,091	2.0	1.8	110
£50,000+	9,701	4.8	4.3	112
Use of Multiple Stores in Last Year				
Dept. stores (not groceries)	324,256	78.9	78.5	100
Ladies' outfitters	227,738	55.4	53.5	104
Gentlemen's outfitters	274,062	66.7	64.0	104
DIY	259,612	63.2	60.5	104
Furniture, appliances, durables	270,942	65.9	64.6	102
Shoes	297,175	72.3	70.1	103
Visits to Licensed Premises (at least weekly)				
Pubs	121,517	29.6	26.3	112
Licensed clubs	45,844	11.2	11.6	96
Wine bars	7,702	1.9	1.4	134

© CACI Limited, 1998.   Tel: 0171 602-6000 (London) / 0131 557-0123 (Edinburgh).
Note: [1] PayCheck data. Please see Chapter 3 for details.
Source: © BMRB International Limited, 1997. Buying potential info. modelled using data from TGI 4/96-3/97.

WEST SUSSEX

Derived using **CACI's Population Projections for 1998**   Data refers to **adults** except where indicated

Base: All GB		Total for Area	As a Percentage of:		Index (GB av. = 100)
			Area	GB Base	
Total Resident Population		740,644	100.0	100.0	100
of whom female		383,690	51.8	50.8	102
By age:	*of whom female (%)*				
0– 4	48.4	42,540	5.7	6.5	89
5– 9	47.7	44,506	6.0	6.6	92
10–14	47.7	43,262	5.8	6.3	92
15–19	48.0	41,396	5.6	6.2	91
20–24	50.4	41,246	5.6	5.9	95
25–34	49.0	100,051	13.5	15.4	88
35–44	50.1	98,934	13.4	14.3	93
45–54	50.5	100,356	13.5	13.1	103
55–64	51.7	76,044	10.3	9.9	103
65–74	55.2	73,408	9.9	8.4	118
75+	65.2	78,901	10.7	7.4	144
Cost of Car (of only or most recently obtained car)					
Up to £2,999		159,405	26.1	22.9	114
£3,000– £4,999		88,933	14.6	13.5	108
£5,000– £6,999		70,526	11.6	11.1	104
£7,000– £9,999		67,459	11.1	11.1	99
£10,000–£19,999		96,673	15.8	12.8	124
£20,000+		7,068	1.2	1.1	103
Owner of a Company Car		57,767	9.5	7.7	124
Income Level of Households[1]					
Up to £4,999		26,836	8.7	10.9	80
£5,000– £9,999		42,556	13.7	16.3	85
£10,000–£14,999		51,966	16.8	18.1	93
£15,000–£19,999		48,945	15.8	15.7	101
£20,000–£24,999		39,814	12.9	12.0	108
£25,000–£29,999		29,800	9.6	8.5	113
£30,000–£34,999		21,285	6.9	5.9	118
£35,000–£39,999		14,823	4.8	4.0	121
£40,000–£44,999		10,199	3.3	2.7	123
£45,000–£49,999		6,992	2.3	1.8	124
£50,000+		16,306	5.3	4.3	124
Use of Multiple Stores in Last Year					
Dept. stores (not groceries)		508,713	83.3	78.5	106
Ladies' outfitters		323,649	53.0	53.5	99
Gentlemen's outfitters		373,259	61.2	64.0	96
DIY		400,407	65.6	60.5	108
Furniture, appliances, durables		405,214	66.4	64.6	103
Shoes		427,265	70.0	70.1	100
Visits to Licensed Premises (at least weekly)					
Pubs		130,466	21.4	26.3	81
Licensed clubs		57,900	9.5	11.6	82
Wine bars		5,292	0.9	1.4	62

© CACI Limited, 1998. Tel: 0171 602-6000 (London) / 0131 557-0123 (Edinburgh).
Note: [1] PayCheck data. Please see Chapter 3 for details.
Source: © BMRB International Limited, 1997. Buying potential info. modelled using data from TGI 4/96-3/97.

WILTSHIRE

Derived using **CACI's Population Projections** for 1998   Data refers to **adults** except where indicated

Base: All GB	Total for Area	As a Percentage of: Area	As a Percentage of: GB Base	Index (GB av. = 100)
Total Resident Population	606,274	100.0	100.0	100
of whom female	304,161	50.2	50.8	99
By age: *of whom female (%)*				
0– 4 49.4	39,322	6.5	6.5	100
5– 9 48.3	39,856	6.6	6.6	100
10–14 48.7	38,898	6.4	6.3	101
15–19 48.1	34,462	5.7	6.2	92
20–24 48.7	33,378	5.5	5.9	94
25–34 47.3	95,053	15.7	15.4	102
35–44 48.6	89,616	14.8	14.3	103
45–54 49.9	82,304	13.6	13.1	103
55–64 50.2	59,617	9.8	9.9	99
65–74 52.9	49,857	8.2	8.4	98
75+ 63.3	43,911	7.2	7.4	98
Cost of Car (of only or most recently obtained car)				
Up to £2,999	123,753	25.3	22.9	111
£3,000– £4,999	78,394	16.1	13.5	119
£5,000– £6,999	56,937	11.7	11.1	105
£7,000– £9,999	59,888	12.3	11.1	110
£10,000–£19,999	66,068	13.5	12.8	106
£20,000+	6,513	1.3	1.1	119
Owner of a Company Car	42,297	8.7	7.7	113
Income Level of Households[1]				
Up to £4,999	19,970	8.3	10.9	76
£5,000– £9,999	33,879	14.0	16.3	86
£10,000–£14,999	42,356	17.6	18.1	97
£15,000–£19,999	40,066	16.6	15.7	106
£20,000–£24,999	32,193	13.4	12.0	112
£25,000–£29,999	23,497	9.7	8.5	115
£30,000–£34,999	16,232	6.7	5.9	115
£35,000–£39,999	10,890	4.5	4.0	114
£40,000–£44,999	7,213	3.0	2.7	111
£45,000–£49,999	4,765	2.0	1.8	109
£50,000+	10,087	4.2	4.3	98
Use of Multiple Stores in Last Year				
Dept. stores (not groceries)	378,367	77.5	78.5	99
Ladies' outfitters	266,880	54.7	53.5	102
Gentlemen's outfitters	314,882	64.5	64.0	101
DIY	302,358	61.9	60.5	102
Furniture, appliances, durables	317,266	65.0	64.6	101
Shoes	343,090	70.3	70.1	100
Visits to Licensed Premises (at least weekly)				
Pubs	133,183	27.3	26.3	104
Licensed clubs	57,264	11.7	11.6	101
Wine bars	5,560	1.1	1.4	82

© CACI Limited, 1998.   Tel: 0171 602-6000 (London) / 0131 557-0123 (Edinburgh).
Note: [1] PayCheck data. Please see Chapter 3 for details.
Source: © BMRB International Limited, 1997. Buying potential info. modelled using data from TGI 4/96-3/97.

CLWYD

Derived using **CACI's Population Projections for 1998**   Data refers to **adults** except where indicated

Base: All GB	Total for Area	As a Percentage of: Area	GB Base	Index (GB av. = 100)
Total Resident Population	422,133	100.0	100.0	100
of whom female	217,069	51.4	50.8	101
By age: *of whom female (%)*				
0– 4 49.1	24,971	5.9	6.5	92
5– 9 49.2	26,891	6.4	6.6	97
10–14 48.6	27,295	6.5	6.3	102
15–19 48.5	24,442	5.8	6.2	94
20–24 47.8	24,658	5.8	5.9	99
25–34 49.2	57,867	13.7	15.4	89
35–44 50.4	55,442	13.1	14.3	92
45–54 50.8	58,709	13.9	13.1	106
55–64 50.9	45,434	10.8	9.9	108
65–74 53.9	39,494	9.4	8.4	111
75+ 65.1	36,930	8.7	7.4	118
Cost of Car (of only or most recently obtained car)				
Up to £2,999	87,366	25.5	22.9	111
£3,000– £4,999	50,990	14.9	13.5	110
£5,000– £6,999	37,251	10.9	11.1	98
£7,000– £9,999	43,190	12.6	11.1	113
£10,000–£19,999	38,918	11.3	12.8	89
£20,000+	3,531	1.0	1.1	92
Owner of a Company Car	26,361	7.7	7.7	100
Income Level of Households[1]				
Up to £4,999	19,952	11.8	10.9	108
£5,000– £9,999	30,185	17.8	16.3	110
£10,000–£14,999	33,230	19.6	18.1	108
£15,000–£19,999	27,899	16.5	15.7	105
£20,000–£24,999	20,231	11.9	12.0	100
£25,000–£29,999	13,560	8.0	8.5	94
£30,000–£34,999	8,737	5.2	5.9	88
£35,000–£39,999	5,540	3.3	4.0	82
£40,000–£44,999	3,506	2.1	2.7	77
£45,000–£49,999	2,231	1.3	1.8	72
£50,000+	4,376	2.6	4.3	61
Use of Multiple Stores in Last Year				
Dept. stores (not groceries)	260,195	75.9	78.5	97
Ladies' outfitters	189,687	55.3	53.5	103
Gentlemen's outfitters	230,714	67.3	64.0	105
DIY	209,534	61.1	60.5	101
Furniture, appliances, durables	226,541	66.1	64.6	102
Shoes	245,658	71.6	70.1	102
Visits to Licensed Premises (at least weekly)				
Pubs	95,382	27.8	26.3	106
Licensed clubs	44,843	13.1	11.6	113
Wine bars	5,829	1.7	1.4	122

© CACI Limited, 1998.   Tel: 0171 602-6000 (London) / 0131 557-0123 (Edinburgh).
Note: [1] PayCheck data. Please see Chapter 3 for details.
Source: © BMRB International Limited, 1997. Buying potential info. modelled using data from TGI 4/96-3/97.

DYFED

Derived using **CACI's** Population Projections for 1998   Data refers to **adults** except where indicated

Base: All GB	Total for Area	As a Percentage of: Area	As a Percentage of: GB Base	Index (GB av. = 100)
Total Resident Population	356,967	100.0	100.0	100
of whom female	182,491	51.1	50.8	101
By age: *of whom female (%)*				
0– 4 48.6	19,328	5.4	6.5	84
5– 9 48.9	21,290	6.0	6.6	91
10–14 48.5	22,655	6.3	6.3	100
15–19 49.9	24,287	6.8	6.2	111
20–24 46.2	19,597	5.5	5.9	93
25–34 49.0	43,421	12.2	15.4	79
35–44 50.5	46,503	13.0	14.3	91
45–54 50.6	49,328	13.8	13.1	105
55–64 50.3	40,879	11.5	9.9	115
65–74 52.8	37,457	10.5	8.4	125
75+ 63.6	32,222	9.0	7.4	122
Cost of Car (of only or most recently obtained car)				
Up to £2,999	81,060	27.6	22.9	120
£3,000– £4,999	49,829	17.0	13.5	125
£5,000– £6,999	32,167	11.0	11.1	99
£7,000– £9,999	33,107	11.3	11.1	101
£10,000–£19,999	32,947	11.2	12.8	88
£20,000+	2,736	0.9	1.1	83
Owner of a Company Car	20,428	7.0	7.7	91
Income Level of Households[1]				
Up to £4,999	18,991	13.3	10.9	122
£5,000– £9,999	27,882	19.5	16.3	120
£10,000–£14,999	29,483	20.6	18.1	114
£15,000–£19,999	23,491	16.4	15.7	105
£20,000–£24,999	16,136	11.3	12.0	94
£25,000–£29,999	10,288	7.2	8.5	85
£30,000–£34,999	6,343	4.4	5.9	76
£35,000–£39,999	3,870	2.7	4.0	68
£40,000–£44,999	2,366	1.7	2.7	62
£45,000–£49,999	1,460	1.0	1.8	56
£50,000+	2,647	1.9	4.3	43
Use of Multiple Stores in Last Year				
Dept. stores (not groceries)	213,038	72.5	78.5	92
Ladies' outfitters	156,103	53.2	53.5	99
Gentlemen's outfitters	183,105	62.3	64.0	97
DIY	168,017	57.2	60.5	94
Furniture, appliances, durables	177,226	60.3	64.6	93
Shoes	201,359	68.6	70.1	98
Visits to Licensed Premises (at least weekly)				
Pubs	78,498	26.7	26.3	102
Licensed clubs	36,355	12.4	11.6	107
Wine bars	2,525	0.9	1.4	62

© CACI Limited, 1998.   Tel: 0171 602-6000 (London) / 0131 557-0123 (Edinburgh).

Note: [1] PayCheck data. Please see Chapter 3 for details.
Source: © BMRB International Limited, 1997. Buying potential info. modelled using data from TGI 4/96-3/97.

GWENT

Derived using **CACI's Population Projections for 1998**   Data refers to **adults** except where indicated

Base: All GB		Total for Area	As a Percentage of:		Index (GB av. = 100)
			Area	GB Base	
Total Resident Population		453,914	100.0	100.0	100
of whom female		230,870	50.9	50.8	100
By age:	*of whom female (%)*				
0– 4	49.6	28,708	6.3	6.5	98
5– 9	48.6	31,555	7.0	6.6	106
10–14	49.0	31,305	6.9	6.3	109
15–19	48.6	26,501	5.8	6.2	95
20–24	47.6	24,258	5.3	5.9	91
25–34	49.0	62,850	13.8	15.4	90
35–44	49.7	62,654	13.8	14.3	96
45–54	49.9	61,700	13.6	13.1	104
55–64	50.5	48,638	10.7	9.9	108
65–74	53.5	41,282	9.1	8.4	108
75+	64.0	34,463	7.6	7.4	103
Cost of Car (of only or most recently obtained car)					
Up to £2,999		104,172	28.7	22.9	125
£3,000– £4,999		57,865	16.0	13.5	118
£5,000– £6,999		34,239	9.4	11.1	85
£7,000– £9,999		35,601	9.8	11.1	88
£10,000–£19,999		31,364	8.7	12.8	68
£20,000+		2,931	0.8	1.1	72
Owner of a Company Car		22,831	6.3	7.7	82
Income Level of Households[1]					
Up to £4,999		23,293	12.8	10.9	118
£5,000– £9,999		34,259	18.9	16.3	116
£10,000–£14,999		36,129	19.9	18.1	110
£15,000–£19,999		29,087	16.0	15.7	102
£20,000–£24,999		20,462	11.3	12.0	94
£25,000–£29,999		13,495	7.4	8.5	88
£30,000–£34,999		8,660	4.8	5.9	82
£35,000–£39,999		5,514	3.0	4.0	77
£40,000–£44,999		3,521	1.9	2.7	72
£45,000–£49,999		2,268	1.3	1.8	69
£50,000+		4,635	2.6	4.3	60
Use of Multiple Stores in Last Year					
Dept. stores (not groceries)		259,613	71.6	78.5	91
Ladies' outfitters		197,633	54.5	53.5	102
Gentlemen's outfitters		229,379	63.3	64.0	99
DIY		210,940	58.2	60.5	96
Furniture, appliances, durables		226,119	62.4	64.6	97
Shoes		247,801	68.4	70.1	98
Visits to Licensed Premises (at least weekly)					
Pubs		100,043	27.6	26.3	105
Licensed clubs		57,995	16.0	11.6	138
Wine bars		3,541	1.0	1.4	70

© CACI Limited, 1998.   Tel: 0171 602-6000 (London) / 0131 557-0123 (Edinburgh).
Note: [1] PayCheck data. Please see Chapter 3 for details.
Source: © BMRB International Limited, 1997. Buying potential info. modelled using data from TGI 4/96-3/97.

GWYNEDD

Derived using **CACI's Population Projections for 1998**   Data refers to **adults** except where indicated

Base: All GB	Total for Area	As a Percentage of: Area	GB Base	Index (GB av. = 100)
Total Resident Population	240,992	100.0	100.0	100
of whom female	123,659	51.3	50.8	101
By age: *of whom female (%)*				
0– 4 48.9	13,634	5.7	6.5	88
5– 9 48.9	14,666	6.1	6.6	93
10–14 47.4	14,857	6.2	6.3	97
15–19 47.4	15,047	6.2	6.2	101
20–24 47.9	13,825	5.7	5.9	98
25–34 47.3	30,692	12.7	15.4	83
35–44 49.9	30,184	12.5	14.3	88
45–54 50.4	31,463	13.1	13.1	99
55–64 51.8	27,346	11.3	9.9	114
65–74 54.7	25,870	10.7	8.4	128
75+ 65.2	23,408	9.7	7.4	131
Cost of Car (of only or most recently obtained car)				
Up to £2,999	51,784	26.2	22.9	114
£3,000– £4,999	32,028	16.2	13.5	119
£5,000– £6,999	21,065	10.6	11.1	96
£7,000– £9,999	24,376	12.3	11.1	111
£10,000–£19,999	22,053	11.1	12.8	87
£20,000+	1,983	1.0	1.1	89
Owner of a Company Car	14,038	7.1	7.7	93
Income Level of Households[1]				
Up to £4,999	14,002	14.2	10.9	131
£5,000– £9,999	19,352	19.7	16.3	121
£10,000–£14,999	19,977	20.3	18.1	112
£15,000–£19,999	15,809	16.1	15.7	102
£20,000–£24,999	10,869	11.0	12.0	92
£25,000–£29,999	6,954	7.1	8.5	83
£30,000–£34,999	4,306	4.4	5.9	75
£35,000–£39,999	2,641	2.7	4.0	68
£40,000–£44,999	1,624	1.7	2.7	62
£45,000–£49,999	1,010	1.0	1.8	56
£50,000+	1,895	1.9	4.3	45
Use of Multiple Stores in Last Year				
Dept. stores (not groceries)	143,751	72.7	78.5	93
Ladies' outfitters	105,161	53.2	53.5	99
Gentlemen's outfitters	122,400	61.9	64.0	97
DIY	112,543	56.9	60.5	94
Furniture, appliances, durables	119,417	60.4	64.6	93
Shoes	135,240	68.4	70.1	98
Visits to Licensed Premises (at least weekly)				
Pubs	53,993	27.3	26.3	104
Licensed clubs	25,705	13.0	11.6	112
Wine bars	1,808	0.9	1.4	65

© CACI Limited, 1998. Tel: 0171 602-6000 (London) / 0131 557-0123 (Edinburgh).
Note: [1] PayCheck data. Please see Chapter 3 for details.
Source: © BMRB International Limited, 1997. Buying potential info. modelled using data from TGI 4/96-3/97.

MID GLAMORGAN

Derived using **CACI's Population Projections for 1998**   Data refers to **adults** except where indicated

Base: All GB		Total for Area	As a Percentage of: Area	As a Percentage of: GB Base	Index (GB av. = 100)
Total Resident Population		547,686	100.0	100.0	100
of whom female		279,056	51.0	50.8	100
By age:	*of whom female (%)*				
0– 4	49.0	35,332	6.5	6.5	100
5– 9	48.7	38,082	7.0	6.6	106
10–14	49.3	38,533	7.0	6.3	111
15–19	47.8	34,731	6.3	6.2	103
20–24	48.0	32,109	5.9	5.9	100
25–34	49.8	78,395	14.3	15.4	93
35–44	49.9	74,801	13.7	14.3	95
45–54	50.0	73,192	13.4	13.1	102
55–64	50.3	57,156	10.4	9.9	105
65–74	54.1	47,260	8.6	8.4	103
75+	65.6	38,095	7.0	7.4	94
Cost of Car (of only or most recently obtained car)					
Up to £2,999		129,311	29.7	22.9	129
£3,000– £4,999		69,127	15.9	13.5	117
£5,000– £6,999		38,144	8.8	11.1	79
£7,000– £9,999		40,574	9.3	11.1	84
£10,000–£19,999		33,618	7.7	12.8	60
£20,000+		2,382	0.5	1.1	49
Owner of a Company Car		24,427	5.6	7.7	73
Income Level of Households[1]					
Up to £4,999		30,042	14.1	10.9	129
£5,000– £9,999		43,597	20.4	16.3	125
£10,000–£14,999		44,363	20.7	18.1	115
£15,000–£19,999		34,333	16.1	15.7	102
£20,000–£24,999		23,185	10.8	12.0	91
£25,000–£29,999		14,655	6.9	8.5	81
£30,000–£34,999		9,000	4.2	5.9	72
£35,000–£39,999		5,481	2.6	4.0	65
£40,000–£44,999		3,349	1.6	2.7	58
£45,000–£49,999		2,067	1.0	1.8	53
£50,000+		3,747	1.8	4.3	41
Use of Multiple Stores in Last Year					
Dept. stores (not groceries)		307,179	70.5	78.5	90
Ladies' outfitters		240,271	55.1	53.5	103
Gentlemen's outfitters		278,637	63.9	64.0	100
DIY		254,238	58.3	60.5	96
Furniture, appliances, durables		272,747	62.6	64.6	97
Shoes		297,515	68.3	70.1	97
Visits to Licensed Premises (at least weekly)					
Pubs		119,935	27.5	26.3	105
Licensed clubs		74,315	17.1	11.6	147
Wine bars		4,347	1.0	1.4	71

© CACI Limited, 1998.   Tel: 0171 602-6000 (London) / 0131 557-0123 (Edinburgh).
Note: [1] PayCheck data. Please see Chapter 3 for details.
Source: © BMRB International Limited, 1997. Buying potential info. modelled using data from TGI 4/96-3/97.

POWYS

Derived using **CACI's Population Projections for 1998**   Data refers to **adults** except where indicated

Base: All GB	Total for Area	As a Percentage of: Area	GB Base	Index (GB av. = 100)
Total Resident Population	122,048	100.0	100.0	100
of whom female	61,366	50.3	50.8	99
By age: *of whom female (%)*				
0– 4 48.9	6,497	5.3	6.5	82
5– 9 47.9	7,432	6.1	6.6	93
10–14 47.6	7,788	6.4	6.3	101
15–19 47.3	7,126	5.8	6.2	95
20–24 44.2	6,567	5.4	5.9	92
25–34 48.6	14,313	11.7	15.4	76
35–44 50.0	16,286	13.3	14.3	93
45–54 50.2	17,574	14.4	13.1	110
55–64 49.9	14,097	11.6	9.9	116
65–74 51.9	13,174	10.8	8.4	128
75+ 61.3	11,194	9.2	7.4	124
Cost of Car (of only or most recently obtained car)				
Up to £2,999	28,521	28.4	22.9	124
£3,000– £4,999	16,793	16.7	13.5	124
£5,000– £6,999	11,708	11.7	11.1	105
£7,000– £9,999	10,890	10.9	11.1	97
£10,000–£19,999	12,233	12.2	12.8	95
£20,000+	919	0.9	1.1	81
Owner of a Company Car	7,125	7.1	7.7	93
Income Level of Households[1]				
Up to £4,999	5,970	11.9	10.9	110
£5,000– £9,999	9,266	18.5	16.3	114
£10,000–£14,999	10,232	20.4	18.1	113
£15,000–£19,999	8,416	16.8	15.7	107
£20,000–£24,999	5,913	11.8	12.0	99
£25,000–£29,999	3,833	7.7	8.5	90
£30,000–£34,999	2,396	4.8	5.9	82
£35,000–£39,999	1,480	3.0	4.0	74
£40,000–£44,999	916	1.8	2.7	68
£45,000–£49,999	572	1.1	1.8	63
£50,000+	1,076	2.1	4.3	50
Use of Multiple Stores in Last Year				
Dept. stores (not groceries)	73,259	73.0	78.5	93
Ladies' outfitters	52,837	52.7	53.5	99
Gentlemen's outfitters	63,089	62.9	64.0	98
DIY	57,726	57.5	60.5	95
Furniture, appliances, durables	60,487	60.3	64.6	93
Shoes	69,006	68.8	70.1	98
Visits to Licensed Premises (at least weekly)				
Pubs	26,126	26.0	26.3	99
Licensed clubs	10,809	10.8	11.6	93
Wine bars	788	0.8	1.4	56

© CACI Limited, 1998. Tel: 0171 602-6000 (London) / 0131 557-0123 (Edinburgh).

Note: [1] PayCheck data. Please see Chapter 3 for details.
Source: © BMRB International Limited, 1997. Buying potential info. modelled using data from TGI 4/96-3/97.

SOUTH GLAMORGAN

Derived using **CACI's Population Projections for 1998**   Data refers to **adults** except where indicated

Base: All GB		Total for Area	As a Percentage of:		Index (GB av. = 100)
			Area	GB Base	
Total Resident Population		424,519	100.0	100.0	100
of whom female		215,983	50.9	50.8	100
By age:	*of whom female (%)*				
0– 4	48.3	28,969	6.8	6.5	106
5– 9	48.8	29,289	6.9	6.6	105
10–14	48.7	27,958	6.6	6.3	104
15–19	50.0	29,190	6.9	6.2	112
20–24	48.2	24,431	5.8	5.9	98
25–34	49.1	70,130	16.5	15.4	107
35–44	49.6	60,547	14.3	14.3	100
45–54	49.9	50,948	12.0	13.1	91
55–64	51.4	38,208	9.0	9.9	91
65–74	53.7	34,593	8.1	8.4	97
75+	64.7	30,256	7.1	7.4	96
Cost of Car (of only or most recently obtained car)					
Up to £2,999		84,797	25.1	22.9	109
£3,000– £4,999		51,226	15.1	13.5	112
£5,000– £6,999		34,137	10.1	11.1	91
£7,000– £9,999		38,306	11.3	11.1	102
£10,000–£19,999		34,570	10.2	12.8	80
£20,000+		4,111	1.2	1.1	108
Owner of a Company Car		24,737	7.3	7.7	95
Income Level of Households[1]					
Up to £4,999		19,040	11.1	10.9	102
£5,000– £9,999		28,649	16.8	16.3	103
£10,000–£14,999		31,848	18.6	18.1	103
£15,000–£19,999		27,303	16.0	15.7	102
£20,000–£24,999		20,431	12.0	12.0	100
£25,000–£29,999		14,252	8.3	8.5	98
£30,000–£34,999		9,609	5.6	5.9	96
£35,000–£39,999		6,392	3.7	4.0	94
£40,000–£44,999		4,242	2.5	2.7	93
£45,000–£49,999		2,827	1.7	1.8	91
£50,000+		6,251	3.7	4.3	86
Use of Multiple Stores in Last Year					
Dept. stores (not groceries)		252,455	74.6	78.5	95
Ladies' outfitters		179,669	53.1	53.5	99
Gentlemen's outfitters		208,138	61.5	64.0	96
DIY		196,943	58.2	60.5	96
Furniture, appliances, durables		208,814	61.7	64.6	96
Shoes		231,865	68.5	70.1	98
Visits to Licensed Premises (at least weekly)					
Pubs		97,270	28.8	26.3	109
Licensed clubs		46,658	13.8	11.6	119
Wine bars		3,246	1.0	1.4	69

© CACI Limited, 1998.   Tel: 0171 602-6000 (London) / 0131 557-0123 (Edinburgh).
Note: [1] PayCheck data. Please see Chapter 3 for details.
Source: © BMRB International Limited, 1997. Buying potential info. modelled using data from TGI 4/96-3/97.

WEST GLAMORGAN

Derived using **CACI's Population Projections for 1998**　　Data refers to **adults** except where indicated

Base: All GB		Total for Area	As a Percentage of: Area	GB Base	Index (GB av. = 100)
Total Resident Population		371,130	100.0	100.0	100
of whom female		189,141	51.0	50.8	100
By age:	*of whom female (%)*				
0– 4	48.8	21,252	5.7	6.5	89
5– 9	48.4	23,111	6.2	6.6	95
10–14	48.8	24,166	6.5	6.3	103
15–19	48.6	25,465	6.9	6.2	111
20–24	47.9	21,417	5.8	5.9	98
25–34	47.1	50,994	13.7	15.4	89
35–44	50.4	49,396	13.3	14.3	93
45–54	50.4	48,527	13.1	13.1	100
55–64	50.7	39,336	10.6	9.9	107
65–74	53.5	35,848	9.7	8.4	115
75+	65.4	31,618	8.5	7.4	115
Cost of Car (of only or most recently obtained car)					
Up to £2,999		83,954	27.7	22.9	121
£3,000– £4,999		48,630	16.1	13.5	119
£5,000– £6,999		29,187	9.6	11.1	87
£7,000– £9,999		30,438	10.1	11.1	90
£10,000–£19,999		26,641	8.8	12.8	69
£20,000+		2,396	0.8	1.1	70
Owner of a Company Car		19,339	6.4	7.7	83
Income Level of Households[1]					
Up to £4,999		19,396	13.0	10.9	119
£5,000– £9,999		28,717	19.2	16.3	118
£10,000–£14,999		30,363	20.3	18.1	112
£15,000–£19,999		24,405	16.3	15.7	104
£20,000–£24,999		17,002	11.4	12.0	95
£25,000–£29,999		11,005	7.4	8.5	87
£30,000–£34,999		6,881	4.6	5.9	79
£35,000–£39,999		4,249	2.8	4.0	72
£40,000–£44,999		2,625	1.8	2.7	66
£45,000–£49,999		1,636	1.1	1.8	60
£50,000+		3,043	2.0	4.3	48
Use of Multiple Stores in Last Year					
Dept. stores (not groceries)		218,832	72.3	78.5	92
Ladies' outfitters		164,053	54.2	53.5	101
Gentlemen's outfitters		189,116	62.5	64.0	98
DIY		175,878	58.1	60.5	96
Furniture, appliances, durables		187,698	62.0	64.6	96
Shoes		206,905	68.4	70.1	98
Visits to Licensed Premises (at least weekly)					
Pubs		83,989	27.8	26.3	105
Licensed clubs		48,846	16.1	11.6	139
Wine bars		2,953	1.0	1.4	70

© CACI Limited, 1998.　Tel: 0171 602-6000 (London) / 0131 557-0123 (Edinburgh).
Note:　　[1] PayCheck data. Please see Chapter 3 for details.
Source:　© BMRB International Limited, 1997. Buying potential info. modelled using data from TGI 4/96-3/97.

BORDERS

Derived using **CACI's Population Projections for 1998**   Data refers to **adults** except where indicated

Base: All GB		Total for Area	As a Percentage of: Area	As a Percentage of: GB Base	Index (GB av. = 100)
Total Resident Population		107,045	100.0	100.0	100
of whom female		55,366	51.7	50.8	102
By age:	*of whom female (%)*				
0– 4	48.9	6,298	5.9	6.5	91
5– 9	48.7	6,449	6.0	6.6	92
10–14	48.8	6,488	6.1	6.3	95
15–19	48.9	6,155	5.7	6.2	93
20–24	49.1	4,958	4.6	5.9	79
25–34	50.6	13,739	12.8	15.4	83
35–44	50.0	15,372	14.4	14.3	100
45–54	50.3	14,817	13.8	13.1	105
55–64	52.2	12,288	11.5	9.9	115
65–74	54.3	10,914	10.2	8.4	121
75+	63.8	9,567	8.9	7.4	121
Cost of Car (of only or most recently obtained car)					
Up to £2,999		15,309	17.4	22.9	76
£3,000– £4,999		13,403	15.3	13.5	113
£5,000– £6,999		12,337	14.0	11.1	127
£7,000– £9,999		9,283	10.6	11.1	95
£10,000–£19,999		10,240	11.7	12.8	91
£20,000+		770	0.9	1.1	78
Owner of a Company Car		3,522	4.0	7.7	52
Income Level of Households[1]					
Up to £4,999		5,244	11.6	10.9	106
£5,000– £9,999		8,209	18.1	16.3	111
£10,000–£14,999		9,032	19.9	18.1	110
£15,000–£19,999		7,474	16.5	15.7	105
£20,000–£24,999		5,345	11.8	12.0	99
£25,000–£29,999		3,558	7.8	8.5	92
£30,000–£34,999		2,294	5.1	5.9	86
£35,000–£39,999		1,464	3.2	4.0	81
£40,000–£44,999		936	2.1	2.7	77
£45,000–£49,999		603	1.3	1.8	73
£50,000+		1,228	2.7	4.3	63
Use of Multiple Stores in Last Year					
Dept. stores (not groceries)		63,618	72.5	78.5	92
Ladies' outfitters		45,701	52.0	53.5	97
Gentlemen's outfitters		57,148	65.1	64.0	102
DIY		50,476	57.5	60.5	95
Furniture, appliances, durables		55,144	62.8	64.6	97
Shoes		58,675	66.8	70.1	95
Visits to Licensed Premises (at least weekly)					
Pubs		27,299	31.1	26.3	118
Licensed clubs		10,549	12.0	11.6	103
Wine bars		1,511	1.7	1.4	123

© CACI Limited, 1998.   Tel: 0171 602-6000 (London) / 0131 557-0123 (Edinburgh).
Note: [1] PayCheck data. Please see Chapter 3 for details.
Source: © BMRB International Limited, 1997. Buying potential info. modelled using data from TGI 4/96-3/97.

CENTRAL

Derived using **CACI's Population Projections for 1998**   Data refers to **adults** except where indicated

Base: All GB		Total for Area	As a Percentage of:		Index (GB av. = 100)
			Area	GB Base	
Total Resident Population		275,348	100.0	100.0	100
of whom female		141,562	51.4	50.8	101
By age:	*of whom female (%)*				
0– 4	49.3	17,473	6.3	6.5	98
5– 9	49.1	17,263	6.3	6.6	96
10–14	48.1	17,197	6.2	6.3	98
15–19	49.3	17,621	6.4	6.2	104
20–24	48.5	16,740	6.1	5.9	103
25–34	49.7	41,161	14.9	15.4	97
35–44	50.4	40,193	14.6	14.3	102
45–54	50.7	36,936	13.4	13.1	102
55–64	52.2	29,260	10.6	9.9	107
65–74	54.9	23,315	8.5	8.4	101
75+	65.1	18,189	6.6	7.4	89
Cost of Car (of only or most recently obtained car)					
Up to £2,999		32,568	14.6	22.9	64
£3,000– £4,999		27,517	12.3	13.5	91
£5,000– £6,999		25,472	11.4	11.1	103
£7,000– £9,999		33,595	15.0	11.1	135
£10,000–£19,999		29,088	13.0	12.8	102
£20,000+		2,556	1.1	1.1	102
Owner of a Company Car		16,298	7.3	7.7	95
Income Level of Households[1]					
Up to £4,999		12,879	11.6	10.9	107
£5,000– £9,999		19,114	17.2	16.3	106
£10,000–£14,999		20,802	18.8	18.1	104
£15,000–£19,999		17,589	15.9	15.7	101
£20,000–£24,999		13,083	11.8	12.0	99
£25,000–£29,999		9,098	8.2	8.5	96
£30,000–£34,999		6,111	5.5	5.9	94
£35,000–£39,999		4,041	3.6	4.0	92
£40,000–£44,999		2,662	2.4	2.7	89
£45,000–£49,999		1,759	1.6	1.8	87
£50,000+		3,769	3.4	4.3	80
Use of Multiple Stores in Last Year					
Dept. stores (not groceries)		174,990	78.3	78.5	100
Ladies' outfitters		117,746	52.7	53.5	99
Gentlemen's outfitters		133,198	59.6	64.0	93
DIY		135,065	60.5	60.5	100
Furniture, appliances, durables		142,689	63.9	64.6	99
Shoes		165,344	74.0	70.1	106
Visits to Licensed Premises (at least weekly)					
Pubs		48,771	21.8	26.3	83
Licensed clubs		28,430	12.7	11.6	110
Wine bars		2,709	1.2	1.4	87

© CACI Limited, 1998.   Tel: 0171 602-6000 (London) / 0131 557-0123 (Edinburgh).
Note: [1] PayCheck data. Please see Chapter 3 for details.
Source: © BMRB International Limited, 1997. Buying potential info. modelled using data from TGI 4/96-3/97.

DUMFRIES AND GALLOWAY

Derived using **CACI's Population Projections for 1998**   Data refers to **adults** except where indicated

Base: All GB		Total for Area	As a Percentage of: Area	As a Percentage of: GB Base	Index (GB av. = 100)
Total Resident Population		148,382	100.0	100.0	100
of whom female		76,124	51.3	50.8	101
By age:	*of whom female (%)*				
0– 4	49.0	8,838	6.0	6.5	92
5– 9	48.5	9,057	6.1	6.6	93
10–14	48.4	9,314	6.3	6.3	99
15–19	48.4	8,783	5.9	6.2	96
20–24	48.0	6,840	4.6	5.9	78
25–34	50.0	19,181	12.9	15.4	84
35–44	50.3	20,948	14.1	14.3	99
45–54	50.4	20,266	13.7	13.1	104
55–64	51.8	17,682	11.9	9.9	120
65–74	53.5	15,514	10.5	8.4	124
75+	63.1	11,959	8.1	7.4	109
Cost of Car (of only or most recently obtained car)					
Up to £2,999		21,174	17.5	22.9	76
£3,000– £4,999		18,486	15.3	13.5	113
£5,000– £6,999		16,960	14.0	11.1	126
£7,000– £9,999		12,837	10.6	11.1	95
£10,000–£19,999		14,180	11.7	12.8	92
£20,000+		992	0.8	1.1	73
Owner of a Company Car		4,518	3.7	7.7	49
Income Level of Households[1]					
Up to £4,999		7,640	12.6	10.9	115
£5,000– £9,999		11,510	18.9	16.3	116
£10,000–£14,999		12,374	20.3	18.1	112
£15,000–£19,999		10,097	16.6	15.7	106
£20,000–£24,999		7,098	11.7	12.0	98
£25,000–£29,999		4,601	7.6	8.5	89
£30,000–£34,999		2,863	4.7	5.9	80
£35,000–£39,999		1,752	2.9	4.0	73
£40,000–£44,999		1,072	1.8	2.7	66
£45,000–£49,999		661	1.1	1.8	60
£50,000+		1,201	2.0	4.3	46
Use of Multiple Stores in Last Year					
Dept. stores (not groceries)		87,093	71.9	78.5	92
Ladies' outfitters		63,263	52.2	53.5	98
Gentlemen's outfitters		79,122	65.3	64.0	102
DIY		69,550	57.4	60.5	95
Furniture, appliances, durables		75,873	62.6	64.6	97
Shoes		81,096	66.9	70.1	95
Visits to Licensed Premises (at least weekly)					
Pubs		36,406	30.0	26.3	114
Licensed clubs		14,197	11.7	11.6	101
Wine bars		1,939	1.6	1.4	115

© CACI Limited, 1998.   Tel: 0171 602-6000 (London) / 0131 557-0123 (Edinburgh).
Note: [1] PayCheck data. Please see Chapter 3 for details.
Source: © BMRB International Limited, 1997. Buying potential info. modelled using data from TGI 4/96-3/97.

FIFE

Derived using **CACI's Population Projections for 1998**   Data refers to **adults** except where indicated

Base: All GB		Total for Area	As a Percentage of: Area	As a Percentage of: GB Base	Index (GB av. = 100)
Total Resident Population		353,869	100.0	100.0	100
of whom female		172,427	48.7	49.2	99
By age:	*of whom female (%)*				
0– 4	49.6	22,029	6.2	6.5	96
5– 9	48.7	22,409	6.3	6.6	97
10–14	48.3	23,049	6.5	6.3	103
15–19	48.7	23,400	6.6	6.2	107
20–24	46.6	21,659	6.1	5.9	104
25–34	49.6	51,973	14.7	15.4	95
35–44	50.3	51,448	14.5	14.3	102
45–54	50.8	46,677	13.2	13.1	100
55–64	52.1	35,933	10.2	9.9	102
65–74	54.9	30,469	8.6	8.4	102
75+	65.0	24,823	7.0	7.4	95
Cost of Car (of only or most recently obtained car)					
Up to £2,999		46,018	16.1	22.9	70
£3,000– £4,999		37,359	13.0	13.5	96
£5,000– £6,999		32,355	11.3	11.1	102
£7,000– £9,999		41,477	14.5	11.1	130
£10,000–£19,999		34,918	12.2	12.8	95
£20,000+		2,406	0.8	1.1	75
Owner of a Company Car		18,949	6.6	7.7	86
Income Level of Households[1]					
Up to £4,999		16,878	11.8	10.9	108
£5,000– £9,999		25,442	17.7	16.3	109
£10,000–£14,999		27,693	19.3	18.1	107
£15,000–£19,999		23,172	16.1	15.7	103
£20,000–£24,999		16,917	11.8	12.0	99
£25,000–£29,999		11,508	8.0	8.5	94
£30,000–£34,999		7,563	5.3	5.9	90
£35,000–£39,999		4,901	3.4	4.0	86
£40,000–£44,999		3,168	2.2	2.7	82
£45,000–£49,999		2,057	1.4	1.8	79
£50,000+		4,205	2.9	4.3	69
Use of Multiple Stores in Last Year					
Dept. stores (not groceries)		221,873	77.5	78.5	99
Ladies' outfitters		149,924	52.4	53.5	98
Gentlemen's outfitters		174,565	61.0	64.0	95
DIY		173,166	60.5	60.5	100
Furniture, appliances, durables		183,046	63.9	64.6	99
Shoes		210,189	73.4	70.1	105
Visits to Licensed Premises (at least weekly)					
Pubs		61,771	21.6	26.3	82
Licensed clubs		36,131	12.6	11.6	109
Wine bars		2,989	1.0	1.4	75

© CACI Limited, 1998. Tel: 0171 602-6000 (London) / 0131 557-0123 (Edinburgh).
Note: [1] PayCheck data. Please see Chapter 3 for details.
Source: © BMRB International Limited, 1997. Buying potential info. modelled using data from TGI 4/96-3/97.

GRAMPIAN

Derived using **CACI's Population Projections for 1998**   Data refers to **adults** except where indicated

Base: All GB		Total for Area	As a Percentage of: Area	As a Percentage of: GB Base	Index (GB av. = 100)
Total Resident Population		539,465	100.0	100.0	100
of whom female		272,452	50.5	50.8	99
By age:	*of whom female (%)*				
0– 4	49.0	34,764	6.4	6.5	100
5– 9	49.0	34,388	6.4	6.6	97
10–14	48.7	33,907	6.3	6.3	99
15–19	49.3	34,689	6.4	6.2	104
20–24	47.9	34,325	6.4	5.9	108
25–34	48.4	84,966	15.8	15.4	102
35–44	49.1	83,169	15.4	14.3	108
45–54	49.3	71,102	13.2	13.1	100
55–64	51.0	52,106	9.7	9.9	97
65–74	54.6	42,475	7.9	8.4	94
75+	65.0	33,574	6.2	7.4	84
Cost of Car (of only or most recently obtained car)					
Up to £2,999		84,667	19.4	22.9	85
£3,000– £4,999		67,869	15.6	13.5	115
£5,000– £6,999		53,773	12.3	11.1	111
£7,000– £9,999		57,532	13.2	11.1	118
£10,000–£19,999		57,226	13.1	12.8	103
£20,000+		2,187	0.5	1.1	45
Owner of a Company Car		22,947	5.3	7.7	69
Income Level of Households[1]					
Up to £4,999		21,517	9.9	10.9	91
£5,000– £9,999		32,960	15.2	16.3	93
£10,000–£14,999		38,060	17.5	18.1	97
£15,000–£19,999		34,185	15.8	15.7	100
£20,000–£24,999		26,819	12.4	12.0	103
£25,000–£29,999		19,540	9.0	8.5	106
£30,000–£34,999		13,686	6.3	5.9	108
£35,000–£39,999		9,396	4.3	4.0	109
£40,000–£44,999		6,400	3.0	2.7	110
£45,000–£49,999		4,355	2.0	1.8	110
£50,000+		10,024	4.6	4.3	108
Use of Multiple Stores in Last Year					
Dept. stores (not groceries)		339,579	77.8	78.5	99
Ladies' outfitters		212,730	48.7	53.5	91
Gentlemen's outfitters		279,255	64.0	64.0	100
DIY		266,131	61.0	60.5	101
Furniture, appliances, durables		274,511	62.9	64.6	97
Shoes		308,278	70.6	70.1	101
Visits to Licensed Premises (at least weekly)					
Pubs		89,558	20.5	26.3	78
Licensed clubs		44,443	10.2	11.6	88
Wine bars		1,442	0.3	1.4	24

© CACI Limited, 1998.   Tel: 0171 602-6000 (London) / 0131 557-0123 (Edinburgh).
Note: [1] PayCheck data. Please see Chapter 3 for details.
Source: © BMRB International Limited, 1997. Buying potential info. modelled using data from TGI 4/96-3/97.

HIGHLAND

Derived using **CACI's Population Projections for 1998**   Data refers to **adults** except where indicated

Base: All GB		Total for Area	As a Percentage of: Area	As a Percentage of: GB Base	Index (GB av. = 100)
Total Resident Population		211,045	100.0	100.0	100
of whom female		107,273	50.8	50.8	100
By age:	*of whom female (%)*				
0– 4	49.0	13,157	6.2	6.5	97
5– 9	47.9	13,691	6.5	6.6	99
10–14	47.7	14,141	6.7	6.3	106
15–19	47.1	13,495	6.4	6.2	104
20–24	46.6	10,444	4.9	5.9	84
25–34	50.1	28,718	13.6	15.4	88
35–44	49.6	30,878	14.6	14.3	102
45–54	49.8	29,900	14.2	13.1	108
55–64	51.7	23,401	11.1	9.9	112
65–74	54.0	18,947	9.0	8.4	107
75+	65.7	14,273	6.8	7.4	92
Cost of Car (of only or most recently obtained car)					
Up to £2,999		32,746	19.3	22.9	84
£3,000– £4,999		26,194	15.4	13.5	114
£5,000– £6,999		21,483	12.6	11.1	114
£7,000– £9,999		23,971	14.1	11.1	127
£10,000–£19,999		22,046	13.0	12.8	102
£20,000+		848	0.5	1.1	44
Owner of a Company Car		8,903	5.2	7.7	68
Income Level of Households[1]					
Up to £4,999		10,266	12.0	10.9	110
£5,000– £9,999		15,560	18.2	16.3	112
£10,000–£14,999		16,928	19.8	18.1	109
£15,000–£19,999		14,063	16.4	15.7	105
£20,000–£24,999		10,122	11.8	12.0	99
£25,000–£29,999		6,741	7.9	8.5	93
£30,000–£34,999		4,315	5.0	5.9	86
£35,000–£39,999		2,716	3.2	4.0	80
£40,000–£44,999		1,705	2.0	2.7	74
£45,000–£49,999		1,075	1.3	1.8	69
£50,000+		2,042	2.4	4.3	56
Use of Multiple Stores in Last Year					
Dept. stores (not groceries)		129,728	76.3	78.5	97
Ladies' outfitters		83,548	49.1	53.5	92
Gentlemen's outfitters		107,947	63.5	64.0	99
DIY		102,132	60.1	60.5	99
Furniture, appliances, durables		105,516	62.0	64.6	96
Shoes		120,552	70.9	70.1	101
Visits to Licensed Premises (at least weekly)					
Pubs		33,288	19.6	26.3	74
Licensed clubs		17,063	10.0	11.6	86
Wine bars		597	0.4	1.4	25

© CACI Limited, 1998. Tel: 0171 602-6000 (London) / 0131 557-0123 (Edinburgh).
Note: [1] PayCheck data. Please see Chapter 3 for details.
Source: © BMRB International Limited, 1997. Buying potential info. modelled using data from TGI 4/96-3/97.

LOTHIAN

Derived using **CACI's Population Projections for 1998**   Data refers to **adults** except where indicated

Base: All GB		Total for Area	As a Percentage of: Area	As a Percentage of: GB Base	Index (GB av. = 100)
Total Resident Population		771,532	100.0	100.0	100
of whom female		396,090	51.3	50.8	101
By age:	*of whom female (%)*				
0– 4	48.5	48,631	6.3	6.5	98
5– 9	49.1	46,739	6.1	6.6	92
10–14	48.5	44,466	5.8	6.3	91
15–19	48.8	45,441	5.9	6.2	96
20–24	49.7	53,233	6.9	5.9	117
25–34	49.2	133,395	17.3	15.4	112
35–44	49.8	115,847	15.0	14.3	105
45–54	51.0	97,266	12.6	13.1	96
55–64	52.0	74,194	9.6	9.9	97
65–74	55.8	62,042	8.0	8.4	96
75+	66.1	50,278	6.5	7.4	88
Cost of Car (of only or most recently obtained car)					
Up to £2,999		86,455	13.7	22.9	60
£3,000– £4,999		75,533	12.0	13.5	88
£5,000– £6,999		73,251	11.6	11.1	104
£7,000– £9,999		97,507	15.4	11.1	139
£10,000–£19,999		83,154	13.2	12.8	103
£20,000+		8,804	1.4	1.1	124
Owner of a Company Car		48,406	7.7	7.7	100
Income Level of Households[1]					
Up to £4,999		33,891	10.4	10.9	96
£5,000– £9,999		52,918	16.3	16.3	100
£10,000–£14,999		59,214	18.2	18.1	100
£15,000–£19,999		51,295	15.8	15.7	100
£20,000–£24,999		39,123	12.0	12.0	101
£25,000–£29,999		27,942	8.6	8.5	101
£30,000–£34,999		19,292	5.9	5.9	101
£35,000–£39,999		13,111	4.0	4.0	102
£40,000–£44,999		8,867	2.7	2.7	102
£45,000–£49,999		6,006	1.8	1.8	101
£50,000+		13,807	4.2	4.3	99
Use of Multiple Stores in Last Year					
Dept. stores (not groceries)		510,064	80.7	78.5	103
Ladies' outfitters		324,083	51.3	53.5	96
Gentlemen's outfitters		370,944	58.7	64.0	92
DIY		378,187	59.9	60.5	99
Furniture, appliances, durables		402,883	63.8	64.6	99
Shoes		469,610	74.3	70.1	106
Visits to Licensed Premises (at least weekly)					
Pubs		150,646	23.8	26.3	91
Licensed clubs		74,457	11.8	11.6	102
Wine bars		9,269	1.5	1.4	105

© CACI Limited, 1998.   Tel: 0171 602-6000 (London) / 0131 557-0123 (Edinburgh).
Note: [1] PayCheck data. Please see Chapter 3 for details.
Source: © BMRB International Limited, 1997. Buying potential info. modelled using data from TGI 4/96-3/97.

STRATHCLYDE

Derived using **CACI's Population Projections for 1998**   Data refers to **adults** except where indicated

Base: All GB		Total for Area	As a Percentage of: Area	GB Base	Index (GB av. = 100)
Total Resident Population		2,264,360	100.0	100.0	100
of whom female		1,171,653	51.7	49.2	102
By age:	*of whom female (%)*				
0– 4	48.8	145,170	6.4	6.5	99
5– 9	48.8	144,887	6.4	6.6	98
10–14	49.0	145,741	6.4	6.3	101
15–19	48.8	147,202	6.5	6.2	106
20–24	49.2	137,271	6.1	5.9	103
25–34	50.0	351,458	15.5	15.4	101
35–44	50.6	334,143	14.8	14.3	103
45–54	50.8	280,487	12.4	13.1	94
55–64	52.7	235,730	10.4	9.9	105
65–74	56.1	195,967	8.7	8.4	103
75+	66.9	146,304	6.5	7.4	87
Cost of Car (of only or most recently obtained car)					
Up to £2,999		260,072	14.2	22.9	62
£3,000– £4,999		193,552	10.6	13.5	78
£5,000– £6,999		183,003	10.0	11.1	90
£7,000– £9,999		245,356	13.4	11.1	120
£10,000–£19,999		204,019	11.2	12.8	87
£20,000+		17,111	0.9	1.1	83
Owner of a Company Car		114,079	6.2	7.7	81
Income Level of Households[1]					
Up to £4,999		128,745	13.9	10.9	127
£5,000– £9,999		180,163	19.4	16.3	119
£10,000–£14,999		180,864	19.5	18.1	107
£15,000–£19,999		142,342	15.3	15.7	98
£20,000–£24,999		100,384	10.8	12.0	90
£25,000–£29,999		67,306	7.2	8.5	85
£30,000–£34,999		44,104	4.7	5.9	81
£35,000–£39,999		28,666	3.1	4.0	78
£40,000–£44,999		18,643	2.0	2.7	75
£45,000–£49,999		12,198	1.3	1.8	72
£50,000+		25,703	2.8	4.3	65
Use of Multiple Stores in Last Year					
Dept. stores (not groceries)		1,417,965	77.5	78.5	99
Ladies' outfitters		950,209	52.0	53.5	97
Gentlemen's outfitters		1,092,274	59.7	64.0	93
DIY		1,084,713	59.3	60.5	98
Furniture, appliances, durables		1,174,968	64.3	64.6	99
Shoes		1,343,048	73.4	70.1	105
Visits to Licensed Premises (at least weekly)					
Pubs		410,461	22.4	26.3	85
Licensed clubs		239,954	13.1	11.6	113
Wine bars		18,196	1.0	1.4	71

© CACI Limited, 1998.   Tel: 0171 602-6000 (London) / 0131 557-0123 (Edinburgh).
Note: [1] PayCheck data. Please see Chapter 3 for details.
Source: © BMRB International Limited, 1997. Buying potential info. modelled using data from TGI 4/96-3/97.

TAYSIDE

Derived using **CACI's Population Projections for 1998**   Data refers to **adults** except where indicated

Base: All GB		Total for Area	As a Percentage of: Area	GB Base	Index (GB av. = 100)
Total Resident Population		396,523	100.0	100.0	100
of whom female		204,737	51.6	50.8	102
By age:	of whom female (%)				
0– 4	48.7	24,112	6.1	6.5	94
5– 9	48.5	24,318	6.1	6.6	94
10–14	49.2	25,041	6.3	6.3	99
15–19	48.9	24,599	6.2	6.2	101
20–24	47.6	23,462	5.9	5.9	101
25–34	49.6	55,783	14.1	15.4	91
35–44	50.6	55,702	14.0	14.3	98
45–54	51.0	52,036	13.1	13.1	100
55–64	52.2	42,736	10.8	9.9	108
65–74	55.0	37,837	9.5	8.4	114
75+	65.5	30,897	7.8	7.4	105
Cost of Car (of only or most recently obtained car)					
Up to £2,999		61,691	19.1	22.9	83
£3,000– £4,999		45,253	14.0	13.5	103
£5,000– £6,999		36,020	11.2	11.1	100
£7,000– £9,999		37,849	11.7	11.1	105
£10,000–£19,999		35,933	11.1	12.8	87
£20,000+		1,300	0.4	1.1	36
Owner of a Company Car		14,667	4.5	7.7	59
Income Level of Households[1]					
Up to £4,999		20,862	12.5	10.9	115
£5,000– £9,999		31,193	18.7	16.3	115
£10,000–£14,999		32,886	19.7	18.1	109
£15,000–£19,999		26,597	16.0	15.7	102
£20,000–£24,999		18,902	11.3	12.0	95
£25,000–£29,999		12,624	7.6	8.5	89
£30,000–£34,999		8,200	4.9	5.9	84
£35,000–£39,999		5,276	3.2	4.0	80
£40,000–£44,999		3,397	2.0	2.7	76
£45,000–£49,999		2,201	1.3	1.8	73
£50,000+		4,506	2.7	4.3	63
Use of Multiple Stores in Last Year					
Dept. stores (not groceries)		246,451	76.3	78.5	97
Ladies' outfitters		155,648	48.2	53.5	90
Gentlemen's outfitters		203,818	63.1	64.0	99
DIY		193,246	59.8	60.5	99
Furniture, appliances, durables		202,143	62.6	64.6	97
Shoes		225,415	69.8	70.1	100
Visits to Licensed Premises (at least weekly)					
Pubs		66,976	20.7	26.3	79
Licensed clubs		36,787	11.4	11.6	98
Wine bars		889	0.3	1.4	20

© CACI Limited, 1998. Tel: 0171 602-6000 (London) / 0131 557-0123 (Edinburgh).
Note: [1] PayCheck data. Please see Chapter 3 for details.
Source: © BMRB International Limited, 1997. Buying potential info. modelled using data from TGI 4/96-3/97.

ORKNEY

Derived using **CACI's Population Projections for 1998**   Data refers to **adults** except where indicated

Base: All GB	Total for Area	As a Percentage of: Area	As a Percentage of: GB Base	Index (GB av. = 100)
Total Resident Population	20,067	100.0	100.0	100
of whom female	10,132	50.5	50.8	99
By age: *of whom female (%)*				
0– 4	51.5	1,279	6.4	6.5	99
5– 9	46.9	1,393	6.9	6.6	106
10–14	51.0	1,402	7.0	6.3	110
15–19	46.7	1,183	5.9	6.2	96
20–24	48.8	943	4.7	5.9	80
25–34	49.1	2,672	13.3	15.4	86
35–44	49.0	2,836	14.1	14.3	99
45–54	49.1	2,874	14.3	13.1	109
55–64	50.6	2,346	11.7	9.9	118
65–74	51.9	1,717	8.6	8.4	102
75+	63.4	1,422	7.1	7.4	96
Cost of Car (of only or most recently obtained car)				
Up to £2,999	3,263	20.4	22.9	89
£3,000– £4,999	2,631	16.4	13.5	121
£5,000– £6,999	2,385	14.9	11.1	134
£7,000– £9,999	2,036	12.7	11.1	114
£10,000–£19,999	2,557	16.0	12.8	125
£20,000+	66	0.4	1.1	37
Owner of a Company Car	798	5.0	7.7	65
Income Level of Households[1]				
Up to £4,999	1,071	13.3	10.9	122
£5,000– £9,999	1,481	18.4	16.3	113
£10,000–£14,999	1,575	19.5	18.1	108
£15,000–£19,999	1,296	16.1	15.7	102
£20,000–£24,999	928	11.5	12.0	96
£25,000–£29,999	618	7.7	8.5	90
£30,000–£34,999	397	4.9	5.9	84
£35,000–£39,999	251	3.1	4.0	78
£40,000–£44,999	158	2.0	2.7	73
£45,000–£49,999	100	1.2	1.8	68
£50,000+	190	2.4	4.3	55
Use of Multiple Stores in Last Year				
Dept. stores (not groceries)	12,340	77.2	78.5	98
Ladies' outfitters	7,632	47.7	53.5	89
Gentlemen's outfitters	10,191	63.7	64.0	100
DIY	9,571	59.8	60.5	99
Furniture, appliances, durables	9,671	60.5	64.6	94
Shoes	11,357	71.0	70.1	101
Visits to Licensed Premises (at least weekly)				
Pubs	2,877	18.0	26.3	68
Licensed clubs	1,169	7.3	11.6	63
Wine bars	41	0.3	1.4	18

© CACI Limited, 1998.   Tel: 0171 602-6000 (London) / 0131 557-0123 (Edinburgh).
Note: [1] PayCheck data. Please see Chapter 3 for details.
Source: © BMRB International Limited, 1997. Buying potential info. modelled using data from TGI 4/96-3/97.

SHETLAND

Derived using **CACI's Population Projections for 1998**   Data refers to **adults** except where indicated

Base: All GB		Total for Area	As a Percentage of: Area	As a Percentage of: GB Base	Index (GB av. = 100)
Total Resident Population		23,377	100.0	100.0	100
of whom female		11,520	49.3	50.8	97
By age:	*of whom female (%)*				
0– 4	48.7	1,750	7.5	6.5	116
5– 9	49.8	1,669	7.1	6.6	109
10–14	47.9	1,633	7.0	6.3	110
15–19	46.0	1,592	6.8	6.2	111
20–24	47.7	1,324	5.7	5.9	96
25–34	47.6	3,496	15.0	15.4	97
35–44	47.3	3,437	14.7	14.3	103
45–54	46.8	3,196	13.7	13.1	104
55–64	47.4	2,290	9.8	9.9	99
65–74	54.0	1,573	6.7	8.4	80
75+	68.7	1,417	6.1	7.4	82
Cost of Car (of only or most recently obtained car)					
Up to £2,999		3,947	21.5	22.9	94
£3,000– £4,999		3,082	16.8	13.5	124
£5,000– £6,999		2,333	12.7	11.1	115
£7,000– £9,999		2,365	12.9	11.1	116
£10,000–£19,999		2,457	13.4	12.8	105
£20,000+		78	0.4	1.1	38
Owner of a Company Car		963	5.3	7.7	69
Income Level of Households[1]					
Up to £4,999		581	6.6	10.9	61
£5,000– £9,999		1,065	12.1	16.3	75
£10,000–£14,999		1,436	16.4	18.1	90
£15,000–£19,999		1,455	16.6	15.7	105
£20,000–£24,999		1,237	14.1	12.0	118
£25,000–£29,999		943	10.7	8.5	126
£30,000–£34,999		673	7.7	5.9	131
£35,000–£39,999		462	5.3	4.0	132
£40,000–£44,999		310	3.5	2.7	131
£45,000–£49,999		205	2.3	1.8	128
£50,000+		416	4.7	4.3	111
Use of Multiple Stores in Last Year					
Dept. stores (not groceries)		13,955	76.2	78.5	97
Ladies' outfitters		9,045	49.4	53.5	92
Gentlemen's outfitters		11,901	64.9	64.0	102
DIY		11,259	61.4	60.5	101
Furniture, appliances, durables		11,568	63.1	64.6	98
Shoes		12,930	70.6	70.1	101
Visits to Licensed Premises (at least weekly)					
Pubs		3,479	19.0	26.3	72
Licensed clubs		1,696	9.3	11.6	80
Wine bars		42	0.2	1.4	17

© CACI Limited, 1998.   Tel: 0171 602-6000 (London) / 0131 557-0123 (Edinburgh).

Note: [1] PayCheck data. Please see Chapter 3 for details.

Source: © BMRB International Limited, 1997. Buying potential info. modelled using data from TGI 4/96-3/97.

WESTERN ISLES

Derived using **CACI's Population Projections for 1998**   Data refers to **adults** except where indicated

Base: All GB		Total for Area	As a Percentage of:		Index (GB av. = 100)
			Area	GB Base	
Total Resident Population		28,718	100.0	100.0	100
of whom female		14,436	50.3	50.8	99
By age:	*of whom female (%)*				
0– 4	48.7	1,640	5.7	6.5	88
5– 9	46.8	1,901	6.6	6.6	101
10–14	49.8	1,965	6.8	6.3	108
15–19	48.7	1,915	6.7	6.2	108
20–24	41.1	1,395	4.9	5.9	83
25–34	50.3	3,736	13.0	15.4	84
35–44	48.1	3,828	13.3	14.3	93
45–54	46.5	3,870	13.5	13.1	103
55–64	50.7	3,251	11.3	9.9	114
65–74	52.2	2,747	9.6	8.4	114
75+	67.2	2,470	8.6	7.4	116
Cost of Car (of only or most recently obtained car)					
Up to £2,999		4,828	20.8	22.9	91
£3,000– £4,999		3,683	15.9	13.5	117
£5,000– £6,999		2,712	11.7	11.1	105
£7,000– £9,999		3,029	13.1	11.1	117
£10,000–£19,999		2,667	11.5	12.8	90
£20,000+		68	0.3	1.1	26
Owner of a Company Car		1,031	4.4	7.7	58
Income Level of Households[1]					
Up to £4,999		1,253	11.4	10.9	105
£5,000– £9,999		1,943	17.7	16.3	109
£10,000–£14,999		2,192	19.9	18.1	110
£15,000–£19,999		1,861	16.9	15.7	108
£20,000–£24,999		1,348	12.3	12.0	103
£25,000–£29,999		893	8.1	8.5	96
£30,000–£34,999		565	5.1	5.9	88
£35,000–£39,999		350	3.2	4.0	80
£40,000–£44,999		215	2.0	2.7	73
£45,000–£49,999		133	1.2	1.8	66
£50,000+		235	2.1	4.3	50
Use of Multiple Stores in Last Year					
Dept. stores (not groceries)		17,272	74.4	78.5	95
Ladies' outfitters		11,356	48.9	53.5	92
Gentlemen's outfitters		14,823	63.9	64.0	100
DIY		13,841	59.6	60.5	98
Furniture, appliances, durables		14,225	61.3	64.6	95
Shoes		16,242	70.0	70.1	100
Visits to Licensed Premises (at least weekly)					
Pubs		4,530	19.5	26.3	74
Licensed clubs		2,527	10.9	11.6	94
Wine bars		71	0.3	1.4	22

© CACI Limited, 1998.   Tel: 0171 602-6000 (London) / 0131 557-0123 (Edinburgh).
Note: [1] PayCheck data. Please see Chapter 3 for details.
Source: © BMRB International Limited, 1997. Buying potential info. modelled using data from TGI 4/96-3/97.

CHAPTER 6

WHO BUYS WHAT

PRODUCT PROFILE BY ACORN GROUP

This Chapter shows the ACORN Group with highest penetration across TGI and Lifestyle Product Types. For example, 62.2% of adults in ACORN Group A01 have a building society account, whereas only 51.4% of all adults in Great Britain have this type of account.

Refer to Chapter 8 for a fuller description of the consumer characteristics relating to each ACORN Group

			Penetration (%)	
	ACORN Group with Highest Penetration		ACORN Group	GB
FINANCIAL				
Household Income Levels (PayCheck data[1])			**Households**	
Up to £4,999	F16	Council Estate Res.,Greatest Hardship	23.9	10.9
£5,000– £9,999	F16	Council Estate Res.,Greatest Hardship	29.2	16.3
£10,000–£14,999	F16	Council Estate Res.,Greatest Hardship	22.9	18.2
£15,000–£19,999	B05	Well-Off Workers, Family Areas	17.7	15.7
£20,000–£24,999	B04	Affluent Executives, Family Areas	15.5	12.0
£25,000–£29,999	B04	Affluent Executives, Family Areas	13.0	8.5
£30,000–£39,999	B04	Affluent Executives, Family Areas	17.3	9.8
£40,000–£49,999	A01	Wealthy Achievers, Suburban Areas	8.6	4.5
£50,000+	C07	Prosperous Professionals, Metro. Areas	10.8	4.2
TGI Product				
Current Accounts			**Adults**	
Bank account with interest	B04	Affluent Executives, Family Areas	72.8	62.8
Building society account with interest	C06	Affluent Urbanites, Town & City Areas	30.0	26.8
Bank acc. without interest	A03	Prosperous Pensioners, Retirem't Areas	39.2	34.7
Bank account opened in last 6 months	B04	Affluent Executives, Family Areas	4.4	2.6
Deposit or Savings Account			**Adults**	
Bank account	C06	Affluent Urbanites, Town & City Areas	36.2	27.4
Building society account	A01	Wealthy Achievers, Suburban Areas	62.2	51.4
Building society account: any opened in last year	B05	Well-Off Workers, Family Areas	1.1	0.5
Building society account: first opened in last year	B04	Affluent Executives, Family Areas	2.6	1.8
Other Investments			**Adults**	
National Savings Certs.	A01	Wealthy Achievers, Suburban Areas	6.0	3.2
National Savings/P.O. bank	A02	Affluent Greys, Rural Communities	13.7	9.8
Premium Bonds	A01	Wealthy Achievers, Suburban Areas	33.9	23.7
Stocks & shares	A01	Wealthy Achievers, Suburban Areas	31.8	20.3
TESSAs	A01	Wealthy Achievers, Suburban Areas	13.7	8.0
Unit trusts	A01	Wealthy Achievers, Suburban Areas	12.6	6.8
Pensions/Life Assurance Schemes			**Adults**	
Company pension	B05	Well-Off Workers, Family Areas	45.6	36.6
Life assurance	B05	Well-Off Workers, Family Areas	62.6	56.9
Personal pension plan	A02	Affluent Greys, Rural Communities	16.4	13.0
State pension only	A02	Affluent Greys, Rural Communities	50.0	41.2
Insurance			**Adults**	
Building insurance	B05	Well-Off Workers, Family Areas	74.9	60.9
Home contents insurance	B05	Well-Off Workers, Family Areas	75.3	64.6
Mortgage (by Source)			**Adults**	
Building society	B05	Well-Off Workers, Family Areas	41.6	29.2
Other source	B05	Well-Off Workers, Family Areas	18.4	12.8

		Penetration (%)	
		ACORN Group	GB
TGI Product	ACORN Group with Highest Penetration		
Credit & Plastic Card Ownership		**Adults**	
MasterCard	A01 Wealthy Achievers, Suburban Areas	37.2	24.8
Visa	C07 Prosperous Professionals, Metro. Areas	48.2	35.3
Other credit cards	C07 Prosperous Professionals, Metro. Areas	9.3	3.8
Debit card[2]	B04 Affluent Executives, Family Areas	53.7	42.4
Store card	A01 Wealthy Achievers, Suburban Areas	40.8	28.2
Miscellaneous		**Adults**	
Bank loan/overdraft	C07 Prosperous Professionals, Metro. Areas	14.7	12.7
Have made a will	B04 Affluent Executives, Family Areas	20.8	11.4
Hire purchase	B05 Well-Off Workers, Family Areas	10.7	8.3
Telephone banking	B04 Affluent Executives, Family Areas	47.1	38.0
MEDIA			
Daily Newspaper Readership: Broadsheets		**Adults**	
Daily Telegraph	A03 Prosperous Pensioners, Retirem't Areas	13.7	6.0
Financial Times	C06 Affluent Urbanites, Town & City Areas	2.2	2.7
The Guardian	C08 Better-Off Executives, Inner City Areas	7.3	2.5
The Independent	C06 Affluent Urbanites, Town & City Areas	4.1	1.6
The Times	C06 Affluent Urbanites, Town & City Areas	7.0	2.9
Daily Newspaper Readership: Tabloids		**Adults**	
Daily Express	D09 Comfortable Middle-Agers, Mature Home Owning Areas	8.4	5.9
Daily Mail	A03 Prosperous Pensioners, Retirem't Areas	14.7	9.4
Daily Mirror	F16 Council Estate Res., Greatest Hardship	30.8	15.7
Daily Star	F15 Council Estate Res., High Unemployment	8.9	4.0
The Sun	F15 Council Estate Res., High Unemployment	35.1	19.7
Sunday Newspaper Readership: Broadsheets		**Adults**	
Independent on Sunday	C06 Affluent Urbanites, Town & City Areas	5.1	1.4
Sunday Telegraph	A01 Wealthy Achievers, Suburban Areas	7.5	3.6
Sunday Times	C07 Prosperous Professionals, Metro. Areas	14.2	5.9
The Observer	C06 Affluent Urbanites, Town & City Areas	6.7	1.9
Sunday Newspaper Readership: Tabloids		**Adults**	
Glasgow Sunday Mail	F16 Council Estate Res., Greatest Hardship	13.7	4.4
Glasgow Sunday Post	F13 Older People, Less Prosperous Areas	12.5	5.9
News of the World	F15 Council Estate Res., High Unemployment	32.4	18.7
Sunday Express	D09 Comfortable Middle-Agers, Mature Home Owning Areas	8.9	5.8
Sunday Mirror	F15 Council Estate Res., High Unemployment	17.3	10.6
Sunday People	F16 Council Estate Res., Greatest Hardship	13.6	9.0
The Mail on Sunday	A01 Wealthy Achievers, Suburban Areas	15.0	10.4
TV Channels with Advertising – Viewing Intensity		**Adults**	
ITV			
heavy	F16 Council Estate Res., Greatest Hardship	34.2	14.8
medium heavy	F16 Council Estate Res., Greatest Hardship	20.7	15.2
medium	A03 Prosperous Pensioners, Retirem't Areas	31.0	27.9
light	C07 Prosperous Professionals, Metro. Areas	64.5	40.4
never	C08 Better-Off Executives, Inner City Areas	4.3	1.7
Channel 4			
heavy	F17 People in Multi-Ethnic, Low-Income Areas	26.3	17.3
medium	C08 Better-Off Executives, Inner City Areas	33.7	28.1
light	A03 Prosperous Pensioners, Retirem't Areas	54.5	47.2
never	A02 Affluent Greys, Rural Communities	11.3	7.4

		Penetration (%)	
TGI Product	ACORN Group with Highest Penetration	ACORN Group	GB
Independent Local Radio – Listening Intensity		**Adults**	
IBA			
heavy	F15 Council Estate Res., High Unemployment	31.6	19.6
medium	C07 Prosperous Professionals, Metro. Areas	23.3	19.1
LICENSED TRADE			
Alcohol Consumption: Beer & Cider (bottles, cans or pints/week)[2]		**per 100 Adults**	
Beer (not lager)			
bottled	F15 Council Estate Res., High Unemployment	26.4	13.9
canned	C06 Affluent Urbanites, Town & City Areas	72.0	50.3
draught	D10 Skilled Workers, Home Owning Areas	119.4	89.0
Lager			
bottled	C07 Prosperous Professionals, Metro. Areas	88.9	53.0
canned	F16 Council Estate Res., Greatest Hardship	152.3	98.1
draught	C07 Prosperous Professionals, Metro. Areas	114.5	80.3
Cider (incl. low alcohol)	F16 Council Estate Res., Greatest Hardship	63.4	40.2
Alcohol Consumption: Low Alcohol Beer & Lager[3]		**per 100 Adults**	
draught	E11 New Home Owners, Mature Communities	19.3	13.2
Alcohol Consumption: Spirits (measures/week)		**per 100 Adults**	
Brandy	A02 Affluent Greys, Rural Communities	19.9	15.5
Gin	C07 Prosperous Professionals, Metro. Areas	43.0	23.7
Liqueurs	C08 Better-Off Executives, Inner City Areas	21.5	14.1
Rum, dark & golden	C08 Better-Off Executives, Inner City Areas	14.0	8.5
Rum, white	F15 Council Estate Res., High Unemployment	21.3	10.3
Vodka	C08 Better-Off Executives, Inner City Areas	44.4	23.3
Whisky	A02 Affluent Greys, Rural Communities	106.9	71.3
Whisky, not Scotch	D09 Comfortable Middle Agers, Mature Home Owning Areas	12.3	7.4
Alcohol Consumption: Wine (glasses/week)[3]		**per 100 Adults**	
Port	B04 Affluent Executives, Family Areas	10.4	6.0
Sherry	A03 Prosperous Pensioners, Retirem't Areas	52.0	24.8
Vermouth	C06 Affluent Urbanites, Town & City Areas	19.8	10.0
Wine (table)[4]	C07 Prosperous Professionals, Metro. Areas	269.8	153.8
Alcohol Purchase for Home Consumption (once a month or more)		**Adults**	
Beer	C07 Prosperous Professionals, Metro. Areas	42.4	32.4
Spirits	C07 Prosperous Professionals, Metro. Areas	20.1	12.9
Wine	C07 Prosperous Professionals, Metro. Areas	48.8	34.7
Visits to Licensed Premises (at least weekly)[5]		**Adults**	
Licensed clubs	F16 Council Estate Res., Greatest Hardship	16.6	11.6
Pubs	C07 Prosperous Professionals, Metro. Areas	34.1	27.3
Wine bars	C07 Prosperous Professionals, Metro. Areas	5.8	2.1
RESTAURANTS			
Take-Away Food		**Adults**	
Burger bars	C07 Prosperous Professionals, Metro. Areas	19.5	10.7
Chinese	B04 Affluent Executives, Family Areas	52.1	43.8
Fish & chip shops	B04 Affluent Executives, Family Areas	51.0	46.9
Indian	C06 Affluent Urbanites, Town & City Areas	36.7	22.8
Pizza houses	C06 Affluent Urbanites, Town & City Areas	26.5	16.0
Other	C07 Prosperous Professionals, Metro. Areas	24.2	12.1

TGI Product		ACORN Group with Highest Penetration	Penetration (%)	
			ACORN Group	GB
Eat Out at Restaurants			Adults	
At least monthly:	day	C07 Prosperous Professionals, Metro. Areas	36.1	21.3
	evening	C07 Prosperous Professionals, Metro. Areas	46.2	23.1
In last 3 months:	day	C07 Prosperous Professionals, Metro. Areas	57.1	44.8
	evening	C07 Prosperous Professionals, Metro. Areas	74.0	58.2
Eat Out at Restaurants by Type (in last 3 months)			Adults	
Burger bars		C07 Prosperous Professionals, Metro. Areas	19.5	10.7
Chinese		C07 Prosperous Professionals, Metro. Areas	27.5	17.6
English		A02 Affluent Greys, Rural Communities	23.1	18.2
French		C07 Prosperous Professionals, Metro. Areas	17.7	4.2
Greek/Turkish		C07 Prosperous Professionals, Metro. Areas	13.8	3.1
Indian		C07 Prosperous Professionals, Metro. Areas	38.4	18.9
Indonesian/Thai		C07 Prosperous Professionals, Metro. Areas	14.6	2.9
Italian		C07 Prosperous Professionals, Metro. Areas	36.1	13.2
Pizza restaurants		C07 Prosperous Professionals, Metro. Areas	27.8	11.6
Spanish		C07 Prosperous Professionals, Metro. Areas	10.4	1.6
Steak houses				
Beefeater		B04 Affluent Executives, Family Areas	16.9	10.6
Berni		B04 Affluent Executives, Family Areas	3.2	2.3
Harvester		E12 White Collar Workers, Better-Off Multi-Ethnic Areas	12.2	8.3
Other		B04 Affluent Executives, Family Areas	9.8	6.2
Other		C07 Prosperous Professionals, Metro. Areas	24.2	12.1

GARDEN & HOME

			Adults	
Gardening				
No garden or allotment		F15 Council Estate Res., High Unemployment	49.6	16.5
Have garden or allotment		B05 Well-Off Workers, Family Areas	92.9	83.5
Grow flowers		B05 Well-Off Workers, Family Areas	87.1	74.6
Grow vegetables		A02 Affluent Greys, Rural Communities	39.0	20.0
Ownership			Adults	
Barbecue		B04 Affluent Executives, Family Areas	50.4	34.4
Garden furniture		A01 Wealthy Achievers, Suburban Areas	67.3	48.7
Garden shed		A01 Wealthy Achievers, Suburban Areas	50.2	39.9
Greenhouse		A02 Affluent Greys, Rural Communities	25.0	14.4
Lawnmower, hand		A03 Prosperous Pensioners, Retirem't Areas	12.1	9.2
Lawnmower, power		B04 Affluent Executives, Family Areas	72.5	55.1
Trimmer/strimmer		A02 Affluent Greys, Rural Communities	43.9	30.4
Garden Centres (in last year)			Adults	
Visited		A01 Wealthy Achievers, Suburban Areas	80.2	67.4
Bought anything		B04 Affluent Executives, Family Areas	72.3	58.3
Purchases (in last year)				
Spent more than £24		A01 Wealthy Achievers, Suburban Areas	48.7	34.0
Fertiliser		A01 Wealthy Achievers, Suburban Areas	51.8	37.5
Seeds		A02 Affluent Greys, Rural Communities	54.7	39.0
Weedkiller		A01 Wealthy Achievers, Suburban Areas	43.3	33.8

HOME IMPROVEMENT

			Households	
Central Heating				
Installed in the last year		D10 Skilled Workers, Home Owning Areas	2.2	1.7
Electric		A02 Affluent Greys, Rural Communities	16.6	6.7
Gas fired		B04 Affluent Executives, Family Areas	71.9	56.7

TGI Product	ACORN Group with Highest Penetration	Penetration (%) ACORN Group	GB
Oil fired	A02 Affluent Greys, Rural Communities	22.9	2.8
Solid fuel	A02 Affluent Greys, Rural Communities	15.0	2.6
Windows		**Households**	
Double glazing			
own	A01 Wealthy Achievers, Suburban Areas	23.3	18.3
fitted in last year	F17 People in Multi-Ethnic, Low-Income Areas	1.4	0.6
Replacement Windows			
own	B05 Well-Off Workers, Family Areas	50.7	34.9
fitted in last year	A03 Prosperous Pensioners, Retirem't Areas	6.3	3.8
Miscellaneous: Ownership		**Households**	
Conservatory/sunlounge	A03 Prosperous Pensioners, Retirem't Areas	15.8	10.4
Loft conversion	C07 Prosperous Professionals, Metro. Areas	6.9	4.4
Miscellaneous: Purchases (in last year)		**Households**	
Bathroom fittings	C07 Prosperous Professionals, Metro. Areas	11.0	8.1
Vinyl flooring	F16 Council Estate Res., Greatest Hardship	6.0	4.1

LEISURE GOODS

Ownership		**Households**	
CD player	B04 Affluent Executives, Family Areas	58.7	48.7
Record/cassette player	B04 Affluent Executives, Family Areas	81.1	72.6
Purchases (in last year): Books		**Adults**	
Hardback	C07 Prosperous Professionals, Metro. Areas	1.6	1.1
non-fiction	B05 Well-Off Workers, Family Areas	3.2	1.6
fiction	C07 Prosperous Professionals, Metro. Areas	10.4	4.0
Paperback	C07 Prosperous Professionals, Metro. Areas	4.4	2.4
non-fiction	C08 Better-Off Executives, Inner City Areas	5.9	5.0
fiction	C07 Prosperous Professionals, Metro. Areas	28.0	7.9
Through book club	F16 Council Estate Res., Greatest Hardship	9.5	9.4
Purchases (in last year): Audio Tapes, CDs, Records & Video Tapes		**per 10 Adults**	
Audio tapes (pre-recorded)	C08 Better-Off Executives, Inner City Areas	7.4	5.1
CDs			
albums	F14 Council Estate Res., Better-Off Homes	9.4	13.2
singles	C07 Prosperous Professionals, Metro. Areas	5.2	3.7
Records			
albums	C08 Better-Off Executives, Inner City Areas	1.8	0.6
singles	F14 Council Estate Res., Better-Off Homes	1.2	0.6
Video tapes			
blank	E12 White Collar Workers, Better-Off Multi-Ethnic Areas	3.7	3.4
pre-recorded	F15 Council Estate Res., High Unemployment	2.4	1.9
Purchases (in last year): Computer Games Consoles		**Adults**	
Nintendo	F16 Council Estate Res., Greatest Hardship	5.9	2.4
Sega	F16 Council Estate Res., Greatest Hardship	7.1	3.7
Other	E12 White Collar Workers, Better-Off Multi-Ethnic Areas	6.7	4.9
Purchases (in last year): Sports Equipment		**Adults**	
Bicycle	B05 Well-Off Workers, Family Areas	7.2	5.7
Golf clubs	C06 Affluent Urbanites, Town & City Areas	5.2	3.3
Keep fit equipment	C06 Affluent Urbanites, Town & City Areas	2.9	1.9
Ski clothing	C07 Prosperous Professionals, Metro. Areas	4.0	1.7
Sports shoes	C06 Affluent Urbanites, Town & City Areas	31.9	24.9

TGI Product	ACORN Group with Highest Penetration	Penetration (%)	
		ACORN Group	GB
Purchases (in last year): Other Goods		**Adults**	
Camera	C07 Prosperous Professionals, Metro. Areas	13.7	8.0
Electronic calculator	C08 Better-Off Executives, Inner City Areas	4.2	2.9
Home computer	A01 Wealthy Achievers, Suburban Areas	12.8	9.5
Typewriter	C07 Prosperous Professionals, Metro. Areas	1.1	0.6
Video camera	B05 Well-Off Workers, Family Areas	2.8	1.8
Watch	F17 People in Multi-Ethnic, Low-Income Areas	15.1	10.3

SPORTS & LEISURE (PARTICIPATION)

		Penetration (%)	
Adventure Sports		**Adults**	
Climbing	B04 Affluent Executives, Family Areas	3.9	1.9
Sailing	C07 Prosperous Professionals, Metro. Areas	3.3	1.6
Skiing	C07 Prosperous Professionals, Metro. Areas	7.0	2.9
Water skiing	C07 Prosperous Professionals, Metro. Areas	1.4	0.7
Windsurfing	C07 Prosperous Professionals, Metro. Areas	2.7	0.7
Predominantly Outdoor Sports		**Adults**	
Athletics	B04 Affluent Executives, Family Areas	1.9	1.3
Bowls	A02 Affluent Greys, Rural Communities	4.5	3.0
Cricket	F17 People in Multi-Ethnic, Low-Income Areas	8.9	2.4
Cycling	C07 Prosperous Professionals, Metro. Areas	13.1	8.8
Fishing	F16 Council Estate Res., Greatest Hardship	8.2	5.3
Football	F17 People in Multi-Ethnic, Low-Income Areas	11.5	5.4
Golf	B04 Affluent Executives, Family Areas	12.6	7.7
Rugby Union	A02 Affluent Greys, Rural Communities	2.2	1.3
Running	F17 People in Multi-Ethnic, Low-Income Areas	6.8	3.4
Tennis	C07 Prosperous Professionals, Metro. Areas	13.0	5.0
Walking/rambling	A02 Affluent Greys, Rural Communities	32.6	22.6
Predominantly Indoor Sports		**Adults**	
Badminton	F17 People in Multi-Ethnic, Low-Income Areas	11.1	5.7
Dancing	C08 Better-Off Executives, Inner City Areas	16.6	10.0
Darts	F16 Council Estate Res., Greatest Hardship	9.7	5.6
Keeping fit	B04 Affluent Executives, Family Areas	15.6	11.0
Skating	C08 Better-Off Executives, Inner City Areas	3.2	1.7
Snooker	F17 Older people, Less-Prosperous Areas	13.0	7.4
Squash	C07 Prosperous Professionals, Metro. Areas	5.7	3.1
Swimming	C08 Better-Off Executives, Inner City Areas	27.0	19.9
Table tennis	F17 Older people, Less-Prosperous Areas	6.1	3.0
Ten-pin bowling	B04 Affluent Executives, Family Areas	16.9	11.7
Weight training	C08 Better-Off Executives, Inner City Areas	14.9	10.1
Betting		**Adults**	
Bingo	F16 Council Estate Res., Greatest Hardship	27.3	11.9
Game machines	F14 Council Estate Res., Better-Off Homes	12.2	8.6
The National Lottery	D10 Skilled Workers, Home Owning Areas	70.2	64.7
Other scratch cards[6]	F15 Council Estate Res., High Unemployment	28.9	22.1
On football	F15 Council Estate Res., High Unemployment	25.8	19.1
On horses			
in betting shop	F16 Council Estate Res., Greatest Hardship	13.5	6.7
at the course	C06 Affluent Urbanites, Town & City Areas	4.7	1.4
by telephone	A02 Affluent Greys, Rural Communities	0.7	0.4
Leisure Activities		**Adults**	
Art galleries	C07 Prosperous Professionals, Metro. Areas	32.0	9.8
Camping	C08 Better-Off Executives, Inner City Areas	9.9	7.6
Cinemas	C08 Better-Off Executives, Inner City Areas	42.0	22.8

TGI Product	ACORN Group with Highest Penetration	Penetration (%)	
		ACORN Group	GB
Museums	C07 Prosperous Professionals, Metro. Areas	45.4	25.8
Stately homes/castles, etc.	A01 Wealthy Achievers, Suburban Areas	34.2	24.4
Theatres	C07 Prosperous Professionals, Metro. Areas	33.1	16.9
Theme parks	B04 Affluent Executives, Family Areas	26.7	19.1
Zoos/safari parks	B04 Affluent Executives, Family Areas	21.0	15.7

TRAVEL

Holidays in Last Year — Adults

No holiday	F17 People in Multi-Ethnic, Low-Income Areas	56.8	38.2
One holiday	B04 Affluent Executives, Family Areas	35.2	31.0
Two or more holidays	A01 Wealthy Achievers, Suburban Areas	39.7	29.6
Summer holiday	B04 Affluent Executives, Family Areas	58.3	48.2
Winter holiday	C07 Prosperous Professionals, Metro. Areas	19.8	12.4
Holiday of 3 or more weeks	C07 Prosperous Professionals, Metro. Areas	8.2	3.7
Stayed at GB hotel	A01 Wealthy Achievers, Suburban Areas	41.0	30.4

Transport to Last Holiday — Adults

Air	B05 Well-Off Workers, Family Areas	16.0	11.8
Car	B04 Affluent Executives, Family Areas	10.3	6.0
Coach	F13 Older People, Less Prosperous Areas	7.1	5.3
Rail	C07 Prosperous Professionals, Metro. Areas	4.8	2.2
Travelled by air in last 3 years	C07 Prosperous Professionals, Metro. Areas	72.2	50.6

Destination of Last Holiday — Adults

British Isles	D10 Skilled Workers, Home Owning Areas	37.9	34.2
France	C06 Affluent Urbanites, Town & City Areas	8.8	4.1
Germany	C06 Affluent Urbanites, Town & City Areas	2.2	0.9
Mediterranean (excl. France)	B04 Affluent Executives, Family Areas	17.5	13.0
Other Europe	C07 Prosperous Professionals, Metro. Areas	6.1	3.2
Asia/Far East	F17 People in Multi-Ethnic, Low-Income Areas	6.9	1.0
Australia/New Zealand	F17 People in Multi-Ethnic, Low-Income Areas	1.5	0.6
USA/Canada	C07 Prosperous Professionals, Metro. Areas	8.2	3.3
Rest of the World	C07 Prosperous Professionals, Metro. Areas	5.8	2.0

Type of Accommodation of Last Holiday — Adults

Caravan	F16 Council Estate Res., Greatest Hardship	12.4	7.9
Holiday camp	F14 Council Estate Res., Better-Off Homes	9.8	6.9
Holiday home/timeshare	B04 Affluent Executives, Family Areas	7.0	3.3
Hotel or guest house	A01 Wealthy Achievers, Suburban Areas	28.6	23.5
Rented villa/flat/cottage	B04 Affluent Executives, Family Areas	16.6	12.4
Tent	E12 White Collar Workers, Better-Off Multi-Ethnic Areas	3.8	2.5

Travellers Cheques — Adults

Used in last year	B05 Well-Off Workers, Family Areas	27.1	20.5
Purchased from:			
bank	C06 Affluent Urbanites, Town & City Areas	13.4	18.2
other source	B05 Well-Off Workers, Family Areas	18.4	12.8

MOTORING

Miles Driven Each Week — Adults

0–119	C08 Better-Off Executives, Inner City Areas	59.0	49.7
120–239	A02 Affluent Greys, Rural Communities	20.9	14.9

TGI Product	ACORN Group with Highest Penetration	Penetration (%)	
		ACORN Group	GB
240–549	A01 Wealthy Achievers, Suburban Areas	12.0	7.5
550+	B05 Well-Off Workers, Family Areas	3.5	2.2

Cost of Car (of only or most recently obtained car)

		Adults	
Up to £2,999	F14 Council Estate Res., Better-Off Homes	27.1	22.4
£3,000– £4,999	B05 Well-Off Workers, Family Areas	16.7	13.1
£5,000– £6,999	B05 Well-Off Workers, Family Areas	13.7	11.1
£7,000– £9,999	B04 Affluent Executives, Family Areas	16.4	11.4
£10,000–£19,999	A01 Wealthy Achievers, Suburban Areas	23.9	13.3
£20,000+	C07 Prosperous Professionals, Metro. Areas	3.8	1.4

Engine Size (of only or most recently obtained car)

		Adults	
Up to 1000cc	B05 Well-Off Workers, Family Areas	7.0	5.9
1001–1300cc	D10 Skilled Workers, Home Owning Areas	20.0	17.8
1301–1750cc	B04 Affluent Executives, Family Areas	34.0	26.0
1751–2500cc	A03 Prosperous Pensioners, Retirem't Areas	29.0	19.9
2500cc+	C06 Affluent Urbanites, Town & City Areas	4.1	1.9

Length of Ownership (of only or most recently obtained car)

		Adults	
Up to 12 months	B04 Affluent Executives, Family Areas	31.1	25.9
1–2 years	B04 Affluent Executives, Family Areas	28.1	20.6
3–4 years	A02 Affluent Greys, Rural Communities	19.4	15.1
5+ years	A03 Prosperous Pensioners, Retirem't Areas	17.5	12.4

Car Registration (of only or most recently obtained car)

		Adults	
July '88 or earlier (E, etc.)	A03 Prosperous Pensioners, Retirem't Areas	26.0	22.4
Aug. '88–July '90 (F & G)	B05 Well-Off Workers, Family Areas	16.8	13.8
Aug. '90–July '92 (H & J)	B05 Well-Off Workers, Family Areas	14.3	10.8
Aug. '92–July '94 (K & L)	B04 Affluent Executives, Family Areas	17.9	11.4
Aug. '94–July '96 (M & N)	B04 Affluent Executives, Family Areas	20.8	12.8
Aug. '96 or later (P, etc.)	A01 Wealthy Achievers, Suburban Areas	4.8	3.0

Petrol Used (litres/week)

		Adults	
Less than 20	F17 Prosperous Professionals, Metro. Areas	1.8	1.2
20–30	B04 Affluent Executives, Family Areas	25.8	20.1
30+	A02 Affluent Greys, Rural Communities	33.0	24.9

Purchases: In Last 6 Months

		Adults	
Engine oil (1 or more litres)	A02 Affluent Greys, Rural Communities	35.9	28.5

Purchases: In Last 12 Months

		Adults	
Anti-freeze (2 or more litres)	A02 Affluent Greys, Rural Communities	23.0	18.9
Batteries	A02 Affluent Greys, Rural Communities	10.2	7.9
Car radio/cassette or CD	B04 Affluent Executives, Family Areas	78.5	62.9
Spark plugs	D09 Comfortable Middle Agers, Mature Home Owning Areas	16.1	15.5
Tyres	A02 Affluent Greys, Rural Communities	36.9	27.1

Miscellaneous

		Adults	
Owner of a company car	A01 Wealthy Achievers, Suburban Areas	13.3	7.2

© CACI Limited, 1998. Tel: 0171 602-6000 (London) / 0131 557-0123 (Edinburgh).
Notes: ¹ Please refer to Chapter 3 for details of CACI's PayCheck classification. ² For example, Switch, Connect cards, etc. ³ Bottles, cans or pints a week, where applicable. ⁴ Except for table wine which is in terms of bottles a month. ⁵ Not including licensed restaurants. ⁶ Including other types of 'instant win' games.
Source: Target Group Index, © BMRB International Limited, 1997. Buying potential info. modelled using data from TGI 4/96-3/97.

CHAPTER 7

WHO SPENDS HOW MUCH

VERDICT/TGI PRODUCT SPENDING PROFILE BY ACORN GROUP

This Table shows the ACORN Group with the highest average spend per person per year across Verdict and TGI Product Types. For example, the average spend on cigarettes and tobacco per adult in ACORN Group F15 is £296 a year compared to the GB average of £186.

Refer to Chapter 8 for a fuller description of the consumer characteristics relating to each ACORN Group

		Annual Personal Expenditure, £	
TGI Product	ACORN Group with Highest Personal Spend	ACORN Group	GB
CONVENIENCE GOODS			
Cigarettes, tobacco	F15 Council Estate Res., High Unemploy.	296	186
Food (excl. eating-out)	F15 Council Estate Res., High Unemploy.	1,069	815
Household goods	A03 Comfortable Middle Agers, Mature Areas	204	176
Newspapers, mags., etc.	C07 Prosperous Professionals, Metro. Areas	79	68
Alcohol (off licence)	C07 Prosperous Professionals, Metro. Areas	188	124
Total Convenience	**F15 Council Estate Res., High Unemploy.**	**1,737**	**1,368**
COMPARISON GOODS			
Personal Goods			
Children's, infantswear	C06 Affluent Urbanites, Town & City Areas	58	53
Footwear	C07 Prosperous Professionals, Metro. Areas	88	64
Menswear	C07 Prosperous Professionals, Metro. Areas	137	99
Womenswear	C07 Prosperous Professionals, Metro. Areas	245	173
Jewellery, watches, etc.	B04 Affluent Executives, Family Areas	53	40
OTC medicines[1]	A03 Prosperous Pensioners, Retire. Areas	42	38
Toiletries, cosmetics, perf.	A03 Prosperous Pensioners, Retire. Areas	81	69
Home Goods			
Brown goods	C07 Prosperous Professionals, Metro. Areas	78	66
White goods	A02 Affluent Greys, Rural Communities	104	75
Furniture, floorcoverings	F16 Council Estate Res., Greatest Hardship	183	139
H'hold textiles, soft furnish.	C07 Prosperous Professionals, Metro. Areas	70	51
Leisure Goods			
Books	C07 Prosperous Professionals, Metro. Areas	50	30
DIY, gardening	A01 Wealthy Achievers, Suburban Areas	163	145
Eating out	C07 Prosperous Professionals, Metro. Areas	307	183
Photographic	F17 People in Multi-Ethnic, Low-Income Areas	66	27
Records, tapes, CDs, videos	F17 People in Multi-Ethnic, Low-Income Areas	53	42
Sports equipment	C07 Prosperous Professionals, Metro. Areas	58	48
Toys, games, cycles	F16 Council Estate Res., Greatest Hardship	38	31
Total Comparison	**C07 Prosperous Profs., Metro. Areas**	**1,768**	**1,374**
PERSONAL EXPEND.[2]	**C07 Prosperous Profs., Metro. Areas**	**3,373**	**2,742**

© CACI Limited, 1998.   Tel: 0171 602-6000 (London) / 0131 557-0123 (Edinburgh).

Notes: [1] Excludes NHS prescription charges.
           [2] Total annual personal expenditure on the products shown.

Sources: © BMRB International Limited, 1997.
           © Verdict Research Limited, 1997. Buying potential info. modelled using data from Verdict Research.

SPENDING PATTERNS BY MARKETPLACE

This Table shows annual personal expenditure in the 16 largest marketplaces by selected Verdict and TGI Product Types. For example, on average a person will spend £186.69 per year on cigarettes and tobacco in Greater London, and £236.90 per year in Greater Manchester.

Annual personal expenditure (£)

	Greater London	Greater Manchester	Merseyside	South Yorkshire	Tyne and Wear	West Midlands	West Yorkshire	Central Clydeside
CONVENIENCE GOODS								
Cigarettes, tobacco	186.69	236.90	252.39	203.70	199.28	179.17	189.89	243.00
Food (excl. eating-out)	829.62	814.04	822.59	812.02	825.15	784.65	804.64	862.88
Household goods	171.91	172.73	170.82	174.74	168.38	172.70	173.87	161.67
Newspapers, magazines, etc.	69.73	67.14	67.83	65.34	67.87	67.24	64.78	69.60
Alcohol (off-licence trade)	132.32	129.92	127.11	122.51	113.41	129.27	123.51	119.11
COMPARISON GOODS								
Personal Goods								
Children's & infantswear	51.89	55.78	58.05	47.77	54.03	48.95	46.56	57.89
Footwear	67.62	63.56	65.71	60.67	66.09	60.41	61.62	68.39
Menswear	103.85	95.83	92.34	98.15	94.91	91.17	98.46	106.82
Womenswear	174.08	167.26	172.82	162.07	175.57	156.00	165.86	176.40
Home Goods								
Brown goods	66.33	72.35	64.49	66.75	69.53	64.86	68.50	64.63
White goods	68.07	73.96	77.61	81.87	62.65	79.01	84.79	92.45
Furniture, floor coverings	126.75	133.06	132.46	161.96	143.27	140.92	174.29	172.17
H'hold textiles, soft furnishings	50.90	53.91	53.04	54.45	48.90	50.38	57.03	54.10
Leisure Goods								
Books	34.23	27.49	27.82	26.67	22.96	28.56	26.97	27.85
DIY, gardening	134.25	136.73	136.44	146.98	127.36	145.44	147.11	149.80
Eating-out	225.77	175.54	171.56	172.11	181.73	166.53	175.74	189.37
Photographic	37.81	28.37	26.24	27.84	24.27	21.16	29.37	25.15
Records, tapes, CDs	45.08	41.22	41.61	40.94	38.91	44.80	42.25	47.84
Sports equipment	48.45	48.30	49.11	46.38	50.28	46.02	46.57	51.52
Toys, games, bicycles	27.33	34.95	35.92	33.10	33.12	30.78	32.08	28.72

SPENDING PATTERNS BY MARKETPLACE (Cont.)

Annual personal expenditure (£)

	Edinburgh	Bristol	Cardiff	Leicester	Nottingham	Kingston upon Hull	Stoke on Trent	Plymouth
CONVENIENCE GOODS								
Cigarettes, tobacco	204.75	164.14	156.42	187.35	192.67	226.39	192.96	188.84
Food (excl. eating-out)	905.75	846.91	798.59	749.25	801.05	805.18	789.91	758.30
Household goods	168.63	173.28	169.59	171.71	175.91	175.10	183.15	170.12
Newspapers, magazines, etc.	72.88	66.54	65.02	66.45	67.22	63.76	67.88	61.36
Alcohol (off-licence trade)	135.88	112.08	111.42	133.63	130.25	118.93	133.72	111.68
COMPARISON GOODS								
Personal Goods								
Children's & infantswear	55.61	47.37	47.04	48.89	48.93	47.97	52.41	52.17
Footwear	73.83	63.56	63.14	58.22	59.27	59.06	59.05	57.90
Menswear	120.87	97.04	95.47	92.26	89.82	93.18	92.70	82.95
Womenswear	191.86	184.99	185.28	144.87	148.77	153.81	154.03	160.95
Home Goods								
Brown goods	69.38	63.21	62.43	64.55	62.17	66.24	64.50	62.21
White goods	102.27	66.83	66.44	75.56	80.69	87.16	78.14	70.27
Furniture, floor coverings	166.80	126.46	122.84	134.55	134.18	164.06	137.83	129.54
H'hold textiles, soft furnishings	55.96	41.67	39.47	45.99	49.43	54.32	50.06	47.04
Leisure Goods								
Books	34.73	31.33	29.82	27.83	29.45	25.64	27.32	29.88
DIY, gardening	149.34	143.00	141.77	143.15	137.20	141.05	147.95	142.53
Eating-out	237.08	175.74	166.64	161.84	173.45	169.51	166.18	153.68
Photographic	28.83	24.53	23.93	20.38	22.71	26.85	20.18	21.65
Records, tapes, CDs	47.74	41.39	40.28	45.00	43.60	41.72	43.77	45.15
Sports equipment	54.70	50.36	50.35	45.52	45.89	46.12	46.60	48.63
Toys, games, bicycles	25.15	29.47	28.96	30.34	30.11	33.67	33.63	31.26

© CACI Limited, 1998.   Tel: 0171 602-6000 (London) / 0131 557-0123 (Edinburgh).
Sources: © BMRB International Limited, 1997.
© Verdict Research Limited, 1997. Buying potential info. modelled using data from Verdict Research.

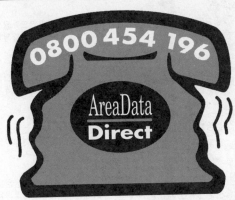

CHAPTER 8

ACORN GROUP PROFILES

This Chapter gives a fuller description of the consumer characteristics relating to each of the 17 Groups in the ACORN classification.

Group A01 – Wealthy Achievers, Suburban Areas

The majority of people in this Group live in a large detached house and have access to two or more cars. They are typically well-educated professional people, corporate managers in their middle-age, enjoying the fruits of their labour. These are the consumers with the money and the space to enjoy very comfortable lifestyles.

ACORN Group A01 accounts for:

demographics
- 16.0% of total 1998 GB population (projected);
- 15.4% of total 1998 GB population (projected) aged 0–14;
- 14.6% of total 1998 GB population (projected) aged 15–24;
- 14.3% of total 1998 GB population (projected) aged 25–44;
- 19.8% of total 1998 GB population (projected) aged 45–64;
- 15.6% of total 1998 GB population (projected) aged 65+.

economics
- 22.8% of people earning over £20,000 p.a.[#];
- 17.6% of people buying their home with a mortgage[*];
- 29.2% of people owning unit trust stocks and shares.

media
- 7.8% of people with heavy ITV viewing.

Top Twenty Products by ACORN Group A01

Ranked in terms of the index

			Penetration (%)		
Category	Product Type	Product	ACORN Group	GB	Index
Motoring	Cost of car	£20,000+	3.5	1.4	251
Home Improvement[1]	Central heating	Oil fired	6.5	2.8	232
Media	Daily newspaper	Daily Telegraph	12.6	6.0	209
Media	Sunday newspaper	Sunday Telegraph	7.5	3.6	207
Media	Sunday newspaper	Sunday Times	11.9	5.9	202
Financial[#]	Income level (h'hold)	£30,000+	22.1	11.1	199
Restaurants	Eating-out[2]	French	7.9	4.2	190
Financial	Investments	Nat. Savings Certs.	6.0	3.2	188
Financial	Investments	Unit trusts	12.6	6.8	185
Motoring	Ownership	Company car	13.3	7.2	185
Financial	Plastic cards	Other credit cards[3]	7.0	3.8	183
Motoring	Cost of car	£10,000–£20,000	23.9	13.3	180
Media	Daily newspaper	The Times	5.1	2.9	177
Travel	Last holiday	France	7.1	4.1	173
Financial	Investments	TESSA	13.7	8.0	171
Motoring	Car registration	L or M reg.	20.1	12.4	163
Sports & Leisure	Adventure sports	Windsurfing	1.1	0.7	163
Motoring	Miles driven	400–549 miles/week	12.0	7.5	160
Motoring	Car registration	P reg.	4.8	3.0	160
Media	Sunday newspaper	The Ind. on Sunday	2.3	1.4	159

© CACI Limited, 1998. Tel: 0171 602-6000 (London) / 0131 557-0123 (Edinburgh).

Notes: **Please note that the above list is not definitive but is intended to give an indication of key characteristics of the ACORN Group. See previous Chapter for Product definitions.**
Penetration: Refers to adults unless otherwise indicated. Figures do not necessarily indicate the ACORN Group with the highest penetration, but highlight particular characteristics of each Group.
Index: Shows the extent of the variation of the percentage penetration for the TGI Product by ACORN Group from the Base for GB as a whole.
[#] PayCheck data. Please see Chapter 3 for details.   [*] From a building society or other source.
[1] Households.   [2] In the last 3 months.   [3] Not MasterCard or Visa.

Source: Target Group Index, © BMRB International Limited, 1997.
Buying potential information modelled using data from TGI 4/96-3/97.

Group A02 – Affluent Greys, Rural Communities

This Group covers Britain's better-off farming communities – residents here are twelve times more likely than Base to be involved in agriculture. Many are self-employed and work long hours. The very high incidence of visitors and households which are not the main residence show that these areas also include many holiday homes.

ACORN Group A02 accounts for:

demographics
- 2.4% of total 1998 GB population (projected);
- 2.2% of total 1998 GB population (projected) aged 0–14;
- 2.1% of total 1998 GB population (projected) aged 15–24;
- 2.1% of total 1998 GB population (projected) aged 25–44;
- 3.0% of total 1998 GB population (projected) aged 45–64;
- 2.9% of total 1998 GB population (projected) aged 65+.

economics
- 1.9% of people earning over £20,000 p.a.#;
- 1.8% of people buying their home with a mortgage*;
- 2.5% of people owning unit trust stocks and shares.

media
- 2.3% of people with heavy ITV viewing.

Top Twenty Products by ACORN Group A02

Ranked in terms of the **index**

Category	Product Type	Product	Penetration (%) ACORN Group	GB	Index
Home Improvement[1]	Central heating	Oil fired	22.9	2.8	824
Home Improvement[1]	Central heating	Solid fuel	15.0	2.6	582
Home Improvement[1]	Central heating	Electric	16.6	6.7	247
Media	Sunday newspaper	Sunday Post	11.6	5.9	195
Garden & Home	Gardening	Grow vegetables	38.9	20.0	194
Motoring	Car engine size	Over 2500cc	3.6	1.9	188
Media	ITV viewing	Never	3.1	1.7	184
Sports & Leisure	Outdoor sports	Hockey	1.7	0.9	181
Sports & Leisure	Outdoor sports	Rugby Union	2.0	1.1	180
Garden & Home	Ownership	Greenhouse	25.0	14.4	173
Media	Sunday newspaper	Sunday Mail	7.2	4.4	162
Motoring	Miles driven	400–549 miles/week	11.6	7.5	155
Media	Sunday newspaper	Sunday Telegraph	5.6	3.6	154
Media	C4 viewing	Never	11.3	7.4	153
Sports & Leisure	Outdoor sports	Bowls	4.5	3.0	151
Sports & Leisure	Adventure sports	Sailing	2.3	1.6	147
Garden & Home	Ownership	Grass trimmer	43.8	30.4	144
Sports & Leisure	Outdoor sports	Walking/rambling	32.6	22.6	144
Motoring	Car registration	N reg.	9.0	6.4	141
Garden & Home	Gardening	Bought seeds	54.6	39.0	140

© CACI Limited, 1998. Tel: 0171 602-6000 (London) / 0131 557-0123 (Edinburgh).

Notes:
Please note that the above list is not definitive but is intended to give an indication of key characteristics of the ACORN Group. See previous Chapter for Product definitions.
Penetration: Refers to adults unless otherwise indicated. Figures do not necessarily indicate the ACORN Group with the highest penetration, but highlight particular characteristics of each Group.
Index: Shows the extent of the variation of the percentage penetration for the TGI Product by ACORN Group from the Base for GB as a whole.
PayCheck data. Please see Chapter 3 for details. * From a building society or other source. [1] Households.

Source: Target Group Index, © BMRB International Limited, 1997.
Buying potential information modelled using data from TGI 4/96-3/97.

Group A03 – Prosperous Pensioners, Retirement Areas

The better-off senior citizens in society are to be found in Group A03. Living in flats, detached houses or bungalows, these are old folk who can enjoy their retirement in pensioned comfort after their professional or executive careers. They are likely to own their home outright, so they have the disposable income to enjoy themselves.

ACORN Group A03 accounts for:

demographics
- 2.5% of total 1998 GB population (projected);
- 1.3% of total 1998 GB population (projected) aged 0–14;
- 1.6% of total 1998 GB population (projected) aged 15–24;
- 1.5% of total 1998 GB population (projected) aged 25–44;
- 2.7% of total 1998 GB population (projected) aged 45–64;
- 6.0% of total 1998 GB population (projected) aged 65+.

economics
- 2.5% of people earning over £20,000 p.a.[#];
- 2.3% of people buying their home with a mortgage[*];
- 2.9% of people owning unit trust stocks and shares.

media
- 1.5% of people with heavy ITV viewing.

Top Twenty Products by ACORN Group A03

Ranked in terms of the **index**

Category	Product Type	Product	Penetration (%) ACORN Group	GB	Index
Media	Daily newspaper	Daily Telegraph	13.7	6.0	228
Media	Sunday newspaper	Sunday Telegraph	7.4	3.6	203
Sports & Leisure	Adventure sports	Sailing	3.1	1.6	196
Travel	Last holiday (to)	Germany	1.5	0.9	166
Home Improvement[1]	Purchases in last yr.	Replac't. windows[2]	6.2	3.8	163
Media	Daily newspaper	Daily Mail	14.7	9.4	158
Licensed Trade	Drink regularly	Sherry	28.5	18.8	152
Home Improvement[1]	Ownership	Conservatory	15.8	10.4	151
Travel	Last holiday (to)	Med. (not France)	3.8	2.5	150
Motoring	Cost of car	£20,000+	2.1	1.4	148
Motoring	Car engine size	1751cc–2500cc	29.0	19.9	146
Media	Sunday newspaper	Mail on Sunday	14.8	10.4	142
Financial	Investments	Nat. Savings Certs.	4.5	3.2	141
Financial	Miscellaneous	Have made a Will	45.3	32.1	141
Motoring	Miscellaneous	Owned car 5+ yrs	17.5	12.4	141
Motoring	Cost of car	£10,000–£20,000	18.7	13.3	141
Financial	Investments	Building soc. a/c	5.6	4.1	137
Sports & Leisure	Outdoor sports	Bowls	4.1	3.0	137
Travel	Length of holiday	More than 3 weeks	5.1	3.7	137
Sports & Leisure	Purchases in last yr.	Ski clothing	2.3	1.7	135

© CACI Limited, 1998.   Tel: 0171 602-6000 (London) / 0131 557-0123 (Edinburgh).

Notes: **Please note that the above list is not definitive but is intended to give an indication of key characteristics of the ACORN Group. See previous Chapter for Product definitions.**
Penetration: Refers to adults unless otherwise indicated. Figures do not necessarily indicate the ACORN Group with the highest penetration, but highlight particular characteristics of each Group.
Index: Shows the extent of the variation of the percentage penetration for the TGI Product by ACORN Group from the Base for GB as a whole.
[#] PayCheck data. Please see Chapter 3 for details.   [*] From a building society or other source.
[1] Households.   [2] Fitted/purchased in last year.

Source: Target Group Index, © BMRB International Limited, 1997.
Buying potential information modelled using data from TGI 4/96-3/97.

Group B04 – Affluent Executives, Family Areas

These are the well qualified business people, successfully juggling jobs and families. There are lots of working women in this Group. With mortgages, young children and often two or more cars to support, these busy people need their incomes but aren't having too hard a time making ends meet. They are likely to have large, modern detached houses and generally enjoy a good standard of living.

ACORN Group B04 accounts for:

demographics
- 4.0% of total 1998 GB population (projected);
- 5.3% of total 1998 GB population (projected) aged 0–14;
- 3.9% of total 1998 GB population (projected) aged 15–24;
- 5.6% of total 1998 GB population (projected) aged 25–44;
- 2.7% of total 1998 GB population (projected) aged 45–64;
- 1.2% of total 1998 GB population (projected) aged 65+.

economics
- 6.1% of people earning over £20,000 p.a.[#];
- 5.3% of people buying their home with a mortgage[*];
- 5.5% of people owning unit trust stocks and shares.

media
- 2.2% of people with heavy ITV viewing.

Top Twenty Products by ACORN Group B04

Ranked in terms of the **index**

Category	Product Type	Product	Penetration (%) ACORN Group	GB	Index
Sports & Leisure	Outdoor sports	Hockey	2.5	0.9	260
Sports & Leisure	Outdoor sports	Rugby League	0.9	0.4	231
Financial	Plastic cards	Other credit cards[1]	8.4	3.8	220
Travel	Holiday accom.	Holiday home[2]	7.0	3.3	214
Travel	Last holiday (to)	Germany	1.9	0.9	212
Sports & Leisure	Outdoor sports	Climbing	3.9	1.9	206
Sports & Leisure	Purchases in last yr.	Ski clothing	3.3	1.7	198
Sports & Leisure	Adventure sports	Skiing	5.7	2.9	198
Financial[#]	Income level (h'hld)	£25,000–£34,999	22.9	12.2	188
Motoring	Cost of car	£20,000+	2.5	1.4	178
Motoring	Cost of car	£10,000–£20,000	23.3	13.3	176
Financial	Investments	Bank a/c (last 6 mth)	4.3	2.6	170
Motoring	Car ownership	Company car	12.2	7.2	170
Travel	Last holiday (to)	France	7.0	4.1	170
Financial[#]	Income level (h'hld)	£35,000+	18.7	11.1	169
Motoring	Car registration	N reg.	10.6	6.4	166
Sports & Leisure	Indoor sports	Table tennis	5.0	3.0	166
Sports & Leisure	Outdoor sports	Golf	12.6	7.7	164
Travel	Last holiday (to)	USA/Canada	5.4	3.3	163
Motoring	Car registration	L or M reg.	20.1	12.4	162

© CACI Limited, 1998. Tel: 0171 602-6000 (London) / 0131 557-0123 (Edinburgh).

Notes: **Please note that the above list is not definitive but is intended to give an indication of key characteristics of the ACORN Group. See previous Chapter for Product definitions.**
Penetration: Refers to adults unless otherwise indicated. Figures do not necessarily indicate the ACORN Group with the highest penetration, but highlight particular characteristics of each Group.
Index: Shows the extent of the variation of the percentage penetration for the TGI Product by ACORN Group from the Base for GB as a whole.
[#] PayCheck data. Please see Chapter 3 for details. [*] From a building society or other source.
[1] Not MasterCard or Visa. [2] Includes timeshares.

Source: Target Group Index, © BMRB International Limited, 1997.
Buying potential information modelled using data from TGI 4/96-3/97.

Group B05 – Well-Off Workers, Family Areas

In a wide range of well-paid occupations, people in Group B05 are likely to be in couples, often with children aged 0-14. Both Mum and Dad are working hard to pay off the mortgage on their detached or, more probably, semi-detached home. While they are not as highly qualified as people in Group B04, they still have an agreeable lifestyle, often with more than two cars per household.

ACORN Group B05 accounts for:

demographics
- 8.2% of total 1998 GB population (projected);
- 10.1% of total 1998 GB population (projected) aged 0–14;
- 8.0% of total 1998 GB population (projected) aged 15–24;
- 10.2% of total 1998 GB population (projected) aged 25–44;
- 7.3% of total 1998 GB population (projected) aged 45–64;
- 4.0% of total 1998 GB population (projected) aged 65+.

economics
- 10.5% of people earning over £20,000 p.a.[#];
- 11.1% of people buying their home with a mortgage[*];
- 8.2% of people owning unit trust stocks and shares.

media
- 5.8% of people with heavy ITV viewing.

Top Twenty Products by ACORN Group B05

Ranked in terms of the **index**

Category	Product Type	Product	ACORN Group	GB	Index
			Penetration (%)		
Financial	Investments	Building society a/c	1.7	0.9	178
Motoring	Miles driven	700+miles/week	3.5	2.2	158
Financial	Investments	Building society a/c[1]	6.2	4.1	151
Travel	Last holiday (to)	Germany	1.3	0.9	151
Sports & Leisure	Purchases in last yr.	Camcorders	2.8	1.8	150
Financial[#]	Income level (h'hld)	£25,000–£34,999	17.7	12.2	145
Home Improvement[2]	Ownership	Replac't. windows[3]	50.7	34.9	145
Motoring	Car registration	J & K reg.	15.2	10.5	144
Travel	Travellers cheques	From travel agent[4]	18.4	12.8	144
Financial	Income level (h'hld)	£20,000–£24,999	13.9	9.7	143
Financial	Mortgage source	Building society	41.6	29.2	142
Restaurants	Eating-out[5]	Beefeater	14.7	10.6	138
Sports & Leisure	Indoor sports	Squash	4.3	3.1	138
Sports & Leisure	Indoor sports	Badminton	7.8	5.7	137
Home Improvement[2]	Ownership	Conservatory	14.1	10.4	135
Garden & Home	Ownership	Barbecue	46.0	34.4	134
Financial	Mortgage source	Not building soc.	12.4	9.3	133
Motoring	Miles driven	400–549/week	9.9	7.5	132
Travel	Holiday accom.	Hotel	27.1	20.5	132
Media	Television	Satellite/cable TV	21.2	16.2	131

© CACI Limited, 1998. Tel: 0171 602-6000 (London) / 0131 557-0123 (Edinburgh).

Notes: **Please note that the above list is not definitive but is intended to give an indication of key characteristics of the ACORN Group. See previous Chapter for Product definitions.**
Penetration: Refers to adults unless otherwise indicated. Figures do not necessarily indicate the ACORN Group with the highest penetration, but highlight particular characteristics of each Group.
Index: Shows the extent of the variation of the percentage penetration for the TGI Product by ACORN Group from the Base for GB as a whole.
[#] PayCheck data. Please see Chapter 3 for details. [*] From a building society or other source.
[1] Savings account. [2] Households. [3] Fitted/purchased in last year. [4] Or building society. [5] In last 3 months.

Source: Target Group Index, © BMRB International Limited, 1997.
Buying potential information modelled using data from TGI 4/96-3/97.

Group C06 – Affluent Urbanites, Town & City Areas

These are the young couples or single people starting out in life, a few years and a couple of kids behind the people in Group B04! They tend to live in flats, terraced houses or bedsits. There are quite a number of students in this Group. Car ownership is Base, reflecting the urban setting.

ACORN Group C06 accounts for:

demographics
- 2.4% of total 1998 GB population (projected);
- 2.1% of total 1998 GB population (projected) aged 0–14;
- 3.3% of total 1998 GB population (projected) aged 15–24;
- 3.0% of total 1998 GB population (projected) aged 25–44;
- 1.9% of total 1998 GB population (projected) aged 45–64;
- 1.9% of total 1998 GB population (projected) aged 65+.

economics
- 2.8% of people earning over £20,000 p.a.#;
- 2.2% of people buying their home with a mortgage*;
- 3.1% of people owning unit trust stocks and shares.

media
- 1.3% of people with heavy ITV viewing.

Top Twenty Products by ACORN Group C06

Ranked in terms of the **index**

Category	Product Type	Product	Penetration (%) ACORN Group	GB	Index
Media	Sunday newspapers	The Ind. on Sunday	5.1	1.4	353
Media	Sunday newspapers	Observer	6.6	1.9	348
Media	Daily newspaper	Financial Times	2.1	0.7	317
Media	Daily newspaper	The Guardian	6.9	2.5	279
Restaurants	Eating-out[1]	French	11.1	4.2	267
Restaurants	Eating-out[1]	Indonesian/Thai	7.6	2.9	259
Media	Daily newspaper	The Independent	4.1	1.6	258
Travel	Last holiday (to)	Germany	2.1	0.9	238
Media	Daily newspaper	The Times	6.9	2.9	237
Licensed Trade	Licensed premises[2]	Wine bars	4.8	2.1	231
Sports & Leisure	Leisure activities	Art gallery visits	21.5	9.8	221
Media	ITV viewing	Never	3.7	1.7	220
Media	Sunday newspaper	The Sunday Times	12.8	5.9	218
Sports & Leisure	Adventure sports	Skiing	6.3	2.9	217
Travel	Last holiday (to)	France	8.8	4.1	216
Motoring	Car engine size	Over 2500cc	4.1	1.9	211
Restaurants	Eating-out[1]	Spanish	3.1	1.6	194
Restaurants	Eating-out[1]	Italian	25.0	13.2	189
Sports & Leisure	Outdoor sports	Tennis	9.4	5.0	187
Sports & Leisure	Purchases in last yr.	Singles	4.1	2.2	183

© CACI Limited, 1998.   Tel: 0171 602-6000 (London) / 0131 557-0123 (Edinburgh).

Notes: **Please note that the above list is not definitive but is intended to give an indication of key characteristics of the ACORN Group. See previous Chapter for Product definitions.**
Penetration: Refers to adults unless otherwise indicated. Figures do not necessarily indicate the ACORN Group with the highest penetration, but highlight particular characteristics of each Group.
Index: Shows the extent of the variation of the percentage penetration for the TGI Product by ACORN Group from the Base for GB as a whole.
PayCheck data. Please see Chapter 3 for details.   * From a building society or other source.
[1] In last 3 months.   [2] Visit at least weekly.

Source: Target Group Index, © BMRB International Limited, 1997.
Buying potential information modelled using data from TGI 4/96-3/97.

Group C07 – Prosperous Professionals, Metropolitan Areas

People in Group C07 share many characteristics with Group C06. However, they live in more cosmopolitan areas with a higher ethnic mix. They take the train or underground to the office each day, working long hours in fairly senior roles and making the most of their high qualifications.

ACORN Group C07 accounts for:

demographics
- 2.3% of total 1998 GB population (projected);
- 1.8% of total 1998 GB population (projected) aged   0–14;
- 2.4% of total 1998 GB population (projected) aged 15–24;
- 3.0% of total 1998 GB population (projected) aged 25–44;
- 1.8% of total 1998 GB population (projected) aged 45–64;
- 2.0% of total 1998 GB population (projected) aged 65+.

economics
- 3.1% of people earning over £20,000 p.a.[#];
- 2.1% of people buying their home with a mortgage[*];
- 3.4% of people owning unit trust stocks and shares.

media
- 1.0% of people with heavy ITV viewing.

Top Twenty Products by ACORN Group C07

Ranked in terms of the **index**

| | | | Penetration (%) | | |
| | | | ACORN | | |
Category	Product Type	Product	Group	GB	Index
Restaurants	Eating-out[1]	Spanish	10.4	1.6	644
Restaurants	Eating-out[1]	Indonesian/Thai	14.6	2.9	500
Restaurants	Eating-out[1]	Greek/Turkish	13.8	3.1	439
Restaurants	Eating-out[1]	French	17.7	4.2	423
Sports & Leisure	Adventure sports	Windsurfing	2.7	0.7	379
Sports & Leisure	Leisure activities	Art gallery visits	31.9	9.8	327
Travel	Last holiday (to)	Far East	5.8	2.0	285
Licensed Trade	Licensed premises[2]	Wine bars	5.8	2.1	280
Media	Sunday newspaper	The Ind. on Sunday	4.0	1.4	278
Media	Daily newspaper	Financial Times	1.8	0.7	275
Motoring	Cost of car	£20,000+	3.9	1.4	275
Restaurants	Eating-out[1]	Italian	36.0	13.2	273
Media	Daily newspaper	The Guardian	6.5	2.5	264
Media	Sunday newspaper	Observer	5.0	1.9	262
Sports & Leisure	Outdoor sports	Tennis	13.0	5.0	258
Travel	Last holiday (to)	USA/Canada	8.2	3.3	248
Sports & Leisure	Outdoor sports	Skiing	7.0	2.9	244
Media	Sunday newspaper	The Sunday Times	14.3	5.9	243
Financial	Plastic cards	Other credit cards[3]	9.3	3.8	242
Restaurants	Eating-out[1]	Pizza restaurants	27.8	11.6	240

© CACI Limited, 1998.   Tel: 0171 602-6000 (London) / 0131 557-0123 (Edinburgh).

Notes: **Please note that the above list is not definitive but is intended to give an indication of key characteristics of the ACORN Group. See previous Chapter for Product definitions.**
Penetration: Refers to adults unless otherwise indicated. Figures do not necessarily indicate the ACORN Group with the highest penetration, but highlight particular characteristics of each Group.
Index: Shows the extent of the variation of the percentage penetration for the TGI Product by ACORN Group from the Base for GB as a whole.

[#] PayCheck data. Please see Chapter 3 for details.   [*] From a building society or other source.
[1] In last 3 months.   [2] Visit at least weekly.   [3] Not MasterCard or Visa.

Source: Target Group Index, © BMRB International Limited, 1997.
Buying potential information modelled using data from TGI 4/96-3/97.

Group C08 – Better-Off Executives, Inner City Areas

These are well-qualified people over a third of whom are single with no dependants. The age profile here is younger than for Groups 6 and 7 and there are many more students and other characteristics of academic centres. This Group also has a relatively high proportion of professionals and executives and shares many of the cosmopolitan features of Group C07.

ACORN Group C08 accounts for:

demographics
- 3.6% of total 1998 GB population (projected);
- 2.6% of total 1998 GB population (projected) aged 0–14;
- 5.8% of total 1998 GB population (projected) aged 15–24;
- 4.5% of total 1998 GB population (projected) aged 25–44;
- 2.7% of total 1998 GB population (projected) aged 45–64;
- 3.0% of total 1998 GB population (projected) aged 65+.

economics
- 2.8% of people earning over £20,000 p.a.[#];
- 2.3% of people buying their home with a mortgage[*];
- 3.1% of people owning unit trust stocks and shares.

media
- 2.1% of people with heavy ITV viewing.

Top Twenty Products by ACORN Group C08

Ranked in terms of the **index**

Category	Product Type	Product	Penetration (%) ACORN Group	GB	Index
Restaurants	Eating-out[1]	Greek/Turkish	10.4	3.1	332
Restaurants	Eating-out[1]	Spanish	5.2	1.6	322
Restaurants	Eating-out[1]	Indonesian/Thai	8.8	2.9	300
Media	Daily newspaper	The Guardian	7.2	2.5	293
Restaurants	Eating-out[1]	French	11.2	4.2	268
Licensed Trade	Licensed premises[2]	Wine bars	5.3	2.1	254
Media	ITV viewing	Never	4.2	1.7	252
Sports & Leisure	Leisure activities	Art gallery visits	24.2	9.8	248
Garden & Home	Gardening	No garden/allot.	39.6	16.5	239
Sports & Leisure	Outdoor sports	Tennis	11.7	5.0	232
Media	Sunday newspaper	The Ind. on Sunday	3.3	1.4	230
Sports & Leisure	Purchases in last yr.	Singles	4.9	2.2	221
Media	Sunday newspaper	Observer	4.2	1.9	218
Media	Daily newspaper	Financial Times	1.4	0.7	217
Sports & Leisure	Outdoor sports	Rugby League	0.8	0.4	213
Sports & Leisure	Indoor sports	Skating	3.2	1.7	194
Sports & Leisure	Adventure sports	Skiing	5.6	2.9	194
Sports & Leisure	Leisure activities	Visit pop concerts	13.2	6.9	192
Sports & Leisure	Adventure sports	Sailing	3.0	1.6	190
Media	Daily newspaper	The Times	5.5	2.9	188

© CACI Limited, 1998.   Tel: 0171 602-6000 (London) / 0131 557-0123 (Edinburgh).

Notes: **Please note that the above list is not definitive but is intended to give an indication of key characteristics of the ACORN Group. See previous Chapter for Product definitions.**
Penetration: Refers to adults unless otherwise indicated. Figures do not necessarily indicate the ACORN Group with the highest penetration, but highlight particular characteristics of each Group.
Index: Shows the extent of the variation of the percentage penetration for the TGI Product by ACORN Group from the Base for GB as a whole.
[#] PayCheck data. Please see Chapter 3 for details.   [*] From a building society or other source.
[1] In last 3 months.   [2] Visit at least weekly.

Source: Target Group Index, © BMRB International Limited, 1997.
Buying potential information modelled using data from TGI 4/96-3/97.

Group D09 – Comfortable Middle Agers, Mature Home Owning Areas

Mr and Mrs Base are to be found in these areas – they are close to the national 'norm' on just about every key characteristic. Living in a detached or semi-detached house with at least one car, likely to be an older married couple, Group D09 represents middle-of-the-road Britain. They are not particularly well-off but have few problems with unemployment or health.

ACORN Group D09 accounts for:

demographics
- 14.2% of total 1998 GB population (projected);
- 12.7% of total 1998 GB population (projected) aged 0–14;
- 12.4% of total 1998 GB population (projected) aged 15–24;
- 12.7% of total 1998 GB population (projected) aged 25–44;
- 16.2% of total 1998 GB population (projected) aged 45–64;
- 17.1% of total 1998 GB population (projected) aged 65+.

economics
- 16.4% of people earning over £20,000 p.a.[#];
- 15.6% of people buying their home with a mortgage[*];
- 16.3% of people owning unit trust stocks and shares.

media
- 12.5% of people with heavy ITV viewing.

Top Twenty Products by ACORN Group D09
Ranked in terms of the **index**

Category	Product Type	Product	Penetration (%) ACORN Group	GB	Index
Media	Sunday newspaper	Sunday Express	8.8	5.8	151
Garden & Home	Ownership	Greenhouse	21.0	14.4	146
Travel	Last holiday (to)	Australia/N. Zealand	0.9	0.6	146
Home Improvement[1]	Ownership	Conservatory	15.0	10.4	144
Home Improvement[1]	Ownership	Loft conversion	6.2	4.4	141
Media	Daily newspaper	Daily Express	8.4	5.9	141
Financial	Investments	Nat. Savings Certs.	4.5	3.2	139
Financial	Investments	TESSA[*]	10.5	8.0	132
Financial	Miscellaneous	Have made a Will	41.9	32.1	130
Media	Daily newspaper	Daily Mail	12.0	9.4	129
Home Improvement[1]	Central heating	Oil fired	3.5	2.8	127
Restaurants	Eating-out[2]	Berni	3.0	2.3	127
Home Improvement[1]	Central heating	Solid fuel	3.3	2.6	126
Home Improvement[1]	Ownership	Replac't. windows[3]	44.1	34.9	126
Media	Sunday newspaper	Mail on Sunday	13.2	10.4	126
Garden & Home	Gardening	Vegetables	25.0	20.0	125
Restaurants	Eating-out[2]	Beefeater	13.3	10.6	125
Garden & Home	Ownership	Grass trimmer	37.6	30.4	124
Motoring	Car registration	J or K reg.	13.1	10.5	124
Financial[#]	Income level (h'hld)	£25,000–£34,999	15.0	12.2	123

© CACI Limited, 1998. Tel: 0171 602-6000 (London) / 0131 557-0123 (Edinburgh).

Notes: **Please note that the above list is not definitive but is intended to give an indication of key characteristics of the ACORN Group. See previous Chapter for Product definitions.**
Penetration: Refers to adults unless otherwise indicated. Figures do not necessarily indicate the ACORN Group with the highest penetration, but highlight particular characteristics of each Group.
Index: Shows the extent of the variation of the percentage penetration for the TGI Product by ACORN Group from the Base for GB as a whole.
[#] PayCheck data. Please see Chapter 3 for details. [*] From a building society or other source. [1] Households. [2] In last 3 months. [3] Fitted/purchased in last year.

Source: Target Group Index, © BMRB International Limited, 1997.
Buying potential information modelled using data from TGI 4/96-3/97.

Group D10 – Skilled Workers, Home Owning Areas

People in this Group are likely to be found in manufacturing areas, working in skilled occupations. They tend to live in terraced homes and are more likely to be couples with children aged 0-14. Most are homeowners and the majority are buying with a mortgage. Not quite as comfortable as Group D09 – car ownership is lower – people in these areas are also around the midpoint on the social ladder.

ACORN Group D10 accounts for:

demographics
- 11.2% of total 1998 GB population (projected);
- 11.4% of total 1998 GB population (projected) aged 0–14;
- 11.5% of total 1998 GB population (projected) aged 15–24;
- 12.1% of total 1998 GB population (projected) aged 25–44;
- 10.6% of total 1998 GB population (projected) aged 45–64;
- 9.9% of total 1998 GB population (projected) aged 65+.

economics
- 9.1% of people earning over £20,000 p.a.[#];
- 13.3% of people buying their home with a mortgage[*];
- 7.3% of people owning unit trust stocks and shares.

media
- 12.0% of people with heavy ITV viewing.

Top Twenty Products by ACORN Group D10
Ranked in terms of the **index**

Category	Product Type	Product	Penetration (%) ACORN Group	GB	Index
Sports & Leisure	Outdoor sports	Rugby League	0.7	0.4	199
Home Improvement[1]	Purchased in last yr.	Secondary glazing	1.0	0.6	174
Sports & Leisure	Purchased in last yr.	Typewriters	1.0	0.6	150
Travel	Holiday accom.	Caravan	11.6	7.9	147
Media	Daily newspaper	Daily Star	5.6	4.0	142
Sports & Leisure	Purchased in last yr.	Camcorders	2.6	1.8	141
Financial	Investments	Building society a/c	1.3	0.9	138
Travel	Holiday accom.	Holiday camps	9.5	6.9	137
Sports & Leisure	Outdoor sports	Rugby Union	1.5	1.1	135
Sports & Leisure	Purchased in last yr.	Singles	3.0	2.2	134
Media	Sunday newspaper	The People	11.9	11.0	132
Home Improvement[1]	Purchased in last yr.	Central heating	2.2	1.7	131
Sports & Leisure	Betting	Bingo	15.4	11.9	129
Sports & Leisure	Indoor sports	Snooker	9.4	7.4	127
Financial	Mortgage source	Building society	36.6	29.2	125
Licensed Trade	Licensed premises[2]	Licensed clubs	14.6	11.6	125
Media	Sunday newspaper	News of the World	23.4	18.7	125
Media	Sunday newspaper	Sunday Mirror	13.2	10.6	125
Media	ITV viewing	Heavy - Medium	19.0	15.2	125
Motoring	Cost of car	£3,000–£4,999	16.3	13.1	125

© CACI Limited, 1998. Tel: 0171 602-6000 (London) / 0131 557-0123 (Edinburgh).

Notes:
Please note that the above list is not definitive but is intended to give an indication of key characteristics of the ACORN Group. See previous Chapter for Product definitions.
Penetration: Refers to adults unless otherwise indicated. Figures do not necessarily indicate the ACORN Group with the highest penetration, but highlight particular characteristics of each Group.
Index: Shows the extent of the variation of the percentage penetration for the TGI Product by ACORN Group from the Base for GB as a whole.
[#] PayCheck data. Please see Chapter 3 for details. [*] From a building society or other source.
[1] Households. [2] Visit at least weekly.

Source: Target Group Index, © BMRB International Limited, 1997.
Buying potential information modelled using data from TGI 4/96-3/97.

Group E11 – New Home Owners, Mature Communities

These areas are characterised by people who have bought their semi-detached or terraced council houses. They are likely to be older couples, often pensioners. Those still at work tend to be involved in craft or machine-related occupations. While these are not affluent areas, unemployment is only slightly above the national Base.

ACORN Group E11 accounts for:

demographics
- 10.2% of total 1998 GB population (projected);
- 9.6% of total 1998 GB population (projected) aged 0–14;
- 9.7% of total 1998 GB population (projected) aged 15–24;
- 8.8% of total 1998 GB population (projected) aged 25–44;
- 11.0% of total 1998 GB population (projected) aged 45–64;
- 12.7% of total 1998 GB population (projected) aged 65+.

economics
- 6.4% of people earning over £20,000 p.a.#;
- 8.6% of people buying their home with a mortgage*;
- 6.4% of people owning unit trust stocks and shares.

media
- 13.4% of people with heavy ITV viewing.

Top Twenty Products by ACORN Group E11

Ranked in terms of the **index**

Category	Product Type	Product	Penetration (%) ACORN Group	GB	Index
Home Improvement[1]	Central heating	Solid fuel	3.8	2.6	147
Media	Sunday newspaper	Sunday Mirror	15.2	10.6	144
Sports & Leisure	Betting	Bingo	17.2	11.9	144
Sports & Leisure	Outdoor sports	Bowls	4.2	3.0	141
Financial	Income level (h'hld)	£4,999 or less	11.1	8.0	139
Media	ITV viewing	Heavy	20.6	14.8	139
Media	Daily newspaper	Daily Mirror[2]	21.4	15.7	137
Sports & Leisure	Outdoor sports	Fishing	7.3	5.3	137
Media	Daily newspaper	The Sun	26.9	19.7	136
Media	Daily newspaper	Daily Star	5.4	4.0	135
Media	Sunday newspaper	The People	12.2	9.0	135
Media	Sunday newspaper	News of the World	25.1	18.7	134
Licensed Trade	Drink (regularly)[3]	Low alc. beer/lager	6.8	5.2	132
Licensed Trade	Licensed premises[3]	Licensed clubs	14.6	11.6	126
Travel	Holiday accom.	Holiday camps	8.7	6.9	125
Home Improvement[1]	Purchases in last yr.	Central heating	2.1	1.7	124
Media	Television	Satellite/cable TV	19.6	16.2	121
Licensed Trade	Drink (regularly)	Dark/golden rum	6.3	5.3	118
Sports & Leisure	Betting	Football betting	22.5	19.1	118
Financial#	Income level (h'hld)	£5,000–£9,999	17.4	14.8	117

© CACI Limited, 1998. Tel: 0171 602-6000 (London) / 0131 557-0123 (Edinburgh).

Notes: **Please note that the above list is not definitive but is intended to give an indication of key characteristics of the ACORN Group. See previous Chapter for Product definitions.**
Penetration: Refers to adults unless otherwise indicated. Figures do not necessarily indicate the ACORN Group with the highest penetration, but highlight particular characteristics of each Group.
Index: Shows the extent of the variation of the percentage penetration for the TGI Product by ACORN Group from the Base for GB as a whole.
PayCheck data. Please see Chapter 3 for details.   * From a building society or other source.
[1] Households.   [2] Or Daily Record.   [3] Visit at least weekly.

Source: Target Group Index, © BMRB International Limited, 1997.
Buying potential information modelled using data from TGI 4/96-3/97.

Group E12 – White Collar Workers, Better-Off Multi-Ethnic Areas

The relatively high incidence of people from diverse ethnic groups – especially Afro-Caribbean and Indian – characterises these multi-ethnic family areas. Accommodation tends to be either terraced houses or flats. Unemployment is slightly higher than in Group E11, but overall living conditions are reasonable.

ACORN Group E12 accounts for:

demographics
- 4.2% of total 1998 GB population (projected);
- 4.4% of total 1998 GB population (projected) aged 0–14;
- 5.1% of total 1998 GB population (projected) aged 15–24;
- 4.7% of total 1998 GB population (projected) aged 25–44;
- 3.6% of total 1998 GB population (projected) aged 45–64;
- 3.5% of total 1998 GB population (projected) aged 65+.

economics
- 4.0% of people earning over £20,000 p.a.[#];
- 4.1% of people buying their home with a mortgage[*];
- 4.1% of people owning unit trust stocks and shares.

media
- 3.7% of people with heavy ITV viewing.

Top Twenty Products by ACORN Group E12
Ranked in terms of the **index**

| | | | Penetration (%) | | |
| | | | ACORN | | |
Category	Product Type	Product	Group	GB	Index
Travel	Last holiday (to)	Far East	2.7	1.0	269
Media	Daily newspaper	The Guardian	5.1	2.5	207
Media	Sunday newspaper	The Ind. on Sunday	2.6	1.4	180
Media	ITV viewing	Never	2.9	1.7	173
Restaurants	Eating-out[1]	Greek/Turkish	5.0	3.1	160
Media	Daily newspaper	Independent	2.5	1.6	158
Sports & Leisure	Indoor sports	Skating	2.6	1.7	158
Travel	Length of holiday	More than 3 weeks	5.8	3.7	156
Travel	Last holiday (to)	USA/Canada	5.0	3.3	152
Travel	Holiday accom.	Tent	3.8	2.5	151
Sports & Leisure	Purchases in last yr.	Singles	3.3	2.2	149
Restaurants	Take-away food	Pizza houses	22.0	14.9	148
Restaurants	Eating-out[1]	Harvester	12.2	8.3	148
Travel	Holiday transport	Rail	3.3	2.2	147
Garden & Home	Gardening	No garden/allot.	23.9	16.5	144
Restaurants	Eating-out[1]	Pizza restaurants	16.6	11.6	144
Sports & Leisure	Indoor sports	Weight training	14.4	10.1	143
Travel	Last holiday (to)	Other Europe	3.6	2.5	142
Sports & Leisure	Indoor sports	Basketball	2.5	1.8	141
Sports & Leisure	Outdoor sports	Athletics	1.8	1.3	141

© CACI Limited, 1998. Tel: 0171 602-6000 (London) / 0131 557-0123 (Edinburgh).

Notes: **Please note that the above list is not definitive but is intended to give an indication of key characteristics of the ACORN Group. See previous Chapter for Product definitions.**
Penetration: Refers to adults unless otherwise indicated. Figures do not necessarily indicate the ACORN Group with the highest penetration, but highlight particular characteristics of each Group.
Index: Shows the extent of the variation of the percentage penetration for the TGI Product by ACORN Group from the Base for GB as a whole.
[#] PayCheck data. Please see Chapter 3 for details.   [*] From a building society or other source.   [1] In last 3 months.

Source: Target Group Index, © BMRB International Limited, 1997.
Buying potential information modelled using data from TGI 4/96-3/97.

Group F13 – Older People, Less Prosperous Areas

These are the areas of older couples aged 55+ who find the going quite tough. The incidence of limiting long-term illness is high. The majority do not have a car. People are generally living in small terraced houses or purpose-built flats, typically from housing associations. Those still at work tend to be in manual or unskilled occupations; unemployment is above Base.

ACORN Group F13 accounts for:

demographics
- 3.8% of total 1998 GB population (projected);
- 2.8% of total 1998 GB population (projected) aged 0–14;
- 3.3% of total 1998 GB population (projected) aged 15–24;
- 3.1% of total 1998 GB population (projected) aged 25–44;
- 3.8% of total 1998 GB population (projected) aged 45–64;
- 6.7% of total 1998 GB population (projected) aged 65+.

economics
- 2.9% of people earning over £20,000 p.a.[#];
- 3.7% of people buying their home with a mortgage[*];
- 1.9% of people owning unit trust stocks and shares.

media
- 6.8% of people with heavy ITV viewing.

Top Twenty Products by ACORN Group F13

Ranked in terms of the **index**

			Penetration (%)		
Category	Product Type	Product	ACORN Group	GB	Index
Media	Sunday newspaper	Sunday Mail	10.3	4.4	231
Media	Sunday newspaper	Sunday Post	12.5	5.9	210
Media	Daily newspaper	Daily Star	7.5	4.0	188
Media	ITV viewing	Heavy	23.9	14.8	161
Financial[#]	Income level (h'hld)	Less than £4,999	12.7	8.0	159
Garden & Home	Gardening	No garden/allot.	26.1	16.5	158
Media	Daily newspaper	Daily Mirror[1]	24.8	15.7	158
Sports & Leisure	Betting	Betting on horses	10.0	7.2	140
Licensed Trade	Licensed premises[2]	Licensed clubs	15.7	11.6	135
Sports & Leisure	Betting	Bingo	16.1	11.9	135
Travel	Holiday transport	Coach	7.1	5.3	134
Financial[#]	Income level (h'hld)	£5,000–£10,999	19.2	14.8	130
Licensed Trade	Drink (regularly)[2]	Rum	6.7	5.3	127
Sports & Leisure	Purchases in last yr.	Watches	5.0	4.0	126
Media	C4 viewing	Heavy	21.6	17.3	125
Licensed Trade	Licensed premises[2]	Wine bars	2.6	2.1	124
Media	Sunday newspaper	News of the World	23.3	18.7	124
Sports & Leisure	Betting	Football betting	23.7	19.1	124
Media	ITV viewing	Heavy - Medium	18.7	15.2	123
Travel	Holiday accom.	Holiday camps	8.6	6.9	123

© CACI Limited, 1998.   Tel: 0171 602-6000 (London) / 0131 557-0123 (Edinburgh).

Notes: **Please note that the above list is not definitive but is intended to give an indication of key characteristics of the ACORN Group. See previous Chapter for Product definitions.**
Penetration: Refers to adults unless otherwise indicated. Figures do not necessarily indicate the ACORN Group with the highest penetration, but highlight particular characteristics of each Group.
Index: Shows the extent of the variation of the percentage penetration for the TGI Product by ACORN Group from the Base for GB as a whole.
[#] PayCheck data. Please see Chapter 3 for details.   [*] From a building society or other source.
[1] Or Daily Record.   [2] Visit at least weekly.

Source: Target Group Index, © BMRB International Limited, 1997.
Buying potential information modelled using data from TGI 4/96-3/97.

Group F14 – Council Estate Residents, Better-Off Homes

These areas are typified by young couples with young children. Housing tends to be council or housing association terraces, often with cramped living conditions, though families tend to be better-off than those in other Groups in this Category. Unemployment is relatively high and there are many single parents.

ACORN Group F14 accounts for:

demographics
- 12.1% of total 1998 GB population (projected);
- 15.9% of total 1998 GB population (projected) aged 0–14;
- 13.9% of total 1998 GB population (projected) aged 15–24;
- 11.8% of total 1998 GB population (projected) aged 25–44;
- 10.4% of total 1998 GB population (projected) aged 45–64;
- 9.4% of total 1998 GB population (projected) aged 65+.

economics
- 5.7% of people earning over £20,000 p.a.#;
- 7.4% of people buying their home with a mortgage*;
- 3.7% of people owning unit trust stocks and shares.

media
- 17.6% of people with heavy ITV viewing.

Top Twenty Products by ACORN Group F14

Ranked in terms of the **index**

Category	Product Type	Product	Penetration (%) ACORN Group	GB	Index
Media	Sunday newspaper	Sunday Mail	9.3	4.4	209
Media	Sunday newspaper	Sunday Post	11.1	5.9	187
Media	ITV viewing	Heavy	25.2	14.8	170
Media	Television	Satellite/Cable TV	16.3	9.7	168
Media	Daily newspaper	Daily Star	6.6	4.0	166
Sports & Leisure	Betting	Bingo	19.3	11.9	162
Financial#	Income level (h'hld)	Less than £4,999	12.6	8.0	159
Media	Sunday newspaper	News of the World	29.7	18.7	159
Media	Daily newspaper	Daily Mirror[1]	24.4	15.7	155
Media	Daily newspaper	The Sun	30.0	19.7	152
Sports & Leisure	Purchases in last yr.	Singles	3.2	2.2	146
Sports & Leisure	Outdoor sports	Fishing	7.7	5.3	146
Travel	Holiday accom.	Holiday camps	9.9	6.9	142
Sports & Leisure	Miscellaneous	Play video games	12.2	8.6	141
Media	Sunday newspaper	The People	12.7	9.0	140
Sports & Leisure	Betting	Betting on horses	10.0	7.2	140
Sports & Leisure	Purchases in last yr.	LPs	3.1	2.2	137
Media	Sunday newspaper	Sunday Mirror	14.2	10.6	134
Financial#	Income level (h'hld)	£5,000–£10,999	19.4	14.8	131
Sports & Leisure	Purchases in last yr.	Watches	5.2	4.0	131

© CACI Limited, 1998. Tel: 0171 602-6000 (London) / 0131 557-0123 (Edinburgh).

Notes: **Please note that the above list is not definitive but is intended to give an indication of key characteristics of the ACORN Group. See previous Chapter for Product definitions.**
Penetration: Refers to adults unless otherwise indicated. Figures do not necessarily indicate the ACORN Group with the highest penetration, but highlight particular characteristics of each Group.
Index: Shows the extent of the variation of the percentage penetration for the TGI Product by ACORN Group from the Base for GB as a whole.
PayCheck data. Please see Chapter 3 for details.   * From a building society or other source.
[1] Or Daily Record.

Source: Target Group Index, © BMRB International Limited, 1997.
Buying potential information modelled using data from TGI 4/96-3/97.

Group F15 – Council Estate Residents, High Unemployment

Group F15 has a greater ethnic mix and higher unemployment than Group F14. This Group has an older age profile and the highest incidence of limiting long-term illness – almost double the national Base. People live mainly in purpose built council flats. Car ownership is lower in these areas than anywhere else.

ACORN Group F15 accounts for:

demographics
- 2.8% of total 1998 GB population (projected);
- 2.3% of total 1998 GB population (projected) aged 0–14;
- 2.7% of total 1998 GB population (projected) aged 15–24;
- 2.5% of total 1998 GB population (projected) aged 25–44;
- 2.6% of total 1998 GB population (projected) aged 45–64;
- 4.3% of total 1998 GB population (projected) aged 65+.

economics
- 1.6% of people earning over £20,000 p.a.#;
- 1.2% of people buying their home with a mortgage*;
- 1.0% of people owning unit trust stocks and shares.

media
- 4.1% of people with heavy ITV viewing.

Top Twenty Products by ACORN Group F15

Ranked in terms of the **index**

Category	Product Type	Product	Penetration (%) ACORN Group	GB	Index
Garden & Home	Gardening	No garden/allot.	49.5	16.5	299
Media	Daily newspaper	Daily Star	8.9	4.0	223
Media	Sunday newspaper	Sunday Mail	9.4	4.4	211
Financial#	Income level (h'hld)	Less than £4,999	15.3	8.0	192
Media	Daily newspaper	The Independent	3.0	1.6	188
Sports & Leisure	Purchases in last yr.	Singles	4.1	2.2	186
Media	Sunday newspaper	The Ind. on Sunday	2.6	1.4	185
Media	Sunday newspaper	Sunday Post	10.8	5.9	182
Media	Daily newspaper	The Sun	35.1	19.7	178
Licensed Trade	Drink (regularly)[1]	White rum	11.4	6.5	175
Media	Sunday newspaper	News of the World	32.5	18.7	174
Media	Daily newspaper	Daily Mirror[2]	27.3	15.7	174
Media	ITV viewing	Heavy	25.7	14.8	173
Sports & Leisure	Betting	Betting on horses	12.0	7.2	167
Media	Sunday newspaper	Sunday Mirror	17.3	10.6	163
Media	Television	Satellite/cable TV	15.8	9.7	163
Licensed Trade	Drink (regularly)[1]	Dark/golden rum	8.6	5.3	162
Media	IBA listening	Heavy	31.6	19.6	161
Sports & Leisure	Betting	Bingo	19.1	11.9	160
Sports & Leisure	Purchases in last yr.	LPs	3.6	2.2	159

© CACI Limited, 1998. Tel: 0171 602-6000 (London) / 0131 557-0123 (Edinburgh).

Notes: **Please note that the above list is not definitive but is intended to give an indication of key characteristics of the ACORN Group. See previous Chapter for Product definitions.**
Penetration: Refers to adults unless otherwise indicated. Figures do not necessarily indicate the ACORN Group with the highest penetration, but highlight particular characteristics of each Group.
Index: Shows the extent of the variation of the percentage penetration for the TGI Product by ACORN Group from the Base for GB as a whole.
PayCheck data. Please see Chapter 3 for details.   * From a building society or other source.
[1] Visit at least weekly.   [2] Or Daily Record..

Source: Target Group Index, © BMRB International Limited, 1997.
Buying potential information modelled using data from TGI 4/96-3/97.

Group F16 – Council Estate Residents, Greatest Hardship

Two key features characterise this Group: single parents and unemployment, both of which – at roughly three times the national Base – are higher in this Group than in any other. Overall, living conditions are extremely tough. There are lots of young and very young children, with large households in small council flats.

ACORN Group F16 accounts for:

demographics
- 2.9% of total 1998 GB population (projected);
- 5.1% of total 1998 GB population (projected) aged 0–14;
- 3.6% of total 1998 GB population (projected) aged 15–24;
- 2.8% of total 1998 GB population (projected) aged 25–44;
- 1.9% of total 1998 GB population (projected) aged 45–64;
- 1.3% of total 1998 GB population (projected) aged 65+.

economics
- 0.4% of people earning over £20,000 p.a.[#];
- 0.8% of people buying their home with a mortgage[*];
- 0.6% of people owning unit trust stocks and shares.

media
- 4.2% of people with heavy ITV viewing.

Top Twenty Products by ACORN Group F16

Ranked in terms of the **index**

Category	Product Type	Product	Penetration (%) ACORN Group	GB	Index
Media	Sunday newspaper	Sunday Mail	13.6	4.4	306
Media	ITV viewing	Heavy	34.2	14.8	231
Sports & Leisure	Betting	Bingo	27.3	11.9	229
Travel	Holiday transport	Rail	4.7	2.2	212
Media	Daily newspaper	Daily Mirror[1]	31.0	15.7	197
Sports & Leisure	Outdoor sports	Rugby League	0.7	0.4	195
Media	Sunday newspaper	Sunday Post	11.2	5.9	189
Sports & Leisure	Betting	Betting on horses	13.5	7.2	189
Financial[#]	Income level (h'hld)	Less than £4,999	14.9	8.0	188
Travel	Holiday accom.	Caravan	12.3	7.9	155
Sports & Leisure	Outdoor sports	Fishing	8.2	5.3	154
Sports & Leisure	Purchases in last yr.	Typewriters	1.0	0.6	152
Media	Daily newspaper	Daily Star	6.0	4.0	151
Media	Sunday newspaper	The People	13.5	9.0	149
Home Improvement[2]	Purchases in last yr.	Vinyl flooring	6.0	4.1	146
Media	Sunday newspaper	News of the World	27.3	18.7	146
Travel	Holidays in last yr.	No holidays	55.4	38.2	145
Licensed Trade	Licensed premises[3]	Licensed clubs	16.6	11.6	143
Media	Daily newspaper	The Sun	28.2	19.7	143
Media	Channel 4 viewing	Heavy	24.2	17.3	140

© CACI Limited, 1998.   Tel: 0171 602-6000 (London) / 0131 557-0123 (Edinburgh).

Notes: **Please note that the above list is not definitive but is intended to give an indication of key characteristics of the ACORN Group. See previous Chapter for Product definitions.**
Penetration: Refers to adults unless otherwise indicated. Figures do not necessarily indicate the ACORN Group with the highest penetration, but highlight particular characteristics of each Group.
Index: Shows the extent of the variation of the percentage penetration for the TGI Product by ACORN Group from the Base for GB as a whole.
[#] PayCheck data. Please see Chapter 3 for details.   * From a building society or other source.
[1] Or Daily Record.   [2] Households.   [3] Visit at least weekly.

Source: Target Group Index, © BMRB International Limited, 1997.
Buying potential information modelled using data from TGI 4/96-3/97.

Group F17 – People in Multi-Ethnic, Low-Income Areas

The greatest ethnic mix in Britain is found in this Group, especially of Pakistani and Bangladeshi groups which account for over 40% of the population. Single parenting and unemployment are very high. Many people are living in extremely cramped conditions in unmodernised terraced housing or council flats. Whilst relatively poor areas, evidence suggests small pockets of more affluent residents.

ACORN Group F17 accounts for:

demographics
- 2.3% of total 1998 GB population (projected);
- 3.8% of total 1998 GB population (projected) aged 0–14;
- 3.1% of total 1998 GB population (projected) aged 15–24;
- 2.4% of total 1998 GB population (projected) aged 25–44;
- 1.5% of total 1998 GB population (projected) aged 45–64;
- 1.1% of total 1998 GB population (projected) aged 65+.

economics
- 1.1% of people earning over £20,000 p.a.#;
- 0.8% of people buying their home with a mortgage*;
- 0.8% of people owning unit trust stocks and shares.

media
- 1.9% of people with heavy ITV viewing.

Top Twenty Products by ACORN Group F17

Ranked in terms of the **index**

			Penetration (%)		
Category	Product Type	Product	ACORN Group	GB	Index
Travel	Last holiday (to)	Far East	6.9	1.0	680
Sports & Leisure	Outdoor sports	Cricket	9.0	2.4	375
Garden & Home	Gardening	No garden/allot.	43.8	16.5	265
Media	ITV viewing	Never	4.3	1.7	257
Travel	Last holiday (to)	Australia/N. Zealand	1.5	0.6	257
Home Improvement[1]	Purchases in last yr.	Secondary glazing	1.2	0.6	213
Sports & Leisure	Outdoor sports	Football	11.3	5.4	212
Travel	Length of holiday	More than 3 weeks	7.6	3.7	204
Sports & Leisure	Indoor sports	Table tennis	6.1	3.0	202
Sports & Leisure	Outdoor sports	Running	6.9	3.4	201
Sports & Leisure	Indoor sports	Basketball	3.5	1.8	196
Sports & Leisure	Outdoor sports	Jogging	9.5	4.9	194
Sports & Leisure	Indoor sports	Badminton	10.9	5.7	191
Sports & Leisure	Purchases in last yr.	Ski clothing	3.2	1.7	190
Sports & Leisure	Indoor sports	Snooker	13.1	7.4	178
Restaurants	Eating-out[2]	Indonesian/Thai	5.1	2.9	176
Financial#	Income level (h'hld)	£4,999 or less	13.7	8.0	172
Media	Daily newspaper	Financial Times	1.1	0.7	166
Restaurants	Take-away food	Pizza houses	24.6	14.9	165
Restaurants	Eating out	Spanish	2.6	1.6	162

© CACI Limited, 1998. Tel: 0171 602-6000 (London) / 0131 557-0123 (Edinburgh).

Notes: **Please note that the above list is not definitive but is intended to give an indication of key characteristics of the ACORN Group. See previous Chapter for Product definitions.**
Penetration: Refers to adults unless otherwise indicated. Figures do not necessarily indicate the ACORN Group with the highest penetration, but highlight particular characteristics of each Group.
Index: Shows the extent of the variation of the percentage penetration for the TGI Product by ACORN Group from the Base for GB as a whole.
PayCheck data. Please see Chapter 3 for details. * From a building society or other source.
[1] Households. [2] In last 3 months.

Source: Target Group Index, © BMRB International Limited, 1997.
Buying potential information modelled using data from TGI 4/96-3/97.

CHAPTER 9

NORTHERN IRELAND IN PROFILE

CACI UK*ACORN PROFILE OF NORTHERN IRELAND

This table shows the UK*ACORN profile for Northern Ireland. Northern Ireland is classified using CACI's generic 17 ACORN Groups and 54 ACORN Types (plus 1 'unclassified') but with an additional unique Group ('Types only found in Northern Ireland') which is further divided into five Types. The UK*ACORN classification is derived from the Government's 1991 Census of Northern Ireland.

UK*ACORN Groups UK*ACORN Types	Population Distribution	
	Number	Percent of Total
UK*ACORN Category A: THRIVING		
1 **Wealthy Achievers, Suburban Areas**		
1.1 Wealthy suburbs, large detached houses	47,254	3.0
1.2 Villages with wealthy commuters	35,995	2.3
1.3 Mature affluent home owning areas	23,117	1.5
1.4 Affluent suburbs, older families	46,431	2.9
1.5 Mature, well-off suburbs	28,864	1.8
2 **Affluent Greys, Rural Communities**		
2.6 Agricultural villages, home based workers	10,166	0.6
2.7 Holiday retreats, older people, home based workers	–	–
3 **Prosperous Pensioners, Retirement Areas**		
3.8 Home owning areas, well-off older residents	–	–
3.9 Private flats, elderly people	–	–
UK*ACORN Category B: EXPANDING		
4 **Affluent Executives, Family Areas**		
4.10 Affluent working families with mortgages	76,420	4.8
4.11 Affluent working couples with mortgages, new homes	–	–
4.12 Transient workforces, living at their place of work	–	–
5 **Well-Off Workers, Family Areas**		
5.13 Home owning family areas	27,262	1.7
5.14 Home owning family areas, older children	60,772	3.9
5.15 Families with mortgages, younger children	80,449	5.1
UK*ACORN Category C: RISING		
6 **Affluent Urbanites, Town & City Areas**		
6.16 Well-off town & city areas	13,475	0.9
6.17 Flats & mortgages, singles & young working couples	–	–
6.18 Furnished flats & bedsits, younger single people	–	–
7 **Prosperous Professionals, Metropolitan Areas**		
7.19 Apartments, young professional singles & couples	–	–
7.20 Gentrified multi-ethnic areas*	–	–
8 **Better-Off Executives, Inner City Areas**		
8.21 Prosperous enclaves, highly qualified executives	–	–
8.22 Academic centres, students & young professionals	10,986	0.7
8.23 Affluent city centre areas, tenements & flats	–	–
8.24 Partially gentrified multi-ethnic areas*	–	–
8.25 Converted flats & bedsits, single people	–	–
UK*ACORN Category D: SETTLING		
9 **Comfortable Middle Agers, Mature Home Owning Areas**		
9.26 Mature established home owning areas	8,085	0.5
9.27 Rural areas, mixed occupations	27,636	1.8
9.28 Established home owning areas	35,245	2.2
9.29 Home owning areas, council tenants, retired people	22,899	1.5

UK*ACORN Groups UK*ACORN Types	Population Distribution	
	Number	Percent of Total
10 Skilled Workers, Home Owning Areas		
10.30 Established home owning areas, skilled workers	15,049	1.0
10.31 Home owners in older properties, younger workers	9,333	0.6
10.32 Home owning areas with skilled workers	39,387	2.5
UK*ACORN Category E: ASPIRING		
11 New Home Owners, Mature Communities		
11.33 Council areas, some new home owners	44,356	2.8
11.34 Mature home owning areas, skilled workers	12,633	0.8
11.35 Low rise estates, older workers, new home owners	–	–
12 White Collar Workers, Better-Off Multi-Ethnic Areas*		
12.36 Home owning multi-ethnic areas, young families*	16,503	1.0
12.37 Multi-occupied town centres, mixed occupations*	29,725	1.9
12.38 Multi-ethnic areas, white collar workers*	–	–
UK*ACORN Category F: STRIVING		
13 Older People, Less Prosperous Areas		
13.39 Home owners, small council flats, single pensioners	22,947	1.5
13.40 Council areas, older people, health problems	14,179	0.9
14 Council Estate Residents, Better-Off Homes		
14.41 Better-off council areas, new home owners	78,936	5.0
14.42 Council areas, young families, some new home owners	22,865	1.4
14.43 Council areas, young families, many lone parents	21,717	1.4
14.44 Multi-occupied terraces, multi-ethnic areas*	49,823	3.2
14.45 Low rise council housing, less well-off families	62,774	4.0
14.46 Council areas, residents with health problems	45,526	2.9
15 Council Estate Residents, High Unemployment		
15.47 Estates with high unemployment	–	–
15.48 Council flats, elderly people, health problems	–	–
15.49 Council flats, very high unemployment, singles	9,873	0.6
16 Council Estate Residents, Greatest Hardship		
16.50 Council areas, high unemployment, lone parents	70,542	4.5
16.51 Council flats, greatest hardship, many lone parents	9,709	0.6
17 People In Multi-Ethnic, Low-Income Areas*		
17.52 Multi-ethnic, large families, overcrowding*	16,812	1.1
17.53 Multi-ethnic, severe unemployment, lone parents*	–	–
17.54 Multi-ethnic, high unemployment, overcrowding*	22,166	1.4
UK*ACORN Category U: UNCLASSIFIED		
18.55 Unclassified	–	–
UK*ACORN Category N: NORTHERN IRELAND		
19 Types only found in Northern Ireland		
19.56 Affluent rural communities with good communication links & low unemployment	95,761	6.1
19.57 Remote properties & smallholdings with employment in agriculture & tourism	59,008	3.7
19.58 Local occupations, some unemployment & large families	97,696	6.2
19.59 Mixed housing tenures, some unemploy. & smaller families	58,844	3.7
19.60 Terraced council houses, severe unemployment, many lone parents large families	96,616	6.1
TOTAL	**1,577,836**	**100.0**

© CACI Limited, 1996. UK*ACORN is a registered servicemark of CACI Limited.

Note: * Characteristics of the Northern Ireland ACORN Types match those for Great Britain in every way except in terms of ethnicity.

Sources: ONS & GRO(NI) © Crown Copyright 1991 and CONI © Crown Copyright 1994. All rights reserved.

CHAPTER 10

SCOTLAND IN PROFILE

CACI SCOTTISH*ACORN PROFILE

This table identifies the 8 ACORN Groups and 43 ACORN Types (plus 1 'unclassified') that represent the Scottish*ACORN profile for Scotland. Scottish*ACORN is derived from the Government's 1991 Census of Scotland.

CACI's 1998 Population Projections

		Scottish Population Distribution	
		Number	Percent of Total
Group A: AFFLUENT CONSUMERS WITH LARGE HOUSES			

This group contains the most affluent people in Scotland. The majority of people in this Group live in large detached houses, and are more likely to have access to two or more cars. They are typically on high incomes and are employed in professional or managerial jobs in the service sector.

		Number	Percent
1	Wealthy Families, Largest Detached Houses	141,091	2.7
2	Wealthy Older Residents, Home Owning Semis	122,627	2.4
3	Affluent Younger Families with Mortgages	200,777	3.9
4	Affluent Older Couples & Families, Often Rural	247,607	4.8

Group B: PROSPEROUS HOME OWNERS

This Group is typically of middle class Scotland and its residents are likely to live in their own homes. Incomes, car ownership and educational qualifications are above average in these areas. These areas are found throughout Scotland, mainly in city suburbs or in better-off towns and villages.

5	Better-Off Families, Mixed Dwellings	98,722	1.9
6	Younger Families with Mortgages, Commuters	222,859	4.3
7	Younger Families with Mortgages, New Homes	103,725	2.0
8	Older People in Suburban Areas & Small Towns	173,459	3.4
9	Working Couples, Owner Occupied Semi-Detached Houses	113,149	2.2
10	Skilled Workers, Owner Occupied Semi-Detached Houses	125,642	2.4
11	Better-Off Older Residents, Mainly Villages	201,825	3.9

Group C: AGRICULTURAL COMMUNITIES

This Group covers Scotland's better-off farming communities and also the Gaelic speaking Western Isles. Type 12 areas are found throughout Scotland and the residents are more likely to live in large houses, either owned or tied, and car ownership is high. In Type 13, there is a high incidence of households which are not a main residence which indicates these areas include many holiday homes.

12	Home Based Workers, Agricultural Areas	169,793	3.3
13	Gaelic Speakers, Remote Areas & Islands	39,614	0.8

Group D: PRIVATE TENEMENTS & FLATS

These neighbourhoods are found in the centres of Scotland's largest towns and cities. The households are likely to contain people living alone, professional couples and students. Many of these households are owner occupied but there is also a high incidence of private renting. Car ownership is below average and usage of all forms of public transport to travel to work is high.

14	Younger Couples & Families, Owner Occupied Flats	80,535	1.6
15	Skilled Workers, Owner Occupied Flats	114,069	2.2
16	Young Professionals & Students, Private & Rented Flats	60,251	1.2
17	Elderly People, Private Flats	70,155	1.4
18	Professionals & Students, Private & Rented Tenements	72,251	1.4
19	Younger Residents with Mortgages, Tenements	87,719	1.7
20	Younger Residents with Mortgages, Smaller Tenements	62,886	1.2

	Scottish Population Distribution	
	Number	Percent of Total

Group E: BETTER-OFF COUNCIL AREAS, HOMES OFTEN PURCHASED

These areas are characterised by people who have bought their council house or flat. They are most likely to contain older couples or families, although in some instances, younger families have exercised their right to buy. While these are not affluent areas, unemployment is at or below average.

		Number	Percent
21	Older Residents, New Home Owners	201,167	3.9
22	Older Residents, Semi-Detached, New Home Owners	138,196	2.7
23	Retired Residents, New Home Owners	81,315	1.6
24	Older Families, Some New Home Owners	142,401	2.8
25	Older People, Some New Home Owners	78,109	1.5
26	Younger New Home Owners, Often New Towns	158,460	3.1
27	Families in Scottish Homes, Some New Home Owners	138,658	2.7

Group F: COUNCIL ESTATES, LESS WELL-OFF FAMILIES

These areas are typified by families of all ages living in council terraces and flats. There is little overcrowding since homes tend to be larger. Unemployment is above average and those that are at work tend to be in manual and unskilled occupations.

		Number	Percent
28	Younger Families in Flats, Many Children	149,126	2.9
29	Younger Families in Mixed Dwellings, Some Lone Parents	123,707	2.4
30	Younger Large Families, Council Terraces	229,168	4.5
31	Families, Older Children, Terraces	131,885	2.6
32	Older Large Families, Semi-Detached Houses	155,177	3.0

Group G: COUNCIL ESTATES, OLDER RESIDENTS

These areas contain couples or single people aged 55+ living in small council flats or terraced homes. The type and location of these properties and the age of residents means that there is a high incidence of limiting long term illness. Unemployment is above average and there are low levels of car ownership.

		Number	Percent
33	Older Residents, Low Rise Council Flats	73,848	1.4
34	Retired People, Health Problems, Mixed Dwellings	111,348	2.2
35	Retired People, Council Terraces	95,056	1.8
36	Single Pensioners, Health Problems, Larger Flats	85,323	1.7
37	Single Pensioners, Health Problems, City Centres	42,046	0.8

Group H: POOREST COUNCIL ESTATES

This Group comprises those council estates likely to have the most serious social problems, with the highest levels of unemployment, overcrowding, large and single parent families. These estates house large numbers of residents dependent upon the State for provision of basic services. Car ownership is significantly below the Scottish average.

		Number	Percent
38	Poorer Families, High Unemployment, Low Rise Housing	72,218	1.4
39	Singles, Housing Association Flats, Overcrowding	60,715	1.2
40	Older Residents, High Unemployment, High Rise Flats	79,266	1.5
41	High Unemployment, Some High Rise Flats, Scottish Homes	58,108	1.1
42	Many Lone Parents, High Unemployment, Council Flats	111,703	2.2
43	Many Lone Parents, Greatest Hardship, Council Flats	84,024	1.6
44	Unclassified	29,951	0.6
	TOTAL	**5,139,731**	**100.0**

FURTHER READING

For a more detailed introduction into the subject of geodemographics, market analysis and targeting, readers are referred to:

TARGETING CUSTOMERS (2nd ed.)
How to use Geodemographic and Lifestyle Data in Your Business

by Peter Sleight,
Partner, Target Market Consultancy

This straightforward and easily digestible introduction to the subject clearly describes geodemographic systems and their applications.

Targeting Customers has been specially written to encourage marketers new to the subject to see the practical relevance of geodemographic and lifestyle data to their business, and to highlight the latest developments to the more experienced user.

ISBN 1-899314-78-4
Format 297 x 210 mm (A4)
Price £29 (plus £2.60 p&p)

An Introductory Guide To
THE 1991 CENSUS

edited by Barry Leventhal, Corrine Moy and James Griffin from the Market Research Society Census Interest Group

The geodemographics industry is driven primarily by Census information, and **An Introductory Guide to the 1991 Census** is a valuable aid in assessing this rich and detailed source, explaining the wide range of outputs and how they may be applied.

Written with those not familiar with the Census in mind, the experienced user will find that the book succinctly puts the new developments in the Census into context.

ISBN 1-870562-13-5
Format 297 x 210 mm (A4)
Price £26 (plus £1.70 p&p)

Both books are published by and available from:

NTC Publications Ltd, Farm Road, Henley-on-Thames, Oxfordshire RG9 IEJ
Tel: (01491) 411000   Fax: (01491) 571188